WHY COOPERATE?

WHY COOPERATE?

The Incentive to Supply Global Public Goods

Scott Barrett

OXFORD
UNIVERSITY PRESS

OXFORD
UNIVERSITY PRESS

Great Clarendon Street, Oxford ox2 6DP

Oxford University Press is a department of the University of Oxford.
It furthers the University's objective of excellence in research, scholarship,
and education by publishing worldwide in

Oxford New York

Auckland Cape Town Dar es Salaam Hong Kong Karachi
Kuala Lumpur Madrid Melbourne Mexico City Nairobi
New Delhi Shanghai Taipei Toronto

With offices in

Argentina Austria Brazil Chile Czech Republic France Greece
Guatemala Hungary Italy Japan Poland Portugal Singapore
South Korea Switzerland Thailand Turkey Ukraine Vietnam

Oxford is a registered trade mark of Oxford University Press
in the UK and in certain other countries

Published in the United States
by Oxford University Press Inc., New York

British Library Cataloguing in Publication Data

Data available

Library of Congress Cataloging in Publication Data

Data available

Typeset by SPI Publisher Services, Pondicherry, India
Printed in Great Britain
on acid-free paper by
Biddles Ltd., King's Lynn, Norfolk

ISBN 978-0-19-921189-0

1 3 5 7 9 10 8 6 4 2

Contents

List of Figures

List of Tables

Foreword

We live in a world of shared risks and common opportunities, mutual dependence and growing interconnectedness. It is a world in which all people's security, health, and prosperity depend in no small part on the quality of their countries' engagement in international cooperation. As we move into a future in which, hopefully, the world will continue to integrate, international cooperation will be more important than ever. Governments the world over increasingly must work together to align their long-term national interests to achieve common goals. These goals—these global public goods—are assuming ever greater importance on the world stage. Global public goods are, in fact, crucial to the future of world integration and interdependence.

The International Task Force on Global Public Goods that I recently co-chaired considered, over the course of its work, many aspects of global public goods, but especially focused on the potential benefits for all nations that would be brought about by increased and improved international cooperation. It was during my work with the global public goods Task Force that I first had the pleasure of meeting and working with Professor Scott Barrett, one of the preeminent experts in the field. After hearing his valuable contributions during several meetings, and seeing the results of his work with the Secretariat of the Task Force, I invited him to come to the Yale Center for the Study of Globalization as a Distinguished Visiting Fellow. At Yale, Professor Barrett led intelligent and fruitful discussions about these issues as he further developed his thoughts on some of the relevant topics, and we encouraged him to produce a volume that would give voice to his viewpoints.

The result is this fine volume. Scott Barrett writes for the lay reader as well as the informed thinker. He both describes global public goods and recognizes the present inadequacies in their provision. He brings to our attention the many hurdles that must be overcome in order to achieve the common goals contained in these goods. In short, he has produced a primer, yet goes beyond the standard definition of that form. He gives us not only the basic elements of global public goods, assessing their promises and prospects, but he also does address with great skill and enlightenment the thorny question: why is it, in fact, so important to cooperate.

Scott Barrett brings much needed attention and focus to the challenges faced by countries, civil societies and international institutions as they work to secure the cooperation needed to enhance the livelihoods of all the world's people.

Ernesto Zedillo
Director, Yale Center for the Study of Globalization

Preface and Acknowledgements

A nuclear weapon has not been exploded in over 60 years. For 25 years, parents everywhere have not needed to worry about their children dying from smallpox, or suffering complications from the live small-pox vaccine. The ozone layer, far from being depleted to the extent once feared, is expected to recover by around 2050. These three events, or non-events, are among humanity's greatest achievements. They are also examples of the subject of this book. They are all global public goods.

All three achievements also only came to be supplied because of the combined efforts of a large number of countries. They thus serve as a reminder that international cooperation can benefit every country—and every person living in every country.

We could achieve even more. Imagine if "loose nukes" were secured from terrorists; if outbreaks of new diseases were prevented, or their spread contained; if breakthrough energy technologies were developed and diffused globally, permitting economic growth without worsening climate change; and if new discoveries, of special relevance to tropical environments, lifted millions of people out of poverty. As explained in this book, all of these imagined futures are attainable; they are within our reach.

They will not, however, be grasped as if by an invisible hand. To realize any of these better futures will require institutional changes—a restructuring of the relationships among countries, a redirection in the incentives that both power and steer the behavior of states, a deliberative but spirited multilateralism. This book outlines the kinds of institutional changes that are required. My hope is that it will inspire the leadership needed to bring them about.

The book was written at the invitation of the International Task Force on Global Public Goods, which was created by an agreement between France and Sweden, signed on April 9, 2003. The Task Force was established to define and clarify the concept, to explain how global public goods came to be supplied in the past, to identify current gaps in supply, and to make recommendations for closing these gaps. Coming at a time when multilateralism was in retreat if not already in hiding, this effort served as a reminder that, as stated in the terms of reference, "national development goals can often not be met by national policies alone."

In the course of carrying out its work, the Secretariat to the Task Force commissioned over three dozen papers, and convened a number of meetings, involving experts, various stakeholders, and members of the Task Force. It was at this stage that I became involved. Initially, I acted as an adviser to the Task Force. Later I was asked to develop material for a final report. My approach was analytical, however, and the Task Force wanted to publish a more political document.[1] It wasn't obvious what would happen to the material I had prepared as background for the final report.

It was at this time that, while on sabbatical from the Johns Hopkins University School of Advanced International Studies, I took up a visiting position at the Yale Center for the Study of Globalization at Yale University. Ernesto Zedillo, a co-chair of the Task Force, and director of the Yale Center, saw at once that my new position offered an opportunity for me to turn the materials I had prepared earlier into a book. The Task Force endorsed his idea, but it was really at his urging that the present book came to be written.

The Task Force was established as an independent body, free of political influence, and I was accorded the same freedom when invited to write this book. The contents of this book reflect my own views entirely and not those of the Task Force or the sponsors or of any of the other parties connected with that effort.

The material I had prepared previously for the Task Force had a specific purpose and was intended for a special audience. The book, I knew, would have to be different. When I first started writing, I began from scratch. I did not even refer back to the earlier work until the book had already taken its present shape. In the end, I drew very little from the material I had prepared earlier. Mostly I relied on research I had done before (updated and presented differently here), or was in the process of doing, or felt impelled to do because the book demanded it. Much of the content of this book is entirely fresh.

And yet I was only able to proceed in this way because I had engaged with the Task Force and the people connected with it for more than a year before I started to write this book. It was as if I had participated in a long and absorbing conversation, had been made to think hard about this subject, had challenged others about their ideas and suffered criticism for my own mistakes, and after all of this was given the chance to write down what I knew about global public goods—or, rather, to write down what I thought other people should know about global public goods.

Which people? I wrote this book for the non-specialist—for people like the members of the Task Force who were more interested in global problems and how to solve them than in definitions and theorems. The logic underlying the book is rigorous (deriving mainly from simple game theory), and I hope compelling, but the presentation is more in the form of a collection of narratives than a text.[2] It consists of a set of images and stories that can be read in isolation. A fuller reading, however, should show that the different parts are held together by a unified structure: a paradigm of how different global issues relate to one another, of the incentives that cause global problems to arise in the first place, and of the institutions that are needed to change these incentives for the purpose of making people everywhere better off.

Many good people participated in the conversation that preceded the writing of this book. In addition to the Task Force members[3] I was given tremendous support by the Secretariat. I must note especially the assistance of Sven Sandström, the head of the Secretariat, and Katell le Goulven, his deputy, for their general guidance and helpful comments on all the materials I prepared previously. Two other advisers to the Task Force, James Fearon of Stanford University and Paul Collier of Oxford University, also provided helpful and detailed comments on my earlier contributions. More than that, they co-authored two sections of the work I took a lead in preparing for the Task Force, and in the process taught me about subjects that are discussed in a somewhat different way in this book. Paul Collier was a close collaborator from an early stage of the project, and I am particularly indebted to him for his many contributions and astute counsel.

A number of people unconnected with the Task Force helped to shape my thinking on the subjects covered in this book either before or while I was writing. They include Joseph Aldy, Kenneth Arrow,

Bruce Aylward, Curtis Barrett, Bruce Benton, Jagdish Bhagwati, Daniel Bodansky, Partha Dasgupta, Ariel Dinar, Paul Ehrlich, Marco Ferroni, David Fidler, Francis Fukuyama, Theodore Groves, D. A. Henderson, Michael Hoel, Dean Jamison, James Joseph, Patrick Kelley, Lee Lane, Jean Lanjouw, Ramanan Laxminarayan, Joshua Michaud, Mark Miller, Ashoka Mody, William Nordhaus, David Pearce, David Popp, Todd Sandler, Dale Squires, Robert Stavins, Nicholas Stern, Christian Turner, Alan Winters, and Lowell Wood. Previous collaborations with Inge Kaul (a Task Force member) and her colleague, Pedro Conceição, at the United Nations Development Programme inspired me to start thinking about this topic years ago. I am also grateful to Michael Hoel for inviting me to visit the Centre for Advanced Study in Oslo just before I took up my visiting position at Yale.

I owe a special intellectual debt to Thomas Schelling. His influence on my thinking has been so great that, in reviewing the manuscript, I had to check to make sure that I had given him proper credit in the text and footnotes. Upon reading the book a final time, I am sure I have not given him credit enough.

While visiting the Yale Center for the Study of Globalization, I was invited by Ernesto Zedillo to give three seminars to select audiences of the Yale faculty and students. It was in these sessions that some of the ideas in this book took their final shape. I am deeply grateful to Ernesto Zedillo for inviting me to join his Center and for chairing these seminars. I also want to thank Haynie Wheeler, Associate Director of the Yale Center, for making my stay both productive and enjoyable. The Yale faculty and students with whom I interacted the most during my sabbatical, or from whom I learned the most when giving these seminars, include Nayan Chanda, Dan Esty, Durland Fish, Alison Galvani, Nathaniel Keohane, Robert Mendelsohn, William Nordhaus, Sheila Olmstead, Robert Repetto, Jonathan Schell, Derek Smith, Christopher Udry, Ulrich Wagner—and, of course, Ernesto Zedillo himself.

Sarah Caro of Oxford University Press helped to bring this book to publication in the shortest possible time. She also provided very helpful comments on an earlier draft. I am grateful to her and her associate, Jennifer Wilkinson, for their support throughout this project.

Writing the book was easy compared with choosing a title. I asked many people for suggestions, and labored over this myself for a long while, but Frances Cairncross, Rector of Exeter College, Oxford came up with the best title, and in an instant. I am grateful to her for suggesting it to me.

I was not able to finish the book in a single semester, and so took the manuscript to Cape Cod for the summer. Nothing, I am sure, could be more boring than seeing your husband or father stooped over a computer, day after day, in the only living space of a small cottage. My family, however, put up with me. They even helped. My wife, Leah, read and commented on the manuscript; my son, Jackson, checked the references; and my daughter, Kira, invented titles for the book. For me, the summer proved much less boring, and also more productive, than I imagined possible—though I could say the same thing about every day I spend with my family. To these three people I am, as always, especially grateful.

Introduction: the incentives to supply global public goods

Global public goods offer benefits that are both non-excludable and non-rival. Once provided, no country can be prevented from enjoying a global public good; nor can any country's enjoyment of the good impinge on the consumption opportunities of other countries. When provision succeeds, global public goods make people everywhere better off.

Global public goods are thus universally to be desired. But because their provision benefits every country, even the ones that do not help to provide them, global public goods are often under-provided. Some are not provided at all.

Why should we care if global public goods are provided? We should care because our wellbeing, the wellbeing of future generations, and even the fate of the Earth depends on them being provided. Global public goods include the prevention of nuclear proliferation, the suppression of killer pandemics, climate change mitigation, and fundamental scientific knowledge. Failure to supply these global public goods exposes the world to great dangers. Providing them expands human capabilities.

The power of the concept lies not only in helping us to understand why *each* of these global public goods is under-provided, or even how their provision can be improved. It lies also in showing us that *all* these global public goods are under-provided for similar reasons. Preventing an outbreak of a new disease and keeping weapons of mass destruction out of the hands of terrorists—these appear to be unrelated challenges. They are certainly different challenges, but since both are global public goods, they constitute data for a broader analysis. Learning how one kind of global public good has been provided may suggest ways in which another can be provided.

Since global public goods differ in fundamental ways, however, we cannot simply lump them together. We need to classify them. Securing "loose nukes" is more akin to preventing a new pandemic than to discovering a new scientific insight. Climate change mitigation is more like ozone layer protection than nuclear non-proliferation. A classification sensitive to the manner in which global public goods are supplied is especially helpful. It shows that some global public goods can only be supplied if every country cooperates; that many need the cooperation of only certain key countries; that most, but not all, require financing; that some can be supplied by mutual restraint or coordination; and that others demand only a single best effort.

This last kind of global public good—the kind requiring a single best effort—is the easiest to supply. It is therefore a good starting point for an introduction to the concept. I turn to it next.

Single best efforts

Imagine this: an asteroid measuring several kilometers in diameter is heading towards the Earth. It is traveling at a speed of 25 kilometers per second (that's 90,000 km per hour). A collision is expected. Upon impact, or soon thereafter, billions of people will be killed. Many will die from the blast wave caused by the explosive impact. Most, however, will die from environmental changes caused by the blast. Some will die from tsunamis, global wildfires, and earthquakes. Others as a result of a planetary dust cloud that darkens the skies, terminating photosynthesis and cooling temperatures. Still more will die from acid rain and ozone depletion.[1] It is possible, perhaps even likely, that our species, *Homo sapiens*, will become extinct.

Fortunately, because of investments in science and technology made years earlier, the asteroid has been identified early; the collision will not occur for decades; we have time to prepare.

We can prepare for more than death. Given sufficient resources, engineers are confident that a spacecraft could be designed, built, and deployed to avoid a collision. The spacecraft might create a gravitational force capable of changing the asteroid's orbit. It might deflect the sun's energy to create a "natural rocket" that pushes the asteroid off course. It might dock a nuclear-powered rocket to the asteroid, or a "solar sail," to give the needed push. It might simply try to obliterate the asteroid. Whichever approach were tried (and this would be a technical matter, depending partly on the shape and composition of the space object, and its distance from the Earth), a collision could be avoided—the Earth could be saved—provided, that is, that the money needed to pay for asteroid defense were made available.

Preventing an asteroid collision is a global public good: if the Earth is "saved" for one country, it is saved for every country, including those countries that may not have contributed to the effort. Moreover, the satisfaction each country derives from its survival does not diminish the benefits enjoyed by other countries. Global public goods, as noted before, provide benefits that are both non-excludable and non-rival.

Ordinarily, we think of global public goods as being prone to free riding. After all, if every country benefits, whether it contributes or not, why should any country help to provide the good?

When the world's survival is at stake, however, this logic breaks down. Failure to supply this global public good would have such profound consequences that every country would be willing to sacrifice practically everything to secure its provision. Moreover, only a single successful intervention, a *single best effort*, would be required.[2] Indeed, and as I shall explain in Chapter 1, it is very likely that a large country—a country with the means and not only the desire to provide the public good—would be prepared to defend the world against a certain asteroid collision all by itself, even if other countries did nothing.

This example is purely hypothetical. To our knowledge, a space object of this size is not heading towards the Earth—not in the near future, anyway. But knowing this should not offer much comfort. The actual problems we face, including the threat of a *possible* asteroid collision, or the more likely threat of a *smaller* impact—these problems are much more challenging. I discuss them, and other global problems like them, in Chapter 1.

Weakest links

Some global public goods can only be provided with the active participation of *every* country.

If you were born before the late 1970s, then, like me, you probably have a circular scar on your upper arm—an artifact of having been vaccinated in your youth for smallpox. Younger persons, including my own children, lack the scar. This is because smallpox was declared eradicated in 1979, and after that there was no need for people to be vaccinated. The eradication of smallpox was a singular achievement. To pull it off, the virus had to be eliminated within every village, every town, and every city—in every country of the world, all at the same time. Had even one country not eliminated smallpox, the entire effort would have failed.

Smallpox eradication is a *weakest link* global public good. It is a global public good because, like asteroid defense, it yields benefits that are both non-excludable and non-rival. Unlike asteroid defense, however, smallpox eradication required *universal* cooperation.

Though the eradication of smallpox did not "save the world," its benefits have been immense. Persons born after 1979 were spared the pain of the bifurcated needle. They were also shielded from the risks associated with this live vaccine.[3] Children born in the poorest countries benefited the most: few such children used to be vaccinated for smallpox, and so millions of people born in poor countries are alive today because the effort to supply this global public good succeeded. As I explain in Chapter 2, smallpox eradication also proved an incredibly good investment. Indeed, it may be the best collective investment the world has ever made.

Why did we succeed in eradicating smallpox, even though the participation of every country was required? The main reason is that each country had an incentive to play its part in eradicating the disease *once assured that all other countries would play their part*.[4] In contrast to the incentives to defend the Earth from an on-coming asteroid, the incentives to eliminate smallpox within a country's borders were *conditional*. It only made sense for some countries to eliminate smallpox if they believed every other country would eliminate smallpox. Once that assurance had been given, however, the incentives to supply this global public good were strong.

As I shall explain later in this introduction, even with all these advantages, the effort to eradicate smallpox nearly failed. So this example, while inspiring, also serves as a caution. Indeed, despite a quarter century's advancement in science and medicine, a deterioration in security and public order in certain parts of the world means that, were we to attempt to eradicate smallpox today, we could not count on the effort succeeding.

Aggregate efforts

Action to address global climate change, another global public good, is proving extremely difficult. So far, very little has been done to mitigate global climate change.

Why is that? There are many reasons; four are critical:

First, climate change does not threaten the survival of the human species.[5] If unchecked, it will cause other species to become extinct (though biodiversity is being depleted now due to other reasons). It will alter critical ecosystems (though this is also happening now, and for reasons unrelated to climate change). It will reduce land area as the seas rise, and in the process displace human populations. "Catastrophic" climate change is possible, but not certain. Moreover, and unlike an asteroid collision, large changes (such as sea level rise of, say, ten meters) will likely take centuries to unfold, giving societies time to adjust. "Abrupt" climate change is also possible, and will occur more rapidly, perhaps over a decade or two. However, abrupt climate change (such as a weakening in the North Atlantic circulation), though potentially very serious, is unlikely to be ruinous. Human-induced climate change is an experiment of planetary proportions, and we cannot be sure of its consequences. Even in a worse case scenario, however, global climate change is not the equivalent of the Earth being hit by mega-asteroid. Indeed, if it were as damaging as this, and if we were sure that it would be this harmful, then our incentive to address this threat would be overwhelming. The challenge would still be more difficult than asteroid defense, but we would have done much more about it by now.

Second, different countries will be affected in different ways by climate change. Not all of the consequences of climate change will be for the worse. Some regions may benefit, at least from some perspectives (a rise in the productivity of agriculture—again, in some areas), at least through the medium term, provided climate change is "gradual." Other regions may lose badly. The countries most likely to be adversely affected are the poorest countries—the countries least able to mitigate climate change. They will be victims of this unfolding process. Disaggregating the impacts matters because individual countries are causing greenhouse gas concentrations to rise, and only individual countries can slow or reverse this trend. By contrast, no country would benefit from an asteroid collision, just as no country benefited from smallpox. In these cases, the countries most affected also have (had, in the case of smallpox) both the incentive and the wherewithal to act. Climate change is different.

Third, mitigating climate change on a significant scale will also have consequences. It will be costly to reduce greenhouse gas emissions substantially. Doing so will require diverting resources from other good causes, including investments that could insulate the most vulnerable countries from climate change—investments that might yield greater benefits than mitigation. Doing so will also increase other risks, such as those associated with an expansion of nuclear power. As I explain later in this book, asteroid defense also entails opportunity costs and new risks. So did smallpox eradication. But the economics of supplying these global public goods are (were, for smallpox) much more favorable. It is harder to draw "red lines" under the climate problem.

Finally, reducing the world's greenhouse gas emissions depends on the *aggregate effort* of all countries. Unlike asteroid protection, a single country cannot stabilize atmospheric concentrations of greenhouse gases all by itself—certainly not by reducing its emissions unilaterally. And in contrast to smallpox eradication, the contributions by individual countries to stabilizing concentrations do not matter (Somalia's cooperation was essential to the success of the smallpox eradication campaign, but it is irrelevant to mitigating climate change). An assurance that some countries will reduce their greenhouse gas emissions may not inspire other countries to join them. Indeed, it could have the opposite effect. Free riding is likely to be a much bigger problem for climate change mitigation.

Of course, countries can agree to limit their emissions collectively, as some have done in the form of the Kyoto Protocol. But that agreement only disguised the incentives to free ride; it did not correct them. Some countries, including Australia and the United States, declined to ratify the agreement. Others, including China and India, agreed to participate only on the condition that they did not have to reduce their emissions. Of the parties that are required to limit their emissions, some may fail to comply—or they may comply only by means of a loophole that ultimately fails to reduce global emissions, thanks to the treaty's trading mechanism and gift of "hot air."[6] Even by an optimistic assessment, the Kyoto Protocol will reduce global emissions of greenhouse gases very little. Indeed, it was designed to do no more than that.

As explained in Chapter 3, another global public good requiring an aggregate effort—protection of the ozone layer—has been supplied, nearly to the fullest extent possible. So it is not this property alone that determines success and failure. It is really the combination of *all* of the above four properties that makes climate change mitigation so hard to supply.

If one advantage of the concept of global public goods is to show us that different global challenges are related, another is to show us that a single problem like climate change has many dimensions requiring international cooperation. Kyoto's approach focuses only on the imperative to cut emissions. But countries will inevitably need to adapt to climate change, and adaptation is a domestic, regional, and international public good. We also need to undertake research and development into breakthrough energy technologies, and this involves supplying the global public good of knowledge. Once discovered, new energy technologies must be diffused around the world, and this will likely involve the setting of technical standards—another global public good. Finally, concentrations have climbed to a level that makes it necessary for us to contemplate the possibility of counteracting human-induced climate change with deliberate climate modification: another global public good. Discussion of these dimensions of the challenge are scattered throughout this book.

Financing and burden sharing

For each of the global public goods discussed thus far, provision requires that something be done. This something—whether it be asteroid deflection, smallpox eradication, or climate change mitigation—has to be paid for; it must be financed. But how? That is the subject of Chapter 4.

Asteroid deflection can be self-financed by a large country with an incentive to provide the global public good all by itself. Such a country may not actually pay the full cost. Others might also contribute. But if a single country has an incentive to pay for asteroid deflection *even if others do not contribute,* then we can be pretty sure that the global public good will be provided. After all, failure to do so would be suicide.

Smallpox eradication was different. It *required* international financing. Smallpox had to be eliminated everywhere, and dozens of poor countries lacked the resources—and, in some cases, the capability—to rid their populations of the virus. The rich countries had to pay a portion of this cost. Had they not done so, the effort almost certainly would have failed. As it was, the effort came close to failing. The reason was a persistent lack of funding.[7]

Why were the main beneficiaries of smallpox eradication so reluctant to pay for it? As noted before, an assurance that other countries would eliminate smallpox made each country want to participate in the global effort. Financing, however, is a little like climate change mitigation in the sense that it is the total effort—the aggregate of all financial contributions—that determines whether eradication can be fully funded.[8]

Eradication is unlike climate change mitigation in another sense. There can be a little or a lot of climate change mitigation, but eradication is binary, not continuous; it either succeeds or fails. Achieving eradication thus requires a fixed sum of money. If the burden of raising this money were shared so that every contributing state gained, given that eradication succeeded, then each such state would have an incentive to contribute its full share, given an assurance that all others would contribute their full share. By this reasoning, international financing should not have been a problem. And yet we know that it was. Free riding thus appears to be a more complicated and challenging phenomenon than it is commonly taken to be.

The challenge of financing climate change mitigation is much greater. To make a material difference, fundamental new energy technologies will be needed. Moreover, these new technologies will have to be diffused globally. In the richer countries, where there already exists an installed base of capital, investment is especially needed to replace depreciating assets. In fast-growing countries like India and China, an even greater investment is needed in the near term (China is rumored to be adding a new coal-fired power plant every week). To reduce global emissions, the fast-growing poor countries need to be put onto a new kind of development path as a priority, and the richer countries transitioned onto the same path a little more gradually as their capital is replaced. The poor countries cannot be expected to finance this investment all by themselves. A significant share of this cost will have to be financed by rich countries.

Financing this technological transformation will require an aggregate effort by the rich countries, and on a scale many times greater than the world has ever attempted before. Global climate change may or may not be the most important problem facing us today, but it is almost certainly the hardest one for the world to address.

Mutual restraint and coordination

Some global public goods cost nothing, and yet may still be challenging to supply and sustain.

One of the most important global public goods is the norm against the use of nuclear weapons. Continued supply of this vital global public good requires *mutual restraint*, not financing. I discuss it, and other global public goods like it, in Chapter 5.

The global public good of the standard for determining time—a standard that both facilitates and is an expression of the phenomenon we call "globalization"—also costs nothing to supply. Providing it requires only *coordination*. I discuss global public goods of this type in Chapter 6.

Though neither of these types of global public good requires financing, they are otherwise very different challenges. Mutual restraint is much harder to sustain than coordination. The inhibition on the use of the bomb was not inevitable, and we cannot be sure it will last. By contrast, standardization of the measurement of time was to be expected (though the particular standard chosen was not inevitable) and is sure to last (today's standard may be changed, but *a* standard will continue to be chosen). Why the difference? The reason, as always, has to do with the incentives for providing these global public goods. Even if no other country has the bomb, there will be some countries that will seek to acquire it. By contrast, if every country obeys a single standard of time, no country will want to break from this consensus and choose a different standard for itself.[9]

To sum up, global public goods are not all alike, and the differences that distinguish one type from another create contrasting *incentives* for provision.[10]

Leadership

The biggest, the richest, and the mightiest states—the great powers—usually have the greatest incentive to supply global public goods. Their leadership is not always sufficient, but it is almost always necessary.

Which states do I mean? I mean the superpower, the United States, naturally.[11] But I mean other countries, too. Indeed, it is a conceit to believe that the U.S., and only the U.S., can supply most vital global public goods unilaterally.

Countries capable of developing asteroid defense include, in addition to the United States, the members of the European Space Agency, Japan, and Russia (soon other countries, such as China and India, will have a similar capability). The United States contributed more than any country to smallpox eradication, but that effort would never have succeeded without the support of the Soviet Union (indeed, the USSR first proposed that this global public good be supplied), for it took place during the Cold War; and as I explain in Chapter 4, financing of this global public good may also have failed were it not for a last minute intervention by Sweden. Indeed, being a weakest link global public good, smallpox eradication could not have been achieved without the support of the weakest of states, Somalia and Sudan included. Finally, though it is inconceivable that an international effort to mitigate climate change on a significant scale can succeed without the United States, the U.S. will not join in such an effort without the participation of other states, including China, the European Union, India, and Japan, and perhaps more states as well.

In other areas, too, the superpower is not powerful enough. Whether the United Nations Security Council sanctions imposed on North Korea will have any effect depends mainly on China; the U.S. does not trade with North Korea. Cybersecurity also cannot be secured solely through unilateral measures. Users can defend themselves from attack, but it is also essential to go after the attackers. The "I Love You" virus, which attacked 60 million computers, including mine, in May 2000, was launched from the Philippines, which at the time had no cybercrime laws. To be able to prosecute and punish attackers, and so to deter them, global standards are needed, not just national defenses. That is the purpose of the Convention on Cybercrime, adopted in 2001. The United States Senate has an allergic-like reaction to most treaties but it ratified this one in late 2006.

Though the incentives for the great powers to supply global public goods are often strong, they can be overridden by other motivations, or tripped up by free riding. The benefits of supplying global public goods can also be overlooked, or misinterpreted, or neglected for reasons of incompetence or ideology. The leadership of the key states cannot always be relied upon. We know that.

We also know that, when there is a dissonance of interests, when different countries are affected differently by the supply of a global public good, or perceive the challenge differently, more than the interests of the great powers need to be recognized. As Franklin Roosevelt noted in his 1945 State of the Union Address, "International cooperation on which enduring peace must be based is not a one-way street ... In a democratic world, as in a democratic nation, power must be linked with responsibility, and obliged to defend and justify itself within the framework of the general good."[12] Looked at somewhat differently, though the supply of most global public goods requires the active participation of the United States, the U.S. can achieve much more when it has the support of other states. In many cases, as noted before, the support of other states is vital. The important point is this: when the opportunities to supply a global public good are seized by the great powers, motivated only by self-interest, but acting "within the framework of the general good," the entire world benefits.

Development

In many if not most cases this benefit is latent; it is a *potential* benefit. Often, to ensure that the benefit is actually realized, complementary domestic public goods must also be supplied. For example, the discovery of a new vaccine, the knowledge of which is a global public good, promises little benefit to a country that is unable to pay for it, or that lacks the domestic institutions needed to recognize the benefit of paying for it. This is why human progress requires not only improved international institutions, necessary to facilitate the supply of global public goods, but also effective domestic institutions, necessary to ensure that the benefits of this supply are fully exploited and widely shared.

Another problem: human development, even in its most basic of forms, is sometimes held back by the under-supply of *regional and international public goods*—goods that *uniquely* benefit the poor and weak states. In these cases, the great powers lack the incentive to lead. If they are to play a role, their motivation must be compassion, not self-interest. Compassion is always to be applauded, but we know that self-interest is usually the more reliable impulse.

Of course, the great powers would benefit *indirectly* were these shortcomings defeated—strengthening the most fragile states, for example, facilitates provision of weakest link global public goods. But overcoming *these* deficiencies is *itself* a global public good; and one that, because it requires financing, is open to free riding.

When a failed state's own leadership and institutions are the problem, the challenge is even greater. Should its sovereignty be respected? Or should it be challenged when the country's leadership fails to fulfill its responsibilities, to its own people, to its neighbors, and to the rest of the world? And which countries should decide whether sovereignty ought to be respected in particular cases? These are difficult questions. They are particularly difficult because of the need to enforce whatever is agreed. It is usually the enforcement of the decision (or the credible threat to enforce it), rather than the decision itself, that supplies the global public good.

Compounding these problems is another tendency. All states lose when global public goods are under-provided, but the great and even middle powers can often compensate for such failures by investing in substitute public goods at the local and national levels (for example, by building dikes to adapt to climate change rather than by reducing emissions to prevent climate change). Poor and weak states cannot make the same substitutions. When international cooperation fails, it is often the poor and weak states that lose the most—another reason why the challenge of supplying global public goods needs to be seen "within the framework of the general good."

All of these considerations suggest a complex relationship between the supply of global and domestic public goods. I address it in Chapter 7.

Domestic public goods

Incentives are not entirely given; they can be molded and redirected by institutions. Indeed, this is what institutions are meant to do—the reason institutions exist in the first place. But can institutions overcome the incentive problems that block the provision of global public goods?

To understand this, it will help to consider the related challenge of financing a *domestic* public good like national defense. Imagine that this public good had to be financed voluntarily. How much would people—the citizens of a state—contribute? Each person would probably figure (rightly) that his own contribution would make little difference to the overall supply of defense. In a population of, say, a million people, each person's contribution would be such a tiny fraction of the total as not to matter. So, why contribute? Of course, each person would also know that, if everyone failed to contribute, or contributed only a nominal amount, then the nation would be vulnerable to attack, and everyone would be worse off as a consequence. But in the end, each person can only determine his own actions. The temptation to contribute very little would thus be strong. It might prove irresistible.

Free riding is only a tendency. Some people will contribute because they believe it is the right thing to do, whether or not others contribute.

Probably more people will condition their choice on the behavior of others, or on the behavior they expect of others. Each such person may apprehend that others will not contribute enough to justify making a sizable contribution herself. That is, each such person may fear that she will get back (in terms of the value she derives from the *overall* level of defense provided) less than she gives (her *own* contribution). Put more positively, each such person may be inclined to contribute more only if she were assured that others would contribute more. Why do people pay their taxes? One reason is the fear of being fined for not paying, but another is the belief that most other residents are paying *their* taxes.[13] Taxation, reinforced by a system of fines and a compliance norm, is an institution that facilitates the supply of public goods. It helps to overcome the deficiencies of volunteerism.

Consider the challenge of supplying a local public good as simple as the village clock, which in centuries past provided a single measure of time to an entire community, a means by which all its members could coordinate their joint activities. How was maintenance of the village clock financed? Volunteerism proved an unreliable source, as noted by a decree from 1618:

Some years ago in Arzberg [Germany] they had a clock made which strikes a bell. The residents of Nichtewitz and Kaucklitz are supposed to contribute, the owners of a hide of land 1/2 Reichstaler, gardners 1 local taler, but they are unwilling to do so. Previously their excuse was that they couldn't hear the clock. Now they have admitted that they can hear it but still they don't want to pay: they are to pay their share; where they don't the authorities shall make them.[14]

Volunteerism failed even in this village setting.[15] Intervention by the "authorities" was needed to ensure that the public good was provided. In 1618, the authorities represented a duke or prince or the emperor. Today, of course, they represent the state.

Domestic institutions

Assume that tax collection can be relied upon, and consider a different choice. Imagine that voters were asked in a referendum whether to support a tax to finance national defense. It seems likely that many of the same persons who would contribute little if anything voluntarily would vote in favor of the referendum, even though they would have to pay a sizable tax if the referendum passed. Why? The reason is that, in voting yes, the voter not only increases the likelihood that *he* will have to pay the tax. He also increases the likelihood that *everyone else* will have to pay the tax. The combination of the vote and the tax— essential domestic institutions—thus change the incentives facing the citizenry; they make the citizens want to contribute more; they ensure that the national public good is supplied in greater abundance.

Local and national public goods are often supplied by means other than taxation. The public good of clean air, for example, is typically supplied by regulation—by governments commanding polluters to reduce their emissions, backed by the threat to punish violators. And while taxation is needed to finance national defense, in many countries, especially in times of war, this is supplemented by conscription. Similarly, during a public health emergency, individuals suspected of being infected, and of posing a danger to others, can be placed under quarantine. Even in the absence of a crisis, governments routinely require that children be vaccinated. This is not just to protect these children. It is to prevent the conditions that would allow an epidemic to emerge and threaten others: another public good.

So, it is really the government's power of compulsion, prefer-ably held in check by democratic institutions, that causes local and national public goods to be supplied. Together, this combination has the potential to make the members of a society better off *collectively*.

The combination cannot, however, be relied upon to make every member better off *individually*. A mother may choose to have her children vaccinated when the vaccine is safe and the probabil-ity of infection is high. She may decline to do so when the vac-cine poses a greater risk than the disease itself. And yet if every mother chooses in this way, "herd immunity" in the general popu-lation will be compromised. So there is a rationale for government intervention—but grounds also for citizen resistance. The tension is inescapable.

It also has a long history. Use of the world's first vaccine, for smallpox, swept through Europe soon after its "discovery" in 1798, but many parents refused to vaccinate their children, and epidemics recurred. Why would parents decline to vaccinate their children? One important reason is that the vaccine was risky. It killed about one out of every 14,000 people vaccinated.[16] The best outcome, from the perspective of every parent, was for *other* children to be vaccinated. This way, your child would be spared both the risk of infection and the risk of a bad reaction to the live vaccine. The problem, of course, is that if every parent behaved in this way, the disease would continue to be present.

How then to encourage more vaccination? In Britain, an 1840 act offered the vaccine free of charge—the country's first free medical ser-vice. That incentive, however, proved inadequate, and so the author-ities tried a different approach. In 1853, parliament made smallpox vaccination compulsory, with violators being subject to fines. When epidemics continued, the visible and strong hand of the government pressed more firmly. The fines were increased and penalties were added for repeat violations. These responses, however, only hardened social resistance. Eventually, the state backed off. In 1898, parliament passed a new Vaccination Act, giving parents the right to refuse to vaccinate their children. The consequence: a quarter of a million certificates were awarded to "conscientious objectors" in the first year.[17]

The United States government has recently encountered a similar resistance. Of the half million health and emergency workers targeted for smallpox vaccination, fewer than one in ten consented. To these individuals, the risk of the vaccine seemed greater than the risk of a bioterrorist attack.

Conflicts of this kind are to be contrasted with the government's role in enforcing purely private decisions. Contracts restrict the freedoms only of those individuals and other legal persons who consent to be bound by them. Governments do not compel individuals to enter into private contracts, but they do enforce such agreements once they have been voluntarily entered into. In doing so, governments provide a service that even libertarians recognize as being valuable. Contract enforcement allows parties to overcome problems of mistrust that otherwise would prevent them from transacting. Government compulsion is needed to make markets work efficiently. It is only when government enforces outcomes in the public sphere that tensions arise.[18]

Of course, some local and national public goods are supplied without the aid of compulsion. At least seven million people (mainly mothers) volunteered to collect donations from over 100 million Americans to help finance development of the world's first polio vaccine. The March of Dimes, as the campaign was known, provided ten times as much research funding as the government-funded National Institutes of Health.[19]

Such exceptions, however, only prove the rule: there are *some* situations in which government compulsion *is* vastly superior to volunteerism. Indeed, a lesson of the effort to develop and test polio vaccine was the need to strengthen government regulation of the process.[20]

To summarize: the institutions of government, though imperfect, can sometimes improve on volunteerism. When they do, these domestic institutions work by restructuring the relationships among the members of a society, by changing the rules of the game of their interaction.[21] Global public goods must somehow be supplied by a similar means. But that task, as I shall now explain, is much, much harder.

International anarchy

The conditions that apply at the international level are very different: there is no world government with the power to tax, to conscript, to regulate, or to quarantine; there are instead nearly 200 national governments, each recognized by international law as being sovereign. The institutions every society relies on to supply essential national public goods do not exist at the global level. Global public goods must be supplied by alternative means. Sovereignty essentially implies that they must be supplied voluntarily.

I noted previously that volunteerism can be, and sometimes is, effective in supplying domestic public goods. It may even succeed in supplying some *global* public goods. Indeed, the example I gave before applies here as well. The knowledge of how to vaccinate against polio, financed mainly by voluntary contributions rather than by taxes, is actually a global public good (the Salk and Sabin vaccines were not even patented). So the need to supply global public goods voluntarily need not spell disaster. However, sovereignty does make it harder for states to supply global public goods than domestic public goods.

To see this, imagine that climate change were a purely national phenomenon. Then every country would bear the full cost of acting, and reap the full reward. Moreover, no state would need to worry that, as it cut its own emissions, other countries might respond by increasing their emissions—whether for reasons of free riding or by virtue of their trade relations.[22]

There might seem an obvious antidote to sovereignty. If the power of compulsion were given to an international authority, if a world government were established, then global public goods could be supplied by the same means employed domestically. Would we not be better off with a world government?

As an abstract proposition, the answer must be yes (for why else do we have government at the national level?), but the peoples of the world are diverse, and would resist being bound by a single set of institutions. In democracies, minorities do not rise up against the majority so long as the beliefs and values of the majority are similar to their own (of course, giving minorities legal protections also helps). As these differences increase, however, majority rule loses its broad appeal; it becomes a means of oppression, a stimulant to nationalism. It is not necessary for every nation to be represented by its own state, but as more nations are gathered under the control of a single state, it becomes harder for the state to maintain legitimacy and even control.[23] The breakup of the Soviet Union and Yugoslavia, and the more recent independence of East Timor, are all expressions of this tendency. So, in the opposite sense, is the reunification of Germany. Also relevant is evidence showing that local public goods are supplied in greater abundance when there are fewer ethnic divisions.[24]

At the global level, the differences among peoples are, by definition, at their maximum, which is why sovereignty proves a strong attractor in the international system. Sovereignty protects minorities. It requires that global rules be established by unanimity. It demands that other rules be adopted by the consent of the countries to which they apply. So long as values and beliefs are strongly associated with national identity, and so long as these continue to diverge, the number of states is likely to remain large. Similarly, the willingness of states to submit to a global majority will continue to be circumscribed. Of course, in Europe sovereignty has been eroded; some (but not all) decisions today are made by a qualified majority of the European Union member states. But further enlargement is resisted by some members (and championed by others) for the simple reason that, as the Union expands to encompass more countries, reflecting a greater diversity of values, beliefs, and interests, efforts to further *deepen* European Union integration may be set back. At some point, this tradeoff may cause enlargement to stop (especially as enlargement requires unanimous consent). When looked at in this way, the European Union is not so much an exception to the rule as an expression of the same phenomenon.

To be sure, the existing arrangements will not persist indefinitely. The differences that divide people today will probably lessen over time—advances in technology and integration by trade should help see to that. But this process of developing shared values will take time (and may suffer setbacks). There is a reason that the international system is organized the way it is; there is a reason states exist and a supranational authority does not; there is a reason there are almost 200 states and not 20 let alone one.[25] As imperfect as the present arrangement may be, centralization of authority, today, cannot be relied upon to improve global wellbeing. Even if wellbeing could potentially be improved according to some criteria (such as a utilitarian perspective), it will not be embraced any time soon. As matters now stand, too many players have too much to lose from such an arrangement.

The challenge today is thus for countries to increase the supply of global public goods within the *existing* anarchic international setting.

International institutions

Unilateralism, the default *modus operandi* of states in the international arena, can sometimes be effective. So, potentially, can "coalitions of the willing."[26] My main concern in this book, however, lies with those situations in which such responses fail—situations in which wellbeing everywhere could be improved if only the behavior of states could be changed. Lacking a supranational authority capable of compelling states to behave differently, the only alternative available is *international cooperation*—a kind of organized volunteerism.

International cooperation is developed and sustained by international institutions. Like their domestic counterparts, international institutions restructure the incentives that determine individual behavior. The difference is that, in the absence of a world government, international institutions have to do this with one hand tied behind their back.

A variety of institutions fulfill this function:

Customary law is an informal institution; it develops spontaneously rather than by deliberate construction and negotiation. Its great advantage is that it applies generally. Its great disadvantage is that it requires unanimous consent.

Treaties are different. They apply only to the states that consent to be bound by them. They therefore reflect a kind of selective volunteerism. Treaties can be stronger than custom, but at the cost, usually, of applying to a narrower set of countries.

Supply of global public goods can also be promoted by organizations created by treaties, the most important example being resolutions passed by the United Nations Security Council. Resolutions passed under Chapter VII of the United Nations Charter are legally binding on all states. This exception to the rule of consent applies to the limited sphere of peace and security, but is subject to veto by any of the five permanent members. Getting these great powers to agree on a matter of importance can be a colossal challenge. No wonder very few meaningful resolutions escape the veto (or are offered for a vote in the first place). Enforcement of Security Council resolutions is another obstacle.

Regulations adopted by the members of the World Health Organization are more democratic—and for that reason may be considered to be more legitimate. Under Article 22 of the WHO Constitution, regulations are binding on all WHO members except those that specifically reject them (or that insist upon making reservations). In contrast to a treaty, the presumption is therefore that all states are "in," rather than "out." This has real advantages. If there is a coordination aspect

Table I.1. Simple Taxonomy of Global Public Goods

	Single Best Effort	Weakest Link	Aggregate Effort	Mutual Restraint	Coordination
Supply depends on...	The single best (unilateral or collective) effort.	The weakest individual effort.	The total effort of all countries.	Countries not doing something.	Countries doing the same thing.
Examples	Asteroid defense, knowledge, peacekeeping, suppressing an infectious disease outbreak at its source, geoengineering.	Disease eradication, preventing emergence of resistance and new diseases, securing nuclear materials, vessel reflagging.	Climate change mitigation, ozone layer protection.	Non-use of nuclear weapons, non-proliferation, bans on nuclear testing and biotechnology research.	Standards for the measurement of time, for oil tankers, and for automobiles.
International cooperation needed?	Yes, in many cases, to determine what should be done, and which countries should pay.	Yes, to establish universal minimum standards.	Yes, to determine the individual actions needed to achieve an overall outcome.	Yes, to agree on what countries should not do.	Yes, to choose a common standard.
Financing and cost sharing needed?	Yes, when the good is provided collectively.	Yes, in some cases.	Yes, with industrialized countries helping developing countries.	No.	No.
Enforcement of agreement challenging?	Not normally.	Yes, except when provision requires only coordination.	Yes.	Yes.	No, though participation will need to pass a threshold.
International institutions for provision	Treaties in some cases; international organizations, such as the UN, in other cases.	Consensus (World Health Assembly) or Security Council resolutions, customary law.	Treaties.	Treaties, norms, customary law.	Non-binding resolutions; treaties in some cases.

to a regulation, this approach helps to ensure fuller participation. Psychology may also play a role. There is evidence that retirement savings are higher when individuals are enrolled automatically in a savings plan.[27] Perhaps participation in an international agreement is subject to a similar behavioral inertia.

Non-binding resolutions passed by the World Health Assembly and various standards organizations also help to supply global public goods. Lacking legal force, these recommendations may seem shallow. They need not be. When cooperation requires only coordination, non-binding resolutions do not have to be enforced.

Norms, like custom, can be universal; but unlike custom they lack legal force. In legalistic societies, norms can seem quaint. At the international level, they can move mountains: the taboo on the use of nuclear weapons, mentioned previously, is a norm of supreme importance. So is the emerging norm of the " 'responsibility to protect'...people suffering from avoidable catastrophe—mass murder and rape, ethnic cleansing by forcible expulsion and terror, and deliberate starvation and exposure to disease."[28]

All of these institutions, when they work, do so by making it in the *interests* of states to *change* their behavior. To do this, they weaken the incentives that impede the provision of global public goods, and strengthen the incentives that facilitate provision. Understanding how and when international institutions can do this is fundamental to our future success in supplying global public goods. It is the subject of the book's concluding chapter.

Overview

This book addresses many different global public goods, and it is important not only to understand each of these but to see the connections among them. The accompanying table (Table I.1) provides a taxonomy of different global public goods, a summary of the book's main conclusions. It shows where the trees stand in the forest: a guide for the chapters that follow.

CHAPTER ONE

Single best efforts: global public goods that can be supplied unilaterally or minilaterally

> Asteroid impact is a danger to all humanity. Preventive action should appropriately be based on international action. In addition to its direct usefulness, such action may also improve international cooperation.
>
> William Tedeschi and Edward Teller[1]

Some global public goods can be supplied by a single best effort. The knowledge of how to stimulate the human immune system to protect against polioviruses is an example. Another example is of more fundamental knowledge: a test of the Standard Model of particle physics, which describes matter's most basic elements and how they interact. In both cases, only a single effort is required. Nothing can be gained by making these discoveries a second time.

Moreover, both of these efforts are discrete. "Half" of a discovery is of no value (except as an input into making a full discovery).

As noted in the Introduction, the polio vaccines were discovered by the United States. They are used, however, around the world. The United States did not discover these vaccines to help other countries. The U.S. undertook this research to stop an epidemic raging within its own borders. But the discovery has benefited other countries. It is a global public good.

Tests of the Standard Model of particle physics are hugely expensive, and no country can justify paying the full cost unilaterally.

Instead, more than 30 countries are cooperating to construct the Large Hadron Collider for the purpose of carrying out such tests, "the greatest basic science endeavor in history."[2]

This chapter explains why the incentives to supply these global public goods are strong.

It also explains why this tendency can create a problem. If one or a small number of countries have an incentive to supply a global public good, then they may not seek the permission of other countries when deciding whether to supply it. If the global public good were universally to be welcomed, this would not matter. No country has complained about the discovery of the polio vaccines. If, however, provision introduces new risks, or harms some countries even as it benefits others, or affects the incentives to supply related global public goods, then governance becomes an issue. As we shall see, experiments using the Large Hadron Collider, though they promise huge advancements in particle physics, may also pose an existential threat. How should these benefits and risks be balanced? Who should decide?

Averting an asteroid strike

Consider again the scary scenario mentioned in the Introduction of a mega-asteroid threatening to collide with the Earth.

Imagine that it costs an amount of money represented by the letter C to prevent this collision. C might be thought of as the cost of deploying a spacecraft that could push the asteroid into a different orbit. (Later I shall explain that C might be about $1 billion.) Let the letter N denote the number of countries in the world today (N is just short of 200), and assign to each country a number reflecting the ordering of the benefits it derives from the global public good of averting a catastrophic asteroid collision. Country *1* thus derives the greatest absolute benefit, Country 2 the second greatest, and so on down to Country N, which benefits the least, in absolute terms, from provision of this global public good. Let the benefit to Country *1* from this global public good be represented by B_1, the benefit to Country 2 by B_2, and so on. These Bs, like C, are measured in money units (if C is measured in dollars, then the Bs must be measured in dollars). By the assumption about the ordering of the countries, B_1 exceeds B_2, B_2

exceeds B_3, and so on. Using $>$ to represent "greater than" we have $B_1 > B_2 > B_3 > \ldots > B_{N-1} > B_N$.

What determines the Bs—the "values" derived from a global public good? We need not answer that question precisely. It is enough to understand that every country would be willing to devote almost all of its resources towards supplying this public good. The real question here is more qualitative. What counts is the value of the Bs *in relation to C*.

Suppose that the world's "largest" country has resources sufficient to avert disaster (that is, $B_1 > C$). Then we can be pretty sure that the public good will be provided—by Country *1* acting unilaterally, if necessary.

But suppose that Country *1* were not powerful enough to supply this global public good on its own. Suppose that the resources of Country *2* were also needed (that is, suppose $B_1 + B_2 > C > B_1$). In this case, the two countries would need to coordinate their efforts. Coordination is not always assured; but in this case, with catastrophe staring both countries down, the incentives to coordinate would be overwhelming, and we can be sure that the two countries will pool their resources. Indeed, it is very likely that other countries will also be prepared to contribute.

Continuing with this logic, it can be expected that the public good of saving *Homo sapiens* from certain extinction will be supplied provided the aggregate resources of the entire world are sufficient to realize this goal (that is, provided $B_1 + B_2 + \ldots + B_N > C$). The incentives to save the Earth, literally, are so overwhelming, that the only real question becomes one of technical feasibility.

As mentioned in Chapter 1, this is a hypothetical scenario. To our knowledge, an asteroid of Earth-destroying size is not headed our way soon. However, the scenario provides a useful benchmark for thinking about global public goods. If we can supply this global public good, why can't we supply others?

Asteroid risks

Very few space objects have an orbit that passes near the Earth's own (the so-called "near Earth" objects) and are large enough to destroy life on Earth, should they smash into us. There are, however, lots of tiny objects that collide with the Earth's atmosphere all the time. These collisions are not to be feared. Indeed, they are a delight. When a meteor the size of a grain of sand scrapes the Earth's atmosphere, and the sun is hidden, the friction created produces a streak of brilliant light. We call it a falling star.

Meteorites as large as basketballs penetrate the Earth's atmosphere about once a month. Since the Earth's surface is mostly covered in water, most of these meteorites fall into the ocean and are unseen. Many also fall on land, but as most of the Earth's land surface is uninhabited by humans, these are also rarely observed. Occasionally a meteorite lands where it is noticed. On June 12, 2004, one smashed through the roof of Phil and Brenda Archer's home in Ellerslie, New Zealand.[3]

Larger asteroids collide with the Earth less frequently—because, as noted before, they are less common. The last significant collision occurred in 1908 when an asteroid perhaps 50 to 70 meters in diameter created an air burst over Siberia's Tunguska valley, devastating an area the size of Manhattan. No one was killed, because no one lived near the impact site, but the debris cloud thrown up by the blast made the skies over northern Europe glow so brightly "that it was possible to read a newspaper at midnight."[4] Collisions with asteroids of about this size are relatively frequent; the chance of another such encounter this century is about 10 percent.[5] However, and as the Tunguska event illustrates, these asteroids are unlikely to cause great damage. The chances that an asteroid this size would impact an urban area are extremely low.

Collision of the Earth with an asteroid ten kilometers or greater in diameter would cause the extinction of most life forms, including humans. (The extinction of the dinosaurs coincided with the Earth being hit by a ten kilometer wide asteroid 65 million years ago.) It is a terrifying prospect.[6] However, intermediate sized asteroids pose the greater risk.

As shown in Table 1.1, the most frequent events cause the least damage. They need not concern us greatly. The largest events constitute a truly existential threat, but they are so unlikely (over this century) as not to be worth diverting substantial resources away from other possible investments—at least not today. Collisions with asteroids of around one kilometer in diameter deserve more serious attention.[7]

Table 1.1. Risk of Collision by Near Earth Objects

Event	Diameter of impactor	Expected interval between impacts	Expected deaths per impact	Expected deaths per year
High atmosphere break-up	<50 meters	Frequent	Close to zero	Close to zero
Tunguska-like event	50–300 meters	250 years	5,000	20
Large regional events	300–1,500 meters	25,000 years	500,000	20
Low global threshold	>600 meters	70,000 years	1.5 billion	20,000
Nominal global threshold	>1.5 kilometers	500,000 years	1.5 billion	3,000
High global threshold	>5 kilometers	6 million years	1.5 billion	250
Extinction event	>10 kilometers	100 million years	>6 billion	50

Sources: Chapman and Morrison (1994, table 2, p. 36); Task Force on Potentially Hazardous Near Earth Objects (2000: 20).

Costs and benefits

How to respond to these *expected* threats? This is a much more diffi-cult challenge than preventing certain catastrophe—the hypothetical scenario considered previously. It would be irrational to devote *all* of the world's resources to preventing a *possible* future asteroid colli-sion. The expected benefit would be too small. Also, the money spent reducing this risk could be spent reducing other risks.

The framework developed in the previous section still applies, but now the decision will depend on the values of the *B*s. How can these values be estimated? Two approaches stand out. The first is to calculate the opportunity cost of saving a "statistical life"—that is, of reducing the number of deaths per year in a large population by another means, such as gun control, road safety, or medical research. The second is to infer the value of reducing the probability of prema-ture death from the choices people make in their own lives, such as the decision to accept a job that is more dangerous but pays better. This is sometimes called the value of a statistical life.

Estimates exist for both of these measures. The value of the oppor-tunity cost of a statistical life saved, reflecting the cost-effectiveness of government regulation, varies dramatically. In the United States, for example, this value ranges from $100,000 to $100 billion.[8] What this range implies is a great inconsistency in regulation. It is not really of much help to us here.

Estimates of the value of a statistical life saved also vary, but by much less. Estimates for individuals in rich countries range from about $4–$9 million.[9] We know less about the values that apply in developing countries, but the scant evidence that exists says that these values are smaller. Estimates for Taiwan and South Korea are below $1 million.[10] Estimates of the value of reducing mortality associated with air pollution in Santiago, Chile are around $500,000 per life saved.[11]

Why should the value of a statistical life saved be smaller for a person living in a developing country than for her identical twin living in a rich country? The reason is not that persons living in developing countries are worth any less as human beings. It is not even because they are poorer (the value of a statistical life saved is not bounded by income, even lifetime income); recall that these estimates reflect the choices that people make in their daily lives. The values are smaller (on average) in developing countries because persons living in these countries make different choices; and they make different choices (at least partly) because they face different constraints. We may regret that these constraints exist; we may feel them to be unjust. But if we do, then our attention should focus on relieving these constraints, on promoting development and equity, not on using estimates of the value of a statistical life that conform to the world as we wish it to be. Doing that will not help the people who must live in the world as it actually is.

So, which country has the largest B? Which country is Country 1? The United States is an obvious candidate. It has a high income per capita, and therefore a high value of a statistical life. It also has a large population.

But is it in the interests of the U.S. to supply global asteroid defense on its own, in the near future, given that the probability of a collision over, say, the next century, is substantially less than one?

The answer depends on the value of C in relation to B_1. Consider first the value of C. As noted before, there are a number of possible ways to avert an asteroid strike. One of these is to use a "space tug" to push the asteroid off of its collision path. By one calculation, this would cost about $1 billion.[12] Should we take this estimate seriously? NASA's Deep Impact mission, which collided a projectile weighing

362 kilograms (798 pounds) into comet 9P/Temple 1 on July 4, 2005, cost about a third as much. Though the force of the Deep Impact collision was too weak to change the comet's orbital path appreciably, that was not its purpose. A different mission, intended to defect an asteroid, seems feasible. It would cost more than Deep Impact, but probably not many times more. It might cost no more than $1 billion.

What is the benefit to the United States of being prepared to avert a possible future collision? Assume that every person on Earth has an equal probability of dying from an impact (an asteroid could strike anywhere). Assume as well that having the capability to avert a collision can be expected to save 1,000 lives per year—as Table 1.1 shows, a conservative estimate.[13] The population of the U.S. is about 5 percent of the world total. So the U.S. might expect to save around 50 persons per year (I am ignoring population growth). Letting b_1 denote the benefit of saving just one American, the expected annual benefit of asteroid defense to the U.S. would be about $50 \times b_1$.

This value is not the same as B_1. The latter is calculated as a present value; it represents the annual benefit, appropriately discounted, and summed over all the years during which asteroid defense is to be provided. Let us say that the capacity to defend the Earth from a collision lasts in perpetuity. Then we need to discount this infinite series of annual benefits to arrive at a single, present value estimate.[14] If we discount this stream of savings at three percent, the value of B_1 will be $50 \times b_1/0.03 = 1,667 \times b_1$. It would thus be in the interests of the United States to finance this program all on its own provided $1,667 \times b_1 > \$1$ billion or $b_1 > \$600,000$. As mentioned previously, the value of a statistical life in the U.S. is more than ten times greater than this. The U.S., it thus seems, has an incentive to supply this global public good all by itself if necessary.

Complementary global public goods

So, is the United States providing this global public good? It has not done so yet. It has, however, invested in related advancements (such as advanced power and propulsion) that will contribute to the future development of this global public good.

Why has the U.S. not done more? One reason is that a technology capable of preventing a near Earth object impact is only of value if we can identify and track these objects. Identification and deflection are near perfect complements; as regards the largest objects, both capabilities are needed; one without the other is of little use. Indeed, this is why no country is looking today for large objects that may strike the Earth soon. If such an object were discovered, nothing could be done to avert such a catastrophe.[15]

Identification is thus the first priority, and the United States *has* taken the lead in supplying *this* global public good. Its Spaceguard Survey aims to detect 90 percent of the near Earth objects one kilometer or greater in diameter by 2008.[16] (The survey must exclude comets that have orbital periods in excess of 200 years. Most of these are completely unknown to science.)

What about smaller near Earth objects? Identifying and tracking these could be of value even if a collision could not be prevented. Provided the point of impact could be identified, people likely to be affected could be moved to safety. Is the benefit of identifying Tunguska-sized and larger objects worth the cost? A study by NASA concluded that, "the benefits associated with eliminating these risks justify substantial investment in [potentially hazardous objects] search systems."[17] Indeed, the NASA study calculated that the investment would pay for itself, even if only the benefits to the U.S. were counted (the global benefits would, of course, be much larger), within the first year of operation.

To sum up, the incentives for Country *1*—the United States—to supply the global public good of near Earth objects identification and collision-prevention are strong. No wonder the Task Force on Potentially Hazardous Near Earth Objects, established by the United Kingdom, found that the United States was "doing more about Near Earth Objects than the rest of the world put together."[18]

Unilateralism reconsidered

That the United States has an incentive to supply these global public goods is reassuring. It means that free riding should not prevent them from being provided.

It does not mean that the United States will be the only country that contributes. Indeed, other countries have already done so. In late 2005, Japan landed space probe Hayabusa (Falcon) on a potato-shaped asteroid named Itokawa, with the intention of collecting samples and returning these to Earth for study. (Unfortunately, the collector malfunctioned, and Haybusa's thrusters sprang a leak. The spacecraft is now gliding back to Earth; with luck, it will land in Australia in 2010.) Other efforts are being planned. The European Space Agency (today, with 17 member states) is expected to approve an ambitious mission named Don Quijote. Like NASA's Deep Impact mission, Don Quijote will smash a projectile into an asteroid. Don Quijote will not be powerful enough to knock an asteroid off of a collision course with the Earth, but it will be more powerful than Deep Impact. It is intended to demonstrate the feasibility of asteroid deflection: a first step to preparing for a possible future mitigation mission.

Why would Japan and Europe contribute to supplying this global public good when the United States has such a strong incentive to do so unilaterally? Why do these countries not free ride?

One reason is that the economics of asteroid deflection are so attractive that these other countries (certainly Japan and the European Union as a whole) also have an incentive to supply this global public good unilaterally. When a multiple of states have an incentive to supply a global public good, we can be pretty sure that the good will be supplied. What we can't be sure of is *which* country (or countries) will supply it.

Other countries may also feel that they cannot count on the United States to make the best choices for them. Indeed, the U.S. may not even be making the best choice for itself. Richard Posner believes that the United States has miscalculated the threat. "The problem [of under provision by the United States]," he says, "is not free riding; it is that asteroids are not yet perceived [by the U.S.] to be a significant enemy."[19]

Technical errors are also possible. In 1999, NASA's Mars Climate Orbiter was literally lost in space because a NASA contractor failed to convert English units to metric. Would the rest of the world really want to rely on American know-how exclusively?

Of course, other countries may also want to contribute for positive reasons: they may want to learn and explore; they may want to play their part in contributing to the global public good.

Governance

The decision to *use* a deflection device is another concern. As Russell Schweickart, a former NASA astronaut, has observed, intervention to prevent an asteroid strike introduces *new* risks.[20]

Suppose that a Tunguska-sized asteroid were expected to hit San Francisco. An attempt to deflect the object may succeed in avoiding a collision entirely. However, the effort might also fail; it might fail entirely or, perhaps even worse, it might cause the asteroid to hit *another* location, such as Indonesia. Given this risk, should the United States be permitted to make the decision to launch unilaterally? Suppose instead that Accra were the likely point of impact, but that an attempt to save this city would increase the risk that the asteroid may fall over the Atlantic Ocean, triggering an impact tsunami that might damage the eastern United States. Should the United States be allowed to make *that* decision unilaterally?

More horrific uses of a deflection technology, though very unlikely, can be imagined. Writing in 1994 with Steven Ostro, Carl Sagan, the famed astronomer, argued that possession of asteroid deflection technology was a doubled-edged sword. "If we can perturb an asteroid out of impact trajectory," the two scientists wrote, "it follows that we can also transform one on a benign trajectory into an Earth-impactor."[21] Specifically, Sagan and Ostro imagined a doomsday scenario in which an asteroid on an out-of-impact trajectory was deliberately "attacked" by nuclear-loaded missiles, calculated to send the asteroid crashing into Earth. "There is no other way known," they added grimly, "in which a few nuclear weapons could by themselves threaten the global civilization."

A much more plausible scenario is that other countries, perhaps motivated by distrust, might develop an asteroid deflection capability of their own.

Global positioning

Though the analogy is imperfect, similar concerns inspired the development of a rival technology to the Global Positioning System.

The GPS, as it is more commonly known, consists of a constellation of satellites, which enables users with a passive receiver to calculate their precise location in three dimensions (longitude, latitude, and altitude). The GPS was developed for the United States military, which uses it for troop logistics and bomb guidance. However, GPS is also used for civilian purposes, especially navigation and tracking. In the future, more uses are anticipated, such as for advanced air traffic control and "smart" highways. Satellite navigation is quickly becoming an essential component of the global infrastructure.

The United States government supplies GPS signals for free (a superior military system is encrypted), but GPS is *not* a global public good. While access is currently unrestricted, there is no guarantee that it will remain so. As an article in *Wired* magazine put it, "Currently, the U.S. decides what nations use the military GPS signals; the U.S. determines whether civilian signals should be jammed if unfriendly powers try to use them for threatening purposes; and the U.S. dominates the industry that makes the related equipment."[22] To avoid, as one French official put it, remaining "under the yoke of an American monopoly," the European Union has decided to develop its own satellite navigation system.[23] The European system, called Galileo, is due to become operational by around 2008–2010. It will be superior to GPS, meeting the more technical demands of air traffic management. But it will also be compatible with GPS, making the combined system more accurate and robust both to unintentional failure and jamming: a benefit to people everywhere.

A second asteroid defense system may also offer global benefits—not least for reasons of redundancy. Like GPS and Galileo, however, use of rival deflection technologies would need to be coordinated. (To take an obvious example, two deflection technologies deployed simultaneously, might interfere with one each other, causing both systems to fail.) As more countries develop an asteroid deflection capability, the need for coordination will increase.

Dangerous science

Another collision—this one involving very tiny particles—could be as damaging as an asteroid strike. Like the scenario imagined by Carl Sagan, a collision like this would also be unnatural. The difference is that the collision of particles is currently being planned. Indeed, the first of its kind is scheduled to take place sometime in 2007.

The collision will be performed by the world's biggest machine, the Large Hadron Collider—a ring 27 kilometers in circumference and 100 meters below ground on the French–Swiss border. The experiment will smash two particle beams at speeds close to the speed of light. The intention is to create not only high energy but high luminosity—a property needed to search for a particle known as the Higgs boson. If the experiment finds the Higgs boson, it will complete the so-called Standard Model of particle physics; it will explain how particles acquire mass. If it fails to find the Higgs boson, *that* discovery will in turn open up new areas of research. Either way, new knowledge will be created by the experiment—another global public good.

There is, unfortunately, a very small chance that the luminosity needed to find the Higgs boson could trigger a global catastrophe. According to Martin Rees, there is a theoretical possibility that the experiment could create a tiny object called a strangelet—an object that, by a process of contagion, might possibly "transform the entire planet Earth into an inert hyperdense sphere about one hundred metres across."[24] Another possibility is that the particle smashes might create a growing black hole—a phenomenon that might destroy not just the Earth but the entire universe.

Experiments using the Large Hadron Collider thus involve a trade-off. They hold the promise of enriching the world with new knowledge. They also involve a very small chance of planetary destruction. How small? That is impossible to say. A report written for the backers of the Large Hadron Collider concludes that there is "no basis for any conceivable threat."[25] But the likelihood of a strangelet being created is impossible to calculate with certainty, since the experiment has never taken place before. Existing theories are reassuring, but they have not been tested. And do we really want to test them? Are we sure that the global public good of new knowledge outweighs the global public bad of the risk of annihilation?

More importantly, who should decide whether the experiments should go ahead? So far, the decision has been left to the member states of CERN (officially, the European Organization for Nuclear Research), the organization that is building and that will run the Large Hadron Collider. But should other countries have been consulted? Should other countries have a veto?

Planned extinction

It may seem idealistic to suggest that a decision like this should be the subject of wider discussion, but a precedent has recently been established.

The successful eradication of smallpox, mentioned briefly in the introduction and discussed in more detail in the next chapter, offered a dividend to the whole world. It meant that there was no longer a need for people to be vaccinated. Many countries stopped routine vaccination even before eradication was certified in 1979. France was the last country to do so. It stopped vaccinating in 1984.

Unfortunately, reaping this dividend creates a new risk. If smallpox were somehow reintroduced today, the world would be more vulnerable than ever to an epidemic.

On August 11, 1978, Jane Parker, a photographer working at the Birmingham Medical School, developed a fever, a headache, and muscular pains. Days later she developed a rash, and shortly after that she was diagnosed with smallpox. Three days, Jane Parker was dead. An inquiry discovered that Mrs. Parker worked above a smallpox research laboratory. She probably became infected by airborne virus particles transported via a faulty duct.[26]

In Britain, routine vaccination had been discontinued many years before this incident, and Mrs. Parker, like most of the British population, had lost her immunity to the virus. Realizing the potential for an epidemic, the authorities traced the people with whom Mrs. Parker had been in contact, vaccinated them, and placed them under quarantine. Mrs. Parker's mother also contracted the disease, probably as a result of caring for her daughter, but she later recovered. To this day, she remains the last person in the world to have been infected with smallpox.

An inquiry into the incident found that, under the direction of Professor Henry Bedson, the Birmingham laboratory had failed to follow basic safety precautions. Shamed by his role in this tragedy, Professor Bedson committed suicide.[27]

The Birmingham incident alarmed the directors of other laboratories still retaining the virus. If an accident could occur in Birmingham, it could occur anywhere. To reduce the chance of a viral escape, these other laboratories started destroying or transferring their stocks. In the year Jane Parker died, 13 laboratories were known to keep smallpox in their freezers, but by the following year only seven did so and by 1983 smallpox virus was kept by just two World Health Organization (WHO) collaborating centers, one in Atlanta and the other in Moscow. Were these the *only* remaining stocks left? Unfortunately, no one could be sure. Some people suspected that covert stocks might have been retained by other states. That concern persists today.

What to do with the last two known stockpiles? In 1986 and again in 1990, the WHO's Committee on Orthopoxvirus Infections recommended that the stocks held in Atlanta and Moscow be destroyed. By 1990 this was also the official position of the United States government.

Destruction would eliminate the risk of an accident like the one that occurred in Birmingham. If preserved, however, the remaining stocks could be used to develop improved diagnostic tools, antiviral drugs, and a novel vaccine—innovations that would be useful should covert stocks exist and should smallpox virus be released deliberately some day.[28] As in so many other areas, the decision to destroy the remaining stores of smallpox entailed a risk-risk tradeoff.

Again the question: Who should decide? The states that possess the virus obviously have the upper hand, but being WHO collaborating centers, the labs in Atlanta and Moscow are obligated to serve the global interest. Moreover, the U.S. possesses samples that used to be held by other countries. If these states wanted their old stocks destroyed, did the U.S. have the right to retain them?

In 1998, the WHO polled its 190 members. Did they want the last known stocks to be retained or destroyed? The WHO's survey revealed a split. Russia wanted to hold onto its samples; Britain, France, Italy, and the United States were undecided; every other country (74 other countries responded) favored destruction.

In 1999, President Clinton announced that the U.S. had changed its mind. It now wanted to retain its stockpile. Why did the U.S. position change? The reason was the growing threat of terrorism.[29] If terrorists could get access to smallpox virus, they might try to release it within the United States.

When the World Health Assembly met shortly after this, a compromise was worked out. A resolution was proposed that reaffirmed the goal of *eventual* destruction but permitted Russia and the U.S. to retain their stocks for research purposes for a period of three years. The resolution passed by acclamation.

The reprieve was subsequently extended, and today smallpox virus is still kept at the two WHO centers. Inspectors have satisfied the WHO's Advisory Committee on Variola Virus Research that the stocks are secure, and the Committee has verified that the research undertaken at both labs has progressed. They have also confirmed, however, that the job is not yet finished. Their judgment is that there is still reason to retain smallpox for research purposes.

Though this process has longer to run, experience to date demonstrates that all the world's countries can take part in a decision having serious global consequences, even though the power relations among them are vastly unequal. That the process has favored consensus is especially fortunate. Since every country will be affected by whatever is decided, it is as well that each should agree with the decision.

An asteroid treaty?

A consensus is also to be desired in efforts to address the threat posed by near Earth objects. How to proceed?

The Task Force on Potentially Hazardous Near-Earth Objects proposed establishing an Intergovernmental Panel on Threats from Space—a technical body that could report to every country on the science, the impacts, and the mitigation possibilities, much as the Intergovernmental Panel on Climate Change has done for another global threat. This is a sensible first step. Before countries can cooperate in an area like this, they must first have a common understanding of the challenge.

But what should be done after the panel has reported? Edward Teller, the inventor of the hydrogen bomb, has proposed (with coauthor William Tedeschi) establishing a Special Branch of the United Nations, "in control of detection research, experimentation, and defence."[30] Russell Schweickart, by contrast, concedes that the responsibility to act will, for reasons of "practical necessity," remain with a "national entity," a country with the wherewithal to act. He proposes that any such country's freedom to act be subject to "safeguards specified by a treaty regime." In particular, he would establish a "monitoring body to ensure compliance with the safeguard agreements," a body with "full review and veto power over any commands sent to the deflecting spacecraft by the operating agency."[31] Schweickart's proposal is a little like the arrangement that has developed to supervise the use of the world's remaining known stocks of smallpox. The difference—and it is a big one—is the veto.

Would a country possessing (or capable of possessing) the means to move an asteroid agree to be bound in this way? Would it agree to cede the veto? There might be advantages to it doing so. Other countries might agree to help finance asteroid defense (just as other states have cooperated to help pay for the Large Hadron Collider and the International Space Station), provided decision-making were shared as a *quid pro quo*. And should rival systems be developed, each state possessing such a capability might agree to restrain its use of the technology, provided that all others consented to a reciprocal obligation. However, should disaster appear likely and imminent, the incentive for a country to cede the right to defend itself would disappear in an instant; and, knowing this, it seems unlikely that countries would give up this right in advance.[32]

The details of a future near-Earth objects treaty are difficult to envision at this point, but there is one thing of which we can be sure: the treaty will not be undermined by free rider behavior.[33] Indeed, if there is a challenge for international cooperation here, it is probably in getting countries to show restraint and consideration in using a technology that would have profound implications—hopefully, but perhaps not inevitably, positive—for others.

Deliberate climate modification

Climate change does not pose the same existential threat as an imminent collision with a very large near Earth object, but as discussed in Chapter 3, there is a risk that climate change could be abrupt. It could even be catastrophic, though as noted in the Introduction, catastrophic climate change (associated, say, with sea level rise of several meters) would likely take a very long time to unfold, and so would be very different from an asteroid collision.

Suppose that sensors in the ocean detected impending change. Suppose, for example, that the meridional overturning circulation—the ocean system that transports heat from the tropics to the poles—showed signs of sudden collapse. What could we do then?

At that point, reducing emissions of greenhouse gases, or removing them from the atmosphere, would take too long to have a noticeable effect. The climate responds to such changes with a decades-long lag (the process is similar to the lag that causes ocean temperatures to peak each summer long after the solar maximum). Abrupt changes, once begun, would thus continue. Reducing atmospheric concentrations of greenhouse gases may not even help much in the long run, should abrupt climate change prove irreversible. Of course, we could adapt to the change in climate (a policy equivalent to moving people away from the point of impact with a small asteroid), but adaptation is more effective when climate change is gradual than when it is abrupt. Could we do more?

If we were prepared, there is one response that might help. This is to modify the climate deliberately, an intervention known as "geoengineering." For example, aerosols might be blasted into the stratosphere to scatter solar radiation back into space, counteracting the effect of rising atmospheric concentrations on temperature.[34]

The idea of engineering the climate sounds bizarre, but we are already doing this on a modest scale, unwittingly. Aerosols released by burning coal have a similar effect.[35] The difference is that these releases are unintentional and inefficient (for purposes of deliberate climate modification, it would be better to place the aerosols in the stratosphere, and to engineer the particles). Geoengineering of a kind also occurs naturally. The eruption of Mount Pinatubo in the Philippines in 1991 injected huge quantities of sulfur dioxide into the stratosphere, lowering the Earth's surface temperature by about 0.5°C the year following the eruption.[36] An analogy might also help: to counteract the effects of acid rain, ground limestone is routinely added to Sweden's pH-sensitive lakes and soils. Though only reductions in acidic emissions can prevent acid rain, liming preserves pH balance; it prevents acid rain damage, against a background of continued acid deposition. Geoengineering would have a similar effect. It would not address the underlying cause of climate change, but if it worked as intended it would prevent temperatures from rising against a background of elevated atmospheric concentrations of greenhouse gases.

Geoengineering has a number of attractions, in addition to being able to prevent abrupt climate change.

First, it may be cheap. By one estimate, scattering back into space the sunlight needed to offset the warming effect of rising greenhouse gas concentrations by the year 2100 would cost just $1 billion per year.[37] This may be a low estimate; another study suggests a cost of $25–50 billion.[38] Even this higher figure, however, is a tiny fraction of the cost of stabilizing greenhouse gas concentrations at levels that could not be relied upon to prevent abrupt climate change.[39] Helping the economics even more, geoengineering affects temperature quickly; reductions in atmospheric concentrations take a lot longer to lower temperature. Investments in geoengineering will thus pay back much sooner than investments in reducing emissions.[40]

Second, geoengineering essentially constitutes a large project, a single best effort.[41] Like asteroid defense, some country or group of countries has to pay for geoengineering, but free riding is much less likely to undercut financing of a project like this than reductions in atmospheric concentrations. Climate change might cost the United States alone about $82 billion in present value terms.[42] To avoid this loss by paying out just $1 billion per year (if the low estimate were correct) would be in the self-interests of the U.S., even if no other country contributed to the effort.[43] If the costs of geoengineering were higher, use by one country might need to wait until substantial climate damages appear more imminent. Alternatively, a coalition of countries may need to develop a geoengineering scheme.

Third, geoengineering may also offer environmental benefits, the main one being the blocking of harmful UV radiation. Indeed, Edward Teller and colleagues calculate that this health-related benefit for the U.S. alone would exceed the total cost of geoengineering by more than an order of magnitude.[44] If correct, the economics are even more favorable than suggested above. Deliberate climate modification would also allow carbon dioxide concentrations to remain elevated—an aid to agriculture.

Some effects of geoengineering will be mixed. Like volcanic eruptions, geoengineering would change the color of the sky. Volcanic particles whiten the sky by day (an environmental loss, presumably, though one that is already being caused by atmospheric pollution), but make sunsets and sunrises more vibrant.[45]

This may or may not matter but there are more worrying consequences to consider.

First, geoengineering constitutes a large-scale experiment (not unlike the experiment it would be meant to correct, that of rising concentrations of greenhouse gases).[46] Stratospheric aerosols could destroy ozone, as did the aerosols released by Mount Pinatubo, though the damage to the ozone layer could be modest.[47] According to Paul Crutzen, a co-recipient of the 1995 Nobel Prize in chemistry for research on the ozone layer, the geoengineering needed to compensate for a doubling in carbon dioxide concentrations "would lead to larger ozone loss but not as large as after Mount Pinatubo"—and this against a background of expected rising ozone levels overall (see Chapter 3, this volume).[48] As well, the risks from geoengineering would be bounded; aerosols pumped into the stratosphere would survive only a few years, much less than greenhouse gases (some of which can persist for more than a millennia). If we didn't like the effects of geoengineering, we could turn the macro-scale experiment off.

Second, geoengineering may not alter the climate uniformly. Even if the Earth's average temperature were stabilized, the spatial distribution of temperature might be altered (greenhouse gases and sunlight scattering have different radiative forcings). Research indicates that this risk is likely to be small (mainly because the distribution of atmospheric temperature is determined by more fundamental forces), but it remains non-zero.[49]

Third, geoengineering would do nothing to address the related problem of ocean acidification. The oceans absorb a portion of the carbon dioxide pumped into the atmosphere. This decreases the pH level of the oceans and is likely to change the process of calcification, endangering animals such as corals (which may be bleached by rising ocean temperatures long before geoengineering is ever tried) and clams. Limestone could be added to the oceans, just as we have added limestone to acid-sensitive lakes, but liming is likely to be feasible only for certain sensitive areas.[50] It is not a comprehensive answer to the problem.

In short, then, the possibility of geoengineering confronts us with a tradeoff.

Governing the atmosphere

Ironically, the attribute that makes geoengineering attractive also makes it worrying. If it's so economic to use, a large country can do it on its own. For that same reason, more than one country can do it.

Who is to decide whether geoengineering should be deployed? Should a country be allowed to do so unilaterally? Could it be prevented from doing so? Some countries are expected to benefit from climate change, at least gradual climate change into the medium term.[51] Should these countries be allowed to use geoengineering to *absorb*, rather than to scatter, radiation (or to increase their emissions of greenhouse gases)? Would these countries need to be compensated for damages resulting from a geoengineering intervention to mitigate climate change? What about countries that have different attitudes towards risk, or that object to the idea of deliberately altering the climate, however instrumentally helpful that intervention might prove to be. Should their views be heeded? The situation is akin to the world agreeing on an arrangement for asteroid defense.[52]

There is, however, one important difference. Humans are causing the climate to change, and we are not causing asteroids to smash into us. Though actions to reduce atmospheric concentrations of greenhouse gases will not avert abrupt climate change after the signs of sudden change have emerged, if undertaken in advance they could prevent abrupt climate change from occurring in the first place. Geoengineering is thus a *substitute* for reductions in atmospheric concentrations of greenhouse gases. Any effort to make geoengineering appear more (less) attractive will make reducing emissions appear less (more) attractive. It is for this reason that some people would prefer that the possibility of geoengineering not even be discussed publicly.[53]

The risks associated with geoengineering mean that this incentive problem needs to be taken seriously. However, as I mentioned in the Introduction, reducing concentrations also entails risks. More importantly, and as I shall explain in Chapter 3, the prospects of climate change being prevented or even dramatically slowed through reductions in atmospheric concentrations appear dim, whatever the prospects for geoengineering. The failure to contemplate geoengineering thus exposes the world to yet another risk—the risk that, should mitigation fail and climate change prove to be abrupt, we will either not have the technology ready to deploy in the time required or that we will be forced to deploy it without having previously studied its consequences on small scales.

More broadly, since geoengineering should be determined jointly with other climate change policies (including investments in technologies for early detection of abrupt change, another global public good, and a complement to geoengineering) more is needed than a treaty that governs only its study, use, and financing.[54] A geoengineering treaty needs to be part of a coordinated response to the threat of global climate change: a protocol, one of many probably, under a comprehensive umbrella convention on global climate change.[55]

Big science

Radical breakthroughs in technology will be needed if atmospheric concentrations of greenhouse gases are to be stabilized without reducing economic growth substantially. Agreements promoting R&D in this area, yielding the global public good of knowledge, will therefore also be needed as part of a coordinated response.[56] They should form part of a multitrack climate treaty system.

An example of the kind of R&D collaboration needed is the nuclear fusion project (the ITER, or International Thermonuclear Experimental Reactor), supported by the European Union, China, India, Japan, South Korea, Russia, and the United States. A climate R&D agreement (or set of agreements), however, would have to be even more ambitious than this single project.[57] It would have to address more forms of energy, and advance the new technologies to a stage where they could be developed commercially.

This bigger effort will be expensive. It will also be difficult to finance. This is because the willingness to finance R&D derives from the expected benefits to individual countries of the knowledge gained from the R&D. For nuclear fusion, the benefits are substantial, even ignoring the implications for climate change mitigation. We should not be surprised that big science projects like the ITER are fully financed.[58] The knowledge of how to mitigate climate change is different. Its value to any country depends on the prospects of the technologies created from this knowledge being diffused worldwide.[59] That is, the benefits of this R&D will depend on the climate change damages these technologies are capable of avoiding. Currently, the prospects for diffusing climate-friendly technologies appear poor. They are discussed in later chapters.

In other areas, the prospects for big science appear much brighter. Probably the next major high-energy physics facility will be an electron-positron linear collider. This will cost as much as the Large Hadron Collider, but the new collider will need to be operated concurrently with this project, pushing up the total cost. Beyond this, even bigger projects are being contemplated. As noted by an international consultative body on high-energy physics,

it is generally accepted that the next generation of facilities that will be needed to prove physics "beyond the Standard Model" will require a changed paradigm, from national or regional facilities exploited internationally, to inherently global projects that will be fundamentally different in their basic organizational concepts.[60]

As science projects grow bigger and bigger, more and more countries will have to cooperate in their planning, construction, and operation—all for the simple reason that more financing will be needed, and the costs can only be justified when spread over a larger number of countries. There is a bonus to increasing scale. The problems of governance noted earlier in this chapter will recede as the level of participation needed for project financing increases.

Small science

I opened this chapter by referring to a great discovery from the past: the knowledge of how to protect people from polio. The world's two polio vaccines were developed in the United States. So were many other scientific advances. The United States is a leader in science—it is, after all, Country *1*.

The U.S. is not, however, the only country to contribute to science. Smaller states have always done so. Just think of Copernicus's contributions to astronomy (Poland), Linnaeus's invention of taxonomy (Sweden), and Barnard's famous heart transplant (South Africa). Supplying the global public good of knowledge is justified from the perspective of self-interest alone so long as a country's individual benefit exceeds the cost of supply. Even small countries can do small science.

Table 1.2 shows the contributions made by individual countries to the global public good of scientific knowledge as measured by research success—the number of published scientific research papers and their citations. (The table includes the 31 countries accounting for more than 98 percent of the world's most highly cited papers.) As expected, the table shows that the bigger and richer countries tend to lead, though many smaller countries make substantial contributions.[61]

The more striking observation, however, is that contributions to the global public good of basic scientific knowledge are highly concentrated. Most countries contribute very little. The 162 countries not listed in the table each contribute less than tiny Luxembourg. Together, they contribute less than 2 percent of the world total—less, that is, than Spain.

This would not matter if the unlisted countries were simply free riders. The reason it matters is that the research that would be of special benefit to the regions unrepresented or underrepresented in the table is not being done by any country.

Table 1.2. States Responsible for Top 1% of Highly Cited Publications, 1997–2001

Country	Share of Publications	Share of Citations	Share of Most Cited Publications
	Percent World		Percent Group
United States	34.86	49.43	62.76
EU15 (net total)	37.12	39.30	37.30
United Kingdom	9.43	11.39	12.78
Germany	8.76	10.02	10.40
Japan	9.28	8.44	6.90
France	6.39	6.89	6.85
Canada	4.58	5.30	5.81
Italy	4.05	4.39	4.31
Switzerland	1.84	2.95	4.12
Netherlands	2.55	3.46	3.80
Australia	2.84	2.84	2.78
Sweden	2.01	2.50	2.46
Spain	2.85	2.55	2.08
Belgium	1.32	1.55	1.69
Denmark	1.02	1.34	1.51
Israel	1.27	1.33	1.50
Russia	3.40	1.43	1.33
Finland	0.96	1.14	1.10
Austria	0.93	1.00	1.01
China	3.18	1.56	0.99
South Korea	1.53	0.88	0.78
Poland	1.18	0.71	0.61
India	2.13	0.86	0.54
Brazil	1.21	0.71	0.50
Taiwan	1.25	0.69	0.40
Ireland	0.35	0.35	0.36
Greece	0.62	0.41	0.30
Singapore	0.42	0.25	0.26
Portugal	0.37	0.29	0.25
South Africa	0.50	0.31	0.21
Iran	0.13	0.06	0.04
Luxembourg	0.01	0.01	0.01

Source: King (2004, table 1). Adapted by permission from Macmillian Publishers Ltd: *Nature* (vol. 430: 312), copyright 2004.
Note: European Union members before the 2004 accession are in italics. Estimates based on the location of authors' institution. Papers with authors from two or more states are counted more than once. Estimates for the EU15 are net (for example, a paper by a Greek and Italian author would count only once). The second and third columns are shares of the world total. They add to more than 100 because of papers having multiple authors from multiple locations. The shares given in the final column are with respect to the countries listed only, not the world total. Note, however, that the countries listed comprise more than 98 percent of the world total in terms of the top one percent most cited publications.

Neglected science

The polio epidemic peaked in the United States in 1952, when 57,000 cases were recorded, 21,000 people suffered permanent paralysis, and about 3,000 people died.[62] The scale of the epidemic stimulated a race to develop a vaccine, and it took only a short time before Jonas Salk conducted the first wide scale test. Salk's discovery was a major achievement. In David Oshinksy's words, it was "America's gift to the world."[63] It was a global public good.

Malaria is of little consequence to the United States. In 2004, there were 1,324 cases of malaria in the U.S., and only four deaths. Almost all of these people were infected while traveling abroad, and contracted the disease because they had failed to take antimalarial chemoprophylaxis as recommended.[64] In contrast to polio in the 1950s, the U.S. has relatively little incentive to develop a vaccine for malaria today.

Globally, however, there are 350–500 million cases of malaria each year, and more than a million deaths.[65] If malaria were as big a problem for the United States today as polio was in the 1950s, the U.S. would be investing much more money in malaria vaccine R&D. Similarly, if the countries most burdened by malaria responded in the same way as the United States did to polio, *they* would be investing much more in malaria R&D. Sadly—no, tragically—no country is responding in this way. Diseases like malaria that primarily affect poor countries are largely being neglected by science.[66] I shall explain why in Chapter 7.

Conclusions

Not all global public goods are vulnerable to free riding. The incentives to supply global public goods requiring single best efforts are sometimes so strong that countries will supply them unilaterally. Even when countries must cooperate to supply global public goods requiring single best efforts, free riding is unlikely to block provision.

Ironically, this only creates a different problem: a challenge for governance. When one or a few states have an incentive to supply a global public good, these providers cannot be counted on to take into account the interests of other countries. If global public goods were unambiguously to be desired, this would not matter. But the provision of some global public goods may introduce new risks, or harm some countries even while benefiting the providers, or reduce the provision of other global public goods that may be of even greater benefit.

There do not exist general rules for addressing these questions of governance.[67] At best, there exist only *ad hoc* arrangements. In some cases, these arrangements are inadequate. In other cases, they are worrying. For example, there is no global oversight of particle collider experiments.

Though some single best effort global public goods are supplied by smaller and poorer states, as a rule the supply of these global public goods tends to be dominated by larger, more developed countries—the middle and great powers. When these countries supply global public goods, the smaller and weaker states benefit. When they don't, however, and when the smaller and weaker states fail to compensate for this underinvestment, the small and weak states lose out.

There are other situations in which what the small and weak states do affects the larger and stronger states, and not only the other way around. I turn to these situations in the next chapter.

CHAPTER TWO

Weakest links: global public goods that depend on the states that contribute the least

From the time the Intensified Programme began, smallpox eradication staff had speculated as to where the last case might occur—no one had expected that it would be Somalia.

F. Fenner, Henderson, D. A., Arita, I., Jezek, Z., and Ladnyi, I. D.[1]

Some global public goods can only be supplied if every country lends a hand. Should even one country not help, the entire effort may fail. These are weakest link global public goods.

Why might a country not help? There are two reasons:

Some countries may be incapable of helping. These are usually the failed states. If every other country eliminated a disease, the "last" country would (almost) surely want to do so because it could then claim a huge reward: a future free of both infection and the need to vaccinate. Failed states, however, lack the wherewithal to provide even basic services. They may be unable to contribute to the supply of this global public good, however much they would like to do so.

In some cases, countries may lack incentives to help. All countries may gain *collectively* by keeping their nuclear materials out of the hands of terrorists, or by reducing the chance that a new strain of pandemic influenza will emerge. Each country, however, may lose *individually* by contributing to such an effort, since each country can realize just a fraction of the total benefits of providing these global public goods. Provision may thus require some combination of sticks and carrots.

This chapter explains the nature of these challenges, and how the world is seeking to address them.

The last case

To understand how weakest link global public goods are provided, it is best to begin at the end.

On October 22, 1977, Ali Maow Maalin, a 23-year-old hospital cook living in the port town of Merca, Somalia, felt feverish and went to his rented room to rest. Three days later he was admitted to the hospital. At first doctors thought he was suffering from malaria. The next evening, however, he developed a rash and was diagnosed with chickenpox. On October 27, Mr. Maalin was discharged from the hospital. Still ill, he remained at home, where his rash continued to develop. Having previously been a temporary vaccinator in the smallpox eradication program (but, strangely, not having been vaccinated himself), Mr. Maalin suspected that he was infected with smallpox. Fearing that he would be placed under quarantine, however, he kept his suspicions private. Fortunately, a fellow co-worker at the hospital, a male nurse, reported Mr. Maalin to the regional health superintendent, perhaps hoping to claim the reward of 200 Somali shillings (about $32) for reporting a smallpox case. This time, doctors made a correct diagnosis, and Mr. Maalin was placed under 24-hour police guard. Later, he recovered; after a month he was released. Though no one knew it at the time, Ali Maow Maalin was the last person in the world to be infected with endemic smallpox.

How did Mr. Maalin get infected? On October 12, local authorities connected with the smallpox eradication campaign discovered two children with smallpox at a nomadic encampment about 90 kilometers from Merca. Following standard procedures, the children and their mother were taken to an isolation camp outside of the city. Driving at night, the party stopped at Merca Hospital to ask for directions. It was there that they met Mr. Maalin. He offered to lead the party to the home of the local smallpox surveillance team leader, and climbed in the back of the Land Rover, sitting next to the two sick children. He was in the vehicle for less than 15 minutes—long enough to inhale the virus. Of the two sick children, the little boy survived, but his 6-year-old sister, Habiba Nur Ali, died two days after arriving at the camp. She was the last person in the world to die from endemic smallpox.

Who might Mr. Maalin have infected? He was believed to have come into contact with 161 people, some living more than 120 kilometers from Merca. These people, mostly friends and co-workers, had of course been in contact with other people; these other people had been in contact with still more people; and so on. It was impossible to tell how far the disease had spread. Contact tracing is difficult. Indeed, when authorities traced the people whom Miss Ali and her brother had met before arriving at the isolation camp, Mr. Maalin's brief encounter with the children had gone undetected. As members of the World Health Organization (WHO) smallpox eradication team in Somalia later remarked, in retrospect, the world's last known case of endemic smallpox "occurred as the result of a combination of errors and omissions."[2]

To stop the outbreak that infected Miss Ali and her brother, the local WHO team searched the Somali desert for anyone who may have been in contact with the family. They also searched for the people who had been in contact with *these* persons, and so on. They worked outwards in concentric circles, vaccinating every suspected contact. Heavy rains made it impossible for the eradication staff to travel by vehicle, and so, like the nomads they pursued, the officials traveled on foot or on camels and donkeys. Their search ended on October 18 at a water hole named Edi Shabelli.

Officials also needed to be sure that Mr. Maalin had not spread the disease. They traced the people with whom he had been in contact, vaccinated them, and then put them under watch. Merca Hospital was sealed shut, and its staff and patients vaccinated and placed under quarantine. Everyone living near Mr. Maalin's home was vaccinated. After that, everyone living in his ward was vaccinated. These searches, involving WHO staff, a local party leader, and a policeman, were conducted at night, "to achieve the maximum possible vaccination coverage of the population."[3] Police checkpoints were established on the roads and footpaths leading into and out of Merca, and all travelers were stopped and vaccinated. By the time the mop up effort was over, two weeks after Mr. Maalin's confinement, 54,777 people had been vaccinated.

For many months after that, house-to-house searches continued in Merca and the surrounding region. No more cases were found. The search continued for two more years, extending throughout the Horn of Africa. Still, no more cases were found. A global search was carried out over this same period. Again, no more cases (apart from the Birmingham cases of non-endemic smallpox noted in Chapter 1). By late 1979, the conditions established for certifying the global eradication of smallpox had been satisfied. When the World Health Assembly had their next meeting, in May 1980, victory was formally declared. The chain of endemic disease that had begun thousands of years before, and that had claimed many millions of lives, harming every country in the world, had ended at last. It died inside the body of Ali Maow Maalin.

The eradication dividend

Had these final efforts failed, the many years of toil needed to wipe out the disease from every other part of the globe would have achieved little. The disease would have remained endemic in the world. The eradication "dividend" would not have been realized.

What was this dividend? Eradication is an investment.[4] To eradicate a disease, increased costs must be incurred in the near term. These costs are the additional costs of vaccination and surveillance needed to achieve and certify eradication—that is, the costs over and above those that would have been incurred were eradication not attempted and the disease merely controlled. Once achieved, the benefits of eradication are realized indefinitely. These benefits are the costs of the vaccinations, illnesses, and deaths avoided by eradication.

Estimates of these benefits and costs, taken from the official account of the eradication program, are shown in Table 2.1. These were calculated by first estimating the values for India and the United States, and then, assuming that these countries were representative of other developing and industrialized countries, prorating these values across the rest of the world.[5] Adding up then yields the global totals.

The totals are impressive, but the ratios of benefits to costs are even more so. The benefit–cost ratio is 159 : 1 if all costs are included and 483 : 1 if international finance only is counted (the latter is the money given by industrialized countries to finance smallpox elimination programs in developing countries—the additional finance needed

Table 2.1. Benefits and Costs of Smallpox Eradication (Millions of US dollars)

Benefits and Costs	Amount
Annual benefit to India	722
Annual benefit to all developing countries	1,070
Annual benefit to the United States	150
Annual benefit to all industrialized countries	350
Total annual benefit	1,420
Total international expenditure on eradication	98
Total national expenditure by endemic countries	200
Combined total expenditure on eradication	298
Benefit–cost ratio of international expenditure	483 : 1
Benefit–cost ratio of combined total expenditure	159 : 1

Source: Fenner et al. (1988: 1364–1366). Benefit–cost ratios are found by dividing the annual benefit by 0.03 (that is, a 3 percent discount rate), and dividing that number by the relevant cost estimates (costs are assumed to be incurred in a single year).

to eradicate the disease). I am not aware of any public investment offering returns this high. The eradication of smallpox is very likely the greatest collective investment the world has ever made.

The differences between developing and industrialized countries are also striking. For India, 97 percent of the benefit of eradication consisted of a reduction in the value of the lives lost to the disease.[6] For the United States, avoided deaths make up less than one-tenth of 1 percent of the benefit. The main benefit to the U.S. consisted of avoided vaccination costs—including the costs of illnesses associated with vaccination.

While India and the United States both gained from eradication, Table 2.1 shows that India gained more than twice as much as all industrialized countries put together. These estimates should correct a common misperception—namely, that eradication primarily bene-fited rich countries. For example, a working group of the Commission on Macroeconomics and Health claims that,

the enormous financial gains that accrued to the United States in the case of smallpox eradication...were not matched by similar gains in most developing countries. The greatest beneficiaries were likely to be the developed countries that needed eradication to consolidate the gains of their national immunization programmes.[7]

The estimates shown in Table 2.1 tell a different story. The rich countries gained tremendously from smallpox eradication, but the poor countries benefited even more.

In human terms, the difference in the gains to rich and poor countries is even more striking. The last outbreak of smallpox in the United States occurred in 1949. Triggered by an imported case, but with routine vaccination having secured herd immunity in the population, only eight Americans fell ill; and, of these, only one died.[8] In the decades preceding eradication, the bigger risk to a country like the United States came not from the disease but from the live vaccine, which may have killed around nine or so children a year.[9]

The situation in other rich countries was similar. The Scandinavian countries "provided an example for the rest of the world," eliminating smallpox towards the end of the nineteenth century, before any other country had done so.[10] By 1953, all of Europe (including the Soviet Union) was smallpox free. Imported cases were reported, particularly in the countries with colonial ties to the tropics. But with routine vaccination being maintained, imports failed to spark epidemics. Similarly, Canada eliminated smallpox in 1944 and Japan in 1951. Australia and New Zealand, being more isolated and lightly populated, never suffered much from smallpox.

Among poor countries, the situation was mixed. Island states like Madagascar had few cases; like Australia and New Zealand they were more isolated. Elsewhere, effective vaccination programs prevented epidemics. By 1952, smallpox had been vanquished from Central America, including Mexico. Smallpox had been eliminated in Vietnam by 1959, and on the Korean peninsula even earlier. By the time the World Health Assembly voted to eradicate smallpox in 1959, the disease remained endemic in only 59 countries in Africa, South America, and Asia. Some of these countries, however, were on the verge of eliminating the disease. China, for example, did so in 1961. By the time the "intensified" smallpox eradication campaign began in 1967, smallpox remained endemic in just 31 countries. Almost by definition, however, these countries were least able to control let alone to eliminate this disease. In that same year, an estimated 10–15 million people fell ill with smallpox and 1.5–2 million people died.[11] The eradication of smallpox stopped this carnage.

The weakest link

As noted in the quote that introduces this chapter, no one expected that smallpox would make its last stand in the deserts of Somalia. Like fire, an infectious disease requires a fuel source, a steady supply of susceptible hosts, to "burn." This requires a large total population, a high population density to effect transmission, and a sufficiently low level of immunization to keep the chain of transmission going. Somalia, it was thought, satisfied none of these conditions. Most of the country was sparsely populated by nomadic and semi-nomadic pastoralists—groups that never congregated in large numbers. Indeed, Somalia had been declared smallpox free in 1962, without the help of mass vaccination. In 1975, Somalia's national program director reported that 85 percent of the population had been successfully vaccinated—a generous margin, for normally, even in densely populated areas, 80 percent vaccination was believed to be sufficient to prevent epidemics.

The situation "on the ground," as it were, was very different. This was a time of great upheaval in the region. In 1974–1975, drought and famine throughout the Ogaden desert displaced around a quarter of a million people, forcing many into crowded refugee camps. Then, in July 1977, Somalia invaded Ethiopia, hoping to annex the Ogaden and so to create a Greater Somalia (Somalia lost). War swelled the refugee camps even more. Finally, previous vaccination efforts proved less successful than reported. By 1977 it became clear that coverage in settled populations was perhaps 60–80 percent—below the critical level. Among the nomads in the south, coverage was even lower, ranging from 10–20 percent.[12]

Inadequate surveillance and false reporting was another problem—and one that grew worse as the eradication program neared the finish line. WHO officials were convinced that smallpox would make its last stand in Ethiopia. Indeed, the organization's confidence was so high that plans were made to hold a press conference to announce to the world that smallpox had been vanquished.[13] Even as these preparations were underway, however, outbreaks were occurring in Somalia. Local WHO staff in Somalia hoped that they could extinguish the outbreaks without anyone knowing. They wanted Somalia to avoid bearing the stigma of being the last country to be infected with smallpox.[14] As the epidemic persisted, however, officials there realized that discovery was inevitable, and that it would be much worse for this to be made *after* the WHO's Director-General had announced publicly that smallpox had been eradicated. It was only then that more resources were dispatched to Somalia, and the disease was finally vanquished.

Polio

If smallpox were still endemic today, could it be eradicated? It is a sign of the world's uneven progress over the past quarter of a century that we could not be sure of a positive outcome. Somalia has lacked a central, domestic authority since 1991, when the government in charge during the intensified smallpox eradication campaign was ousted from power. Ever since then, Somalia has been the nightmare that Thomas Hobbes imagined an ungoverned society would be, a place of factional fighting, lawlessness, and famine—an environment so hostile that the United Nations humanitarian and peacekeeping mission was forced to withdraw from the country in 1995.

Today, this "collapsed state" is the weakest link of another global eradication campaign—the initiative to eradicate poliomyelitis. As UNICEF's former Executive Director, Carol Bellamy, once said, "If polio can be stopped in Somalia, it can be stopped anywhere."[15]

Since the initiative began in 1988, the number of polio-endemic countries has fallen from 125 to just six. Over this same period, the number of polio cases worldwide has fallen by more than 99 percent. That is a huge achievement from the perspective of control, but eradication succeeds or fails depending on whether incidence can be reduced to *zero*—and kept there, permanently. If the initiative gets close to its goal, but fails to interrupt transmission entirely, it fails. Eradication is a high stakes game.

In 2004, two years after the last case of polio had been recorded, Somalia was removed from the list of polio-endemic countries. UNICEF proudly declared the achievement a "miraculous victory for children over conflict and devastation."[16]

Sadly, the announcement proved premature. Only a few months later, a 15-month-old girl living in Mogadishu was diagnosed with polio.[17] That was in July 2005. Later, more cases were confirmed. By March 2006, a total of 200 polio cases had been identified. Only about one in 200 persons infected with polio suffer paralysis, and so an outbreak of this magnitude implies around 40,000 infections. Even more worryingly, the disease had spread into outlying regions. An epidemic was underway.

Genomic sequencing traced Somalia's first new case of polio to Yemen—a country that, like Somalia, had previously been declared polio-free. The outbreak in Yemen was in turn traced to Chad, and Chad's own outbreak was traced to a case imported from Nigeria. It was here that the problem started.

In 2003, politicians in the Kano state of Nigeria suspended mass vaccinations, claiming that polio eradication was a Western plot, intended to sterilize Muslim girls and spread HIV. Polio was still endemic in the country at this time, and the suspension allowed the disease to spread—rapidly—putting other countries and the entire global initiative at risk. Outbreaks were identified in 21 formerly polio-free states; and, in some of these, transmission became reestablished. Since that low point there has been a partial turn around. Vaccination resumed in Kano in 2004, and supplementary immunization has succeeded in interrupting or substantially curtailing outbreaks in all but one of the 21 countries in which poliovirus was imported. The exception was Somalia.[18]

As indicated in Table 2.2, Somalia has the lowest immunization coverage of any of these states, a consequence of the anarchy that prevails in the country. Botswana also imported a case from Nigeria, but because Botswana maintains very high vaccine coverage, that single import failed to set off an epidemic.

The problem countries, the weakest links, are the "failed states." As suggested by the last column of Table 2.2, the failed states have the poorest immunization coverage.[19] Obviously, immunization depends on more than good governance. For example, in countries with high population density, such as India, higher immunization levels are required to prevent outbreaks. But a desire and ability to implement a sustained vaccination program so intolerant of error is crucial. Without it, eradication is doomed to fail.

This, however, is only a necessary condition; it is not sufficient. Other criteria must also be met.

Sadly, it now appears that, despite the best efforts of the polio eradication initiative, it may not be possible to eradicate this disease, and to deliver a dividend for the whole world to share.[20] There are many reasons for this; five are especially important:

Table 2.2. Polio Eradication Setbacks, 2002–2005

Polio status	Country	Sources of polio imports	No. polio cases	Percent total vaccine coverage	Percent districts with 80% coverage	Failed states index rank
Polio-endemic	Afghanistan		31			10
	Egypt		9			31
	India		2025			93
	Niger		78			44
	Nigeria		2138			22
	Pakistan		274			9
Previously polio-free	Angola	India	10	45	7	37
	Benin	Nigeria	8	83	77	90
	Botswana	Nigeria	1	97	100	96
	Burkina Faso	Nigeria	21	83	43	30
	Cameroon	CAR, Chad, Nigeria	16	73	31	36
	CAR	Chad	31	40	8	13
	Chad	Nigeria	48	48	9	6
	Côte d'Ivoire	Burkina Faso	18	54	20	3
	Eritrea	Sudan	1	83	17	54
	Ethiopia	Sudan	22	52	10	26
	Ghana	Burkina Faso	8	80	48	106
	Guinea	Côte d'Ivoire	7	43	18	11
	Indonesia	Saudi Arabia	299	70	72	32
	Lebanon	India	1	92	100	65
	Mali	Burkina Faso, Côte d'Ivoire, Niger, Nigeria	22	65	43	81
	Nepal	India	4	76	49	20
	Saudi Arabia	Sudan	2	95	100	73
	Somalia	Yemen	154	40	3	6
	Sudan	Chad	146	50	41	1
	Togo	Ghana	1	90	48	37
	Yemen	Sudan	478	66	24	16

Sources: Centers for Disease Control (2006); http://www.ced.gov/mmwr/preview/mmwrhtml/mm5506a1.htm Polio case count for polio-endemic countries from Global Polio Eradication Initiative case count data; http://www.who.int/vaccines/immunization_monitoring/en/diseases/poliomyelitis/afpextract.cfm 2005 failed states index from The Fund for Peace; http://www.fundforpeace.org/programs/fsi/fsindex.php
Notes: As of February 1, 2006, Niger and Egypt were no longer classified as being polio-endemic. CAR stands for the Central African Republic. The countries in italics did not sustain transmission following an imported case.

First, eradication can only be certified if there is effective surveillance, and this can be challenging to achieve in the weakest states. It was only recently discovered, for example, that polioviruses had been circulating in war-ravaged Sudan for years before being detected.[21]

Second, even if transmission of wild polioviruses can be stopped, persons with immunologic disorders can shed (excrete) the viruses, and so continue introducing them into the environment, for years. Reservoirs for the viruses will thus remain. Third, the vaccine of choice in developing countries—the oral vaccine—is also excreted and can revert to a pathologic state, causing new outbreaks. Indeed, this has already happened. Fourth, numerous samples of the virus are likely to exist in laboratories around the world, creating the risk of a future accidental release. Finally, scientists have already shown that poliovirus can be synthesized from scratch. This means that, even if transmission of wild polio can be stopped and all existing sources secured or destroyed, a risk would remain that bioterrorists might reconstruct poliovirus and use it as a weapon.

The terrorist risk

With vaccination having been discontinued for a quarter of a century, the world's overall immunity to smallpox is probably no better today than it was when Edward Jenner demonstrated the world's first vaccine in 1798. Indeed, it may be worse. By one estimate, herd immunity may now be around 18 percent; over time, it will only fall (unless mass vaccination is restarted).[22] To prevent an epidemic, herd immunity would need to be at least 80 percent. Making matters worse, a significant fraction of today's population is immune-compromised. These individuals (including persons with HIV/AIDS and persons taking powerful new anti-cancer drugs) cannot be given the live smallpox vaccine.[23] So, while eradication, accompanied by cessation of vaccination, has yielded the world a huge dividend, it has also made the world exceptionally vulnerable to a new release of the smallpox virus. With hindsight, was eradication really worth doing?

The possibility of a future bioterrorist attack was considered by the WHO's smallpox eradication staff, but the risk at that time was perceived to be small; as the leaders of the eradication unit later noted, "smallpox spreads comparatively slowly, by face-to-face contact. Unless the public health services had completely broken down, the existence of reserve stocks of vaccine...would ensure the containment of any outbreak that followed a deliberate release of variola virus."[24]

After smallpox was eradicated, vaccine was stockpiled in a number of countries. Reserves were also held by the WHO. For a long time, this precaution seemed adequate. Indeed, confidence was so high that the International Health Regulations were amended in 1982 to take smallpox off the list of notifiable diseases. As noted in Chapter 1, negotiations were also initiated to destroy the remaining stocks of variola. Doing so, it was believed, would have made smallpox extinct, shutting the door on this scourge forever.

The terrorist attacks of September 11, 2001 and the anthrax attacks of October 2001 changed this calculation of risk. With a jolt. Since that time, countries have taken a number of steps to reduce the effects of a smallpox attack, should prevention fail. The industrialized countries have vaccinated members of their military and emergency services. They have built up stockpiles of vaccine, or topped up their existing stocks, for added reassurance (the U.S. has stockpiled enough for every American). The WHO has established a Smallpox Vaccine Bank to control outbreaks arising in developing countries. Manufacturers have been encouraged to retain a capacity to produce large quantities of vaccine, should there be a need to ramp up production on short notice. The International Health Regulations have been revised to require that countries once again notify the WHO in the event of a smallpox outbreak. Finally, and as discussed in the previous chapter, the remaining, official stocks of variola virus have been retained. Scientists are continuing to use these to develop improved diagnostic tests, vaccines, and drug treatments.[25]

What is the likelihood of a smallpox attack? Smallpox is different from other biological agents. Unlike anthrax, it does not exist in nature. Unlike polio, it cannot (yet) be engineered using raw materials. Given current technology, smallpox must be acquired from existing stocks. As noted in the last chapter, there is a chance that covert stocks may exist. It is mainly this risk that the stockpiles and related policies are guarding against today.

The decision to eradicate a disease today must take the risk of a terrorist attack seriously. It must also add in the costs of the measures that are needed to limit this risk. Both adjustments make eradication less attractive; they reduce the eradication dividend noted previously. The economics of smallpox eradication, however, are so overwhelming that even in hindsight the decision to eradicate appears wise.[26] Indeed, that must be so because the decision to terminate mass vaccination is reversible. That countries have chosen not to vaccinate their populations is testimony to the enduring benefit of smallpox eradication.

Nuclear security standards

It is, in any event, unlikely that smallpox would be a terrorist's weapon of choice. There are better options.

As a Defense Department official in the Clinton administration, Graham Allison led a scenario planning exercise on the possibility of a terrorist attack on the United States. His team considered the possibility that terrorists might hijack a plane and crash it into a "trophy building." That scenario, however, was less than halfway up the list of the top 100 targets. "Number one on everyone's list," Allison told journalist James Fallows, "was the nuclear detonation in a city... That's the only way you can kill hundreds of thousands of people in an instant."[27]

The attacks of September 11, 2001 killed fewer than 3,000 people. Damage to the World Trade Center was estimated to cost about $83 billion.[28] A single nuclear terrorist attack on, say, a major U.S. seaport would do much more harm. By one estimate, it would kill between 50,000 and one million people, and cost between $300 billion and $1.4 trillion.[29] The losses associated with a nuclear terrorist attack in other countries would be comparable.

How to protect a city from a nuclear terrorist strike? One way is to go after the terrorists, to get them before they get us. Lacking a state, however, terrorists can be hard to identify. And because they are hard to identify, the pursuit of terrorists can injure innocent parties. Another way is to defend against an attack. Complete defense, however, is impossible. (Is every cargo ship to be inspected? Is every part of a state's borders and coastlines to be monitored?) Yet another way is to deter an attack. Deterrence can prevent attacks by another state, but it will be ineffective against stateless terrorists lacking a permanent territory and willing to die for their cause. The most effective way to secure against a nuclear terrorist strike is much simpler. It is to deny terrorists access to nuclear materials. As noted by Graham Allison, "without fissile material, you can't have a nuclear bomb."[30]

Where are terrorists likely to acquire fissile materials? They are almost certain to seek out the easiest source: the weakest link in the global nuclear security chain. Securing these supplies from terrorists should thus be a priority. Doing so will supply a weakest link global public good.

Why is this a *global* public good? One reason is that terrorism is a global phenomenon; any country might be targeted. Another reason is that, even if the fallout from a nuclear explosion did not cross borders, the fallout from the *reaction* to the attack would. Fundamental civil liberties would be curtailed—probably, worldwide. Freedom of travel and immigration would be reduced. There would likely be a violent response, even in the absence of definite evidence about the parties responsible, and *that* response could in turn set off a dangerous spiral of ever increasing hostility. The political reaction to the September 11, 2001 attacks, which has also been global in its reach, would seem muted by comparison.

Nuclear bomb making material is widely available. Around 50 states possess at least five kilograms of weapons-grade material, and an additional 20 metric tons of highly enriched uranium are to be found at some 130 facilities in over 40 countries, including countries as diverse as Chile, Ghana, Iran, and Jamaica.[31] It is widely believed that Russia and Pakistan (ranked 43rd and 9th, respectively, in the 2006 failed states index[32]) are the most likely weakest links—Russia because of the huge quantities of materials left over from the Cold War, widespread corruption, and the government's weak hold on the provinces; Pakistan because of the uncertain chain of command over its nuclear weapons, and its record of having previously supplied the global black market in nuclear materials (through Pakistan's top nuclear scientist, Abdul Qadeer Khan). The true nature of the risk, however, is difficult to calculate and pinpoint, because countries are not legally obligated to report their stockpiles of nuclear materials, and nor is any international agency (including the International Atomic Energy Agency) authorized to monitor stocks.

Minimal protections exist. The Convention on the Physical Protection of Nuclear Material, which entered into force in 1987, requires parties to ensure that civilian nuclear materials are secure when transported internationally. An amendment negotiated in 2005 broadens coverage to include nuclear material in domestic use, storage and transport. It also requires that civilian nuclear facilities be protected from attack and sabotage. This new agreement, however, leaves standard-setting up to individual governments (a party's "physical protection should be based on [its] current evaluation of the threat").

And, like the earlier agreement, the amendment excludes military materials and facilities and contains no provisions for verification or penalties for non-compliance. Like all treaties, it applies only to its parties.[33] Non-parties can do what they like.

This is a toothless response—and one that reveals the inadequacy of the treaty instrument as a means for supplying weakest link global public goods (treaties can be effective at supplying other global public goods). To broaden participation, a treaty may need to allow countries to set their *own* standards—an outcome that will obviously improve little on unilateralism. A treaty can insist on meaningful, binding standards, backed by international inspections and effective enforcement—but only at the cost, perhaps, of key countries choosing not to participate.

United Nations Security Council Resolution 1540, passed in 2004, represents a different approach. It is binding upon all members of the United Nations, and not just those that consent to be bound by it. It is an exceptional action, and lacks the legitimacy of having been approved by a more representative body. However, the motivation behind the resolution should be clear: it is a response to the limitations of treaty-based approaches in supplying this vital global public good.

Like the amendment to the Convention on the Physical Protection of Nuclear Material, Resolution 1540 enjoins states to undertake a broad range of domestic actions to reduce the likelihood that nuclear weapons materials (and materials capable of making of chemical and biological weapons) will fall into the hands of non-state actors having "terrorist purposes." The resolution asks states to establish accounting and physical security mechanisms, border and export controls, and appropriate law enforcement regarding nuclear materials and devices. Like the amendment, however, the resolution's demands are non-specific, making it difficult to determine whether states are in compliance. The resolution recognizes that some states may require assistance in implementing the provisions of the resolution, but it does not obligate more able states to provide any assistance.[34] It thus creates a responsibility but does not provide the resources poorer states will need to implement it. It is also unclear how, or even whether, the resolution will be enforced. Resolution 1540 represents a new approach. Its effectiveness must await a future evaluation but there are reasons to be skeptical of its potential to make a material difference.

International health regulations

The newly revised International Health Regulations are neither a treaty nor a Security Council resolution but something in between.[35] Like a treaty, they require the consent of parties to which they apply. Unlike a treaty, the revised International Health Regulations, set to enter into force in 2007, apply to *all* members of the World Health Organization—essentially, all countries—*except those that reject them*.[36]

The difference is subtle but important. A treaty presumes that a state is bound by its obligations only if it has expressly consented to be bound by them. The International Health Regulations presume that a state is similarly bound unless it has expressly indicated its unwillingness to be bound by them. Essentially, the International Health Regulations shift the *status quo ante*. Unlike a Security Council resolution (made under Chapter VII), they need not be binding upon all countries—any country may opt out. However, precisely for this reason, the International Health Regulations have the advantage of legitimacy. The obligation to comply is accepted by states rather than being imposed on them.

The opt-out design certainly seems to favor full participation. The period during which countries can reject the revised regulations has not ended, as of my writing this book (it will end in December 2006). However, the earlier regulations applied nearly universally. Only one country, Australia, opted out.[37]

Why are the regulations designed in this way? And why do they succeed in sustaining full, or nearly full, participation? As noted in the Introduction, the opt-out design may have a behavioral advantage. Opting out takes effort; staying in, voicing no objection, is easier. More than this, the design of these regulations offers a normative suggestion—that staying in is the "right" thing to do. If not, why would the WHO Constitution have added this principle? Finally, and probably most importantly, the opt-out principle can be looked at as a coordinating device. If it were in each country's self interest to be bound by the regulations *only if all other countries were bound by them*, then the opt-out principle would guide states to this preferred outcome.

This last explanation, of course, would be true only if the International Health Regulations supplied a weakest link global public good—which they do. They supply a weakest link global public good that is the converse of eradication. Rather than focus on the *last* person to have an *established* disease, their attention is directed at the *first* person to contract a *new* disease. Epidemiologists call this person the *index case*.

The index case

On February 21, 2003, Dr. Liu Jianlun traveled from Guangdong province in Southern China to Hong Kong. He had just been treating patients for an atypical form of pneumonia, and was ill himself by the time he arrived at the Metropole Hotel. He was checked into Room 911, and stayed only one night. That was long enough, however, for him to pass his infection on to others. He may have done so while coughing in a crowded elevator, or perhaps while waiting for an elevator. What investigations later proved is that, during his brief stay, Dr. Jianlun infected at least 16 other people, all of whom spent at least some time on the Metropole's ninth floor.

Dr. Jianlun was admitted to a nearby hospital and died there ten days later. He is remembered because the illness that killed him, and that he passed onto others, was entirely unknown to medicine. Dr. Jianlun was the first person to spread internationally a new disease that would later be called "severe acute respiratory syndrome." Dr. Jianlun was the index case for the international spread of SARS.

SARS is an important disease, because it was SARS, and the events surrounding its emergence and spread, that jump-started the negotiations to revise the International Health Regulations. Had it not been for SARS, those negotiations might still be going on today—either that or a watered down version of the revisions might have been accepted.

Spread

How do infectious diseases spread? A disease may be infectious either before or after symptoms first show. With SARS we were lucky. People became ill around four days on average after becoming infected (there is variation around every average I shall mention here), and were generally able to transmit the disease only after this.[38] The peak period for transmission—again, on average—was probably into the second week following the onset of illness. So SARS was spread by people who were ill. That is why medical personnel and family members caring for the sick were particularly vulnerable. It is the reason Dr. Jianlun became infected with SARS in the first place.

Of the people who came into contact with Dr. Jianlun at the Metropole, one person was hospitalized in Singapore on March 1, another was hospitalized in Hong Kong on March 4, and still another died at her home in Toronto on March 5.[39] The Hong Kong patient passed the disease to an astonishingly large number of people—by one count, 138 individuals, most of them healthcare workers.[40] The son of the woman who died in Toronto also got sick. He was admitted to hospital, where he also died, but only after he infected more people. This is how the people Dr. Jianlun infected spread the disease, and this is how the people *they* infected spread the disease. By the time it was all over, a succession of transmission waves spread the disease to 30 countries.[41] A total of 8,422 cases were reported, in countries as geographically dispersed as Brazil, South Africa, Australia, India, and Russia. Only 916 people died from SARS, but that was due at least as much to the nature of this disease as to the measures taken to contain it.[42]

What determines how a disease spreads? A key parameter in epidemiology is the "basic reproductive number" for a disease. This is the number of secondary infections expected when a single infected person is introduced into a population in which everyone is susceptible.

Diseases that spread widely tend to have a high basic reproductive number (though, as we shall see later, other parameters also affect spread). At the Metropole, Dr. Jianlun spread the disease to 16 people: a high number. As noted before, the young man from Hong Kong who visited the Metropole's ninth floor infected more than a hundred people—an extraordinarily high figure. With retrospect, however, we know that both Dr. Jianlun and this young man were "superspreaders." For a combination of reasons—the nature of the hotel and hospital environments, biological factors that make some people prodigious viral shredders, and so on—Dr. Jianlun and the younger man passed the disease on to others at an unusually high rate.

Most people with SARS were not as good at spreading the disease, and the basic reproductive number should reflect the average rather than an extreme value. For SARS, the average basic reproductive number turned out to be around three.[43] This is a relatively small value as most diseases go. Smallpox and polio both have a basic reproductive number close to six; the value for highly infectious measles is around 15.[44] If SARS had been like measles, if Dr. Jianlun were a typical spreader rather than an outlier, SARS would very likely have gone global. We were just lucky that SARS was not like that.

Case fatalities

Another important characteristic of a disease is the case fatality ratio—the fraction of infected persons who die from a disease. For SARS, this was just over 10 percent. For smallpox it was higher—around 30 percent. For the 1918–1919 pandemic influenza it was low by comparison with these diseases (around 2.5 percent) but high in comparison with a typical influenza pandemic (less than 0.1 percent).

The worst disease imaginable would be both lethal *and* highly infectious. The case fatality rate for Ebola can be as high as 80 percent, but Ebola spreads less easily: the basic reproductive number for Ebola is around 1.5, barely above the critical value of 1.0 (the basic reproductive number must be greater than one for a disease to spread).[45] Probably the most disturbing section of Richard Preston's bestselling book, *The Hot Zone*, comes near the end, where he speculates on Ebola's ability to mutate so as to become infectious through the air rather than through intimate, physical contact. If Ebola were to become infectious in the respiratory tract, a disease confined to remote, jungle areas of Africa might become a global horror. As the disease expert C.J. Peters says in Preston's book, Ebola virus spreading in the air is "about the worst thing you can imagine."[46]

Ebola is not the only mutation to fear. The case fatality rate of the H5N1 avian flu among humans is around 60 percent. Should that virus acquire the ability to spread efficiently from human to human the consequences would likely be unprecedented.

The very first case

Retrospective analysis of hospital records indicates that SARS began in the Guangdong province of China in November 2002. We do not know the identity of the first person to be infected—the trail backwards from the Metropole ends in several, seemingly unrelated clusters. But suppose we could identify this first person, the *global* index case. How might *this* person have acquired the disease?

To answer this question, and to know how to treat and protect against this disease, we first need to know something more basic: What is SARS?

At first, scientists thought SARS might be a new form of influenza, possibly of avian origin, or a community-acquired form of pneumonia. After these possibilities were eliminated, researchers discovered that SARS was actually caused by a novel coronavirus, one of the causative agents of the common cold. The World Health Organization made the announcement of this discovery on April 16, 2003.

Coronaviruses are RNA viruses that mutate very rapidly—around a million times faster than their DNA-based hosts. Evolution thus favors the RNA viruses. Somehow, a coronavirus that was resident in one host came into contact with a human and then jumped the species barrier.

Where might SARS reside naturally? Epidemiology sleuths began looking in the exotic wildlife markets and restaurants of southern China, and soon discovered SARS in masked palm civets sold in live animal markets. At first, civets were believed to be the virus's natural host. Follow-up analysis, however, failed to locate the virus in either farmed or wild civets. The civets kept in the market stalls must therefore have been infected by another source, possibly the same source that sparked the human epidemic.

In 2005, two research teams working independently discovered that bats were the likely natural reservoir. They also learned that the kind of SARS found in bats is different from the strain transmitted by civets and humans. The trail for the search of the origins of the SARS epidemic thus ends with three possibilities: either the human epidemic was started by an extremely rare mutation, or the virus jumped first to an intermediate host before being passed to humans, or the human form of SARS originated from a different, as yet undiscovered host rather than from bats. Perhaps in the future researchers will discover the actual source of the 2002–2003 epidemic. For now, it remains a mystery.

Reporting outbreaks

The WHO first learned of a serious outbreak of the disease we now call SARS from unofficial sources, transmitted electronically and linked to its Global Outbreak Alert and Response Network. This was on February 10, 2003. It was not until the next day that the Chinese government reported the outbreak of respiratory illness in Guangdong Province. The timing of China's reporting was not by coincidence. SARS first emerged in mid-November 2002. Previous to the unofficial leak, the Chinese government had been covering up the outbreak. In doing so it had put the entire world at risk.

This might seem astonishing, but governments try to conceal outbreaks all the time. Indeed, it was to prevent such cover ups that the International Health Regulations were negotiated in the first place. These regulations not only imposed a duty upon countries to report. They also tried to remove the disincentive to report, by making it harder for other countries to restrict trade with the country harboring an outbreak. It is the fear of trade restrictions that creates the incentive for countries not to report.

More astonishing than China's failure to report, in my view, is that *China was under no legal obligation to report*. At that time, the International Health Regulations only applied to three diseases—cholera, plague, and yellow fever (as noted previously, smallpox used to be on the list, but was taken off after being eradicated). They did not apply to other diseases, including the most important of all: entirely new diseases like SARS. Emerging diseases like SARS are of particular concern because they leave *every* country vulnerable.

In 2007, when the revised International Health Regulations enter into force, this will change. The revised regulations require notification of all "events that may constitute a public health emergency of international concern." Had these rules been in force in 2003, China would have been legally obligated to report the SARS epidemic. The rules were changed because the SARS outbreak showed the world what can happen when countries hide their outbreaks.[47]

This change is particularly to be welcomed because the next newly emerging disease may be much worse than SARS. Certainly, worse diseases have emerged before.

Pandemic influenza, 1918–1919

One of the two most important diseases to emerge in the last century—the pandemic influenza outbreak of 1918–1919, sometimes known as the "Spanish flu"—"spread rapidly along the conduits of war and commerce to engulf the entire world in a matter of weeks."[48]

How many people died from this epidemic? Estimates vary. The figure most often cited is 20 million deaths worldwide, but other estimates are as high as 30 million people or even 50–100 million.[49] Influenza pandemics emerging after this have been less lethal. The Asian flu of 1957–1958 killed about one million people, and the 1968–1969 Hong Kong flu killed between one and four million people.[50] Future influenza pandemics could be as deadly as these, or much worse. Published estimates of the deaths that could result from a new strain of pandemic influenza top 100 million people, but the death toll could be even higher than this.[51]

Why did the 1918–1919 influenza spread so rapidly? Estimates of the basic reproductive rate for pandemic influenza are as high as 20.[52] Two recent and careful studies, however, suggest a much lower value. A study of U.S. cities suggests a value not greater than four.[53] A study of the outbreak in Geneva suggests a value of just 1.5 for the first wave of the pandemic, and a value of less than four for the second wave.[54] Other research points to a value of 1.7–2.0 for the first wave.[55] Overall, the evidence suggests that the basic reproductive number for the 1918–1919 influenza pandemic was about the same as, or perhaps even lower than, for SARS.

This is surprising. How could a disease with such a low reproductive value spread so rapidly? One reason is that persons infected with this influenza strain were infectious for only three or four days. On a per-day basis, the disease was thus very infectious. Another reason is that, in between a third and a half of all cases, transmission occurred *before* symptoms showed.[56] In contrast to SARS, people infected with the pandemic influenza were transmitting it through the air (and perhaps also through direct contact) without knowing that they were doing so. The people most likely to be infected were not hospital workers or the families of the sick, people who could learn to take precautions, but ordinary people going about their normal business. Finally, the incubation period for this influenza strain was only about two days. This meant that, by the time a person's illness had been expressed, the people with whom she had been in contact would already have transmitted the disease to others. SARS was stopped, and very quickly, by the age-old interventions of quarantine and contact tracing. These methods would not have been effective against the 1918–1919 influenza pandemic.

While this much is known, the origins of the 1918–1919 pandemic remain a mystery. No one knows where the disease first emerged. Nor is the biological origin of the disease understood, though it is likely to have avian roots.[57]

Preventing emergence

Today, the world is concerned about another influenza having avian roots: a mutation of the H5N1 bird flu that spreads from person to person.[58]

A new disease is more likely to emerge in countries that take the least effort to guard against the possibility, making prevention of emergence a weakest link global public good.

When news broke of an outbreak of H5N1 in migratory flocks of wild birds, Dutch authorities ordered commercial poultry indoors. Nigeria also had an emergency plan to deal with a bird flu outbreak, but just days before the minister responsible assured the *New York Times* that avian flu was under control, an international team of health experts reported that the government lacked even the basic tools for response; indeed, "officials had yet to produce a map showing the location of poultry farms there and were hearing reports from large farms that they had no idea even existed."[59] It is possible that the mutation everyone fears will emerge in the Netherlands rather than in Nigeria, but the odds of that seem low. Of the two countries, Nigeria seems the weaker link.[60]

How to strengthen this link? From the perspective of the world as whole, what is required are collectively agreed minimum standards. International standards already exist in some areas—an example being the World Organization for Animal Health's Terrestrial Animal Health Code, which aims "to assure the sanitary safety of international trade in terrestrial animals and their products." However, a broader set of standards is needed. It is not just trade in products that need to be regulated, but the sources of free trade in pathogens. Currently, minimum standards in this area are lacking. Indeed, even the European Union's approach to this problem is fragmented. There is an obvious analogy here to the standards needed to safeguard nuclear facilities.

Establishing standards, however, is only a first step. Countries must also have the capacity to implement internationally agreed standards. Nigeria plainly lacks that capacity.

Finally, minimum standards need to be enforced. In June 2005, reports surfaced that farmers in China had used an antiviral drug, amantadine, to suppress major bird flu outbreaks, in violation of international livestock guidelines.[61] Suppression of an outbreak is a global public good, but the use of this drug caused the H5N1 virus to become resistant. This means that, today, every country relying on this drug to treat humans must now turn to more expensive antivirals such as Tamiflu (developing countries have been the most affected). Maintaining the efficacy of a drug that may be prone to resistance is another weakest link global public good. I discuss this challenge in Chapter 7.

Overfishing and reflagging

Fisheries conservation is not a global public good, since countries can be excluded from certain fisheries jurisdictions.[62] Today, however, the distinction is more of a technical matter, since opportunities for nationalizing the seas seem to have been exhausted. Today, the similarities between over-fishing and the under-provision of global public goods stand out more than do the differences.

In the 1970s, the rights to the oceans changed dramatically. The territorial sea increased from three to 12 miles and a new property right concept, the exclusive economic zone, was created, giving coastal states rights to all the resources of the ocean above the seabed extending out to 200 miles from shore. These changes—all reflected in customary international law (as well as the Convention on the Law of the Sea)—were responses to over-fishing in "international" waters. They were aimed at taking these resources out of the hands of every state and putting them into the hands exclusively of coastal states.

The new property rights arrangements have been only partially successful. Many commercial species migrate. Some fisheries overlap two or more jurisdictions. Others are located entirely in the high seas, or overlap with the high seas.

To limit harvesting of these fish, a large number of international agreements have been brought into force.[63] Unfortunately, nearly all of these efforts have failed. According to the United Nations Food and Agriculture Organization, in the 1970s around one-tenth of the world's fish stocks were overexploited; today, about a quarter of the world's stocks are overfished.[64]

Why the failure? The problem is this: if some countries succeed in limiting their harvests collectively, but all countries possess the legal right to enter the fishery, then any collective effort to conserve only encourages entry by third parties. Often, entry takes the form of fishing vessels changing their country of registration—a loophole known as reflagging.

Reflagging is made especially easy when countries happily register vessels owned by the nationals of other states. According to a recent study, 29 states maintain open registries; and while only around one tenth of the global fleet is registered in this way, these vessels can have "a disproportionately negative impact on fisheries conservation and management measures."[65]

Reflagging makes fisheries management a weakest link collective action problem. So long as there is just one state willing to offer open registration, and this is permitted by international law, the collective conservation efforts of even a large number of states will be vulnerable. For that same reason, fisheries conservation may not even be attempted.

International agreements have been negotiated to try to address this problem, including the 1995 Agreement on the Conservation and Management of Straddling Fish Stocks and Highly Migratory Fish Stocks and the 1993 Agreement to Promote Compliance with International Conservation and Management Measures by Fishing Vessels on the High Seas. Both agreements help, not least by emphasizing that states have a responsibility not to undermine the conservation efforts undertaken by other states. However, neither can solve the problem. The treaty is the wrong instrument. Treaties, as I have noted before, can only be binding on the countries that ratify them. If reflagging is to be prevented from undermining international fisheries conservation efforts, a more general approach to restricting state freedoms will be required.

Which approach? United Nations Security Council Resolutions under Chapter VII apply to "threats to the peace, breaches of the peace, or acts of aggression." They do not apply to overfishing. The Food and Agriculture Organization (FAO) of the United Nations is to ocean fishing what the World Health Organization is to global health, but the FAO is not authorized to issue regulations. The concept of an exclusive economic zone was established through customary law, but custom cannot be created in the same way as a treaty or a resolution or a regulation.

We therefore know what needs to be done: the reflagging loophole must be closed; access to the world's fisheries must be restricted. What we lack are the means for doing these things. Providing the means will require fundamental institutional change.

Conclusions

Whether the supply of weakest link global public goods succeeds or fails depends on the country that does the least. The treaty is therefore an inappropriate instrument. Participation in a treaty is voluntary; if just one country chooses not to participate, that country, if it is the weakest link, can make cooperation by all the other countries pointless.

To supply weakest link global public goods requires other kinds of institutions. Examples include United Nations Security Council resolutions, adopted under Chapter VII; the revised International Health Regulations, which apply to all countries that do not explicitly reject them; and changes in customary law, which by definition apply universally.

All of these institutions help, but only partially. Security Council resolutions may lack legitimacy. Often, they are not enforced. The revised International Health Regulations are a substantial improvement over the old ones, but as I shall explain in Chapter 7, they fall far short of what is really required. Customary law still recognizes the freedom of the seas, blocking efforts to interdict international shipments of nuclear materials as well as efforts to curb entry to the world's most productive fishing grounds.

These institutions work when the underlying incentives are favorable. Smallpox eradication was in every country's interests. If other countries eliminated smallpox, each country would gain the eradication dividend by doing so. Fisheries conservation is different. If some states limit their harvests, others have an incentive to take their place. Enforcement is essential to the supply of many weakest link global public goods.

So, also, is the capability to fulfill a state's responsibilities. The weakest links are usually the failed states. By definition, these are states that lack the wherewithal to provide even basic government services. Even when global minimum standards are agreed, failed states cannot be counted on to meet them. How to address this challenge is another subject for later chapters.

The supply of other global public goods depends not on the best effort nor on the weakest but on the aggregate effort. I turn to these next.

CHAPTER THREE

Aggregate efforts: global public goods that depend on the combined efforts of all states

> Perhaps the single most successful international environmental agreement to date has been the Montreal Protocol, in which states accepted the need to phase out the use of ozone-depleting substances.
>
> Kofi Annan, Secretary General of the United Nations[1]

> I would like us to study now with our European partners the principle of a carbon tax on the import of industrial products from countries that refuse to commit themselves to the Kyoto Protocol after 2012. The environment is a global issue. Our efforts will be worthless if we are the only ones fighting for the future of the planet.
>
> Dominique de Villepin, Prime Minister of France[2]

Imagine a group of rowers trying to propel a boat. Their speed depends not on the weakest rower, nor on the strongest, but on the efforts of all the rowers. Some global public goods likewise depend on the total efforts of all countries. Environmental issues are typically of this type. Pollution is determined by aggregate emissions, over-fishing by the fishing efforts of all countries.

Today, the most important global public good requiring an aggregate effort is global climate change mitigation—the reduction in greenhouse gas concentrations in the atmosphere. Twenty years ago it was ozone depletion. This chapter contrasts these two challenges. It explains why our efforts to protect the ozone layer have succeeded, and why our efforts to limit climate change—so far, anyway—have failed.

There are many reasons for these differences, of course, but one is fundamental. This is the extent of the free rider problem and the ability of countries to overcome it. Ozone depletion is more resistant to free riding, and the treaty aiming to protect the ozone layer overcame these modest free rider incentives. Efforts to reduce greenhouse gas emissions are much more vulnerable to free riding, and the treaty trying to limit global climate change has been much less successful at promoting collective action.

Ozone depletion

One of the ironies of science and technology is that chlorofluorocarbons, or CFCs as they are better known, were first developed, and later marketed, for their perceived safety (the refrigerants they replaced beginning in the 1930s were toxic, corrosive, and flammable). Indeed, Thomas Midgley, soon after discovering this new compound, famously demonstrated its safety at a news conference by inhaling a lungful of CFC-12 and blowing out a candle.

CFCs, we now know, are only safe in the lower atmosphere. When CFCs escape—from a refrigerator, say—they slowly rise in the atmosphere, eventually reaching the stratosphere, 10–40 kilometers above the Earth. Here they are broken down by the sun's ultraviolet radiation and release chlorine. It is the liberated chlorine atoms and not the CFCs themselves that deplete stratospheric ozone.

The process of ozone depletion is slow: start to finish it takes about 50 years.[3] And depletion does not occur directly above the original source of emission; CFC molecules mix in the atmosphere. Indeed, that is why CFCs are abundant even at the South Pole, far from the northern hemisphere where most CFCs have been released.

But why, if CFCs mix in the atmosphere, is *depletion* greatest over Antarctica? Why is there an "ozone hole"? These questions are worth asking because the sudden loss in ozone over Antarctica surprised atmospheric scientists. The discovery of the ozone hole is a reminder that we, humans, are adding new stresses to the environment; and that, because they are new, and also massive in scale, we cannot be sure of their impact. Uncertainty and surprise go with this territory.

Here, then, is the reason: During the long Antarctic winter, strong winds (known as the polar vortex) isolate the Antarctic atmosphere. Special chemical reactions, possible only at very cold temperatures, then delay the time it takes for the chlorine atoms to join with other atoms and become stabilized. They also allow inactive chlorine atoms to be converted into more active forms. The two effects together allow chlorine to accumulate in great volume. When the sun shines again on Antarctica in the spring, ultraviolet rays set all this chlorine free. The result is a burst of depletion (usually reaching a maximum in September of each year) not seen elsewhere.[4] The effect is to create an "ozone hole" (a temporary thinning of the ozone layer). As the temperature warms, and the vortex weakens, the air over Antarctica mixes with the surrounding atmosphere, and the ozone layer over Antarctica stabilizes once again. And then the annual cycle begins all over again.

Because CFCs mix in the atmosphere, depletion everywhere depends on the total quantity of CFCs released, not the amounts released by individual countries. For this same reason, of course, the aggregate efforts of all countries are needed to slow and reverse the depletion. Ozone layer protection is a global public good requiring an aggregate effort.

Why should we care about the ozone layer? What is the benefit of supplying the global public good of ozone layer protection? The ozone layer blocks biologically harmful ultraviolet radiation from reaching the Earth's surface. When we deplete the ozone layer, we lose this protection; we expose all life on Earth to new dangers.

Increased exposure to harmful ultraviolet radiation would retard plant growth, harm plankton and other marine life that live near the ocean's surface, and damage polymers. Worse, it would cause cataracts, immune suppression, and, most worrying of all, skin cancers, including deadly melanomas. Indeed, this may be why the United States signed the Montreal Protocol—the treaty designed to protect the ozone layer—despite the objections of its Interior Secretary (who dismissed the threat by saying, "People who don't stand out in the sun—it doesn't affect them.").[5] In August 1987, a month before the Montreal Protocol was adopted, President

Ronald Reagan had a skin cancer removed from the tip of his nose.

The ozone treaties

The Montreal Protocol is the central ozone treaty.[6] The first, the Vienna Convention, was more of a framework agreement. It did not limit the emission of any ozone-destroying substances. Indeed, it mentions CFCs by name only in an annex. The Montreal Protocol was different. It limited the production and consumption of the most important (by volume) CFCs. These limits, though differentiated, applied to all countries that ratified the agreement, developing and industrialized countries alike. From its creation, this was a global treaty. Moreover, the limits imposed by Montreal lasted indefinitely. Montreal was meant to be a permanent answer to the threat of ozone depletion.

The agreement was designed to be flexible; its greatest achievement was to provide a platform upon which broader and deeper cuts could be adopted over time through a sequence of adjustments and amendments (see Table 3.1).

The adjustments lowered the pre-existing limits. They also brought forward the date by which these tighter limits had to be met. Under the terms of the agreement, adjustments were to be agreed by consensus if possible, but by a two-thirds vote of the parties (representing at least half of the total consumption of controlled substances of all parties) if necessary. Once accepted, the adjustments applied to all parties and not only the countries that positively voted in their favor.

The amendments broadened the scope of the treaty. They added more chemicals to the list of controlled substances and made other changes that increased the effectiveness of the treaty. Amendments are like new treaties. They apply only to the countries that ratify them. Once they enter into force, however, they alter the original treaty. Any country that ratified Montreal after an amendment had entered into force was bound by that amendment as well. Essentially, the amendment process allowed the original agreement to be ratcheted up and up. Over time, new parties to the Montreal Protocol as well as the existing parties were made to do more and more.

Table 3.1. The Ozone Treaties

Year adopted	Treaty	Year entered into force	No. parties	What the treaty/adjustment/amendment does
1985	Vienna Convention for the Protection of the Ozone Layer	1988	190	Countries agree to take "appropriate measures ... to protect human health and the environment against the adverse effects resulting or likely to result from human activities which modify or are likely to modify the Ozone Layer."
1987	Montreal Protocol on Substances that Deplete the Ozone Layer	1989	189	Requires that production and consumption of 5 CFCs be cut in half and that of 3 halons be stabilized.
1990	London Adjustment	1991		Reduction schedules agreed previously in Montreal were accelerated and tightened.
1990	London Amendment	1992	182	Number of controlled substances increased from 8 to 20. Industrial country parties agreed to pay for the "incremental costs" of compliance by developing country parties. Adjustment accelerated reductions in Montreal Protocol.
1992	Copenhagen Adjustment	1993		Further tightened earlier controls.
1992	Copenhagen Amendment	1994	173	Number of controlled substances increased from 20 to 94.
1995	Vienna Adjustment	1996		Tightened earlier controls.
1997	Montreal Adjustment	1998		Tightened earlier controls.
1997	Montreal Amendment	1999	145	Added requirement for a licensing system to allow control and monitoring of trade in controlled substances.
1999	Beijing Adjustment	2000		Revised allowances for meeting "basic domestic needs" of developing country parties.
1999	Beijing Amendment	2002	112	Adds one more substance, bringing the total number of controlled substances to 95.

Source: http://ozone.unep.org/Treaties_and_Ratification/index.asp

Two kinds of discovery drove this process: new scientific discoveries showing that ozone depletion was worse than had previously been expected, and new technological discoveries showing that substitution away from the harmful substances was easier than had previously been expected. The first discovery changed the benefits of ozone protection. The second changed the costs.

Benefits and costs

Table 3.2 summarizes the estimates available of the costs and benefits of the ozone treaties. Only the top two rows can be compared directly. The other rows draw from different studies, evaluating the treaties at different stages, over different periods of time, using different base years and currencies (also calculated in different years). The qualitative impression is what matters, however, and it is overwhelming: the Montreal Protocol and its associated adjustments and amendments have given the world, and individual countries as well, a benefit far in excess of the cost.

Table 3.2. Cost–Benefit Analyses of the Ozone Treaties (Benefits and Costs in Billions)

Study	Benefit	Cost	Net Benefit	B : C ratio
For U.S. only; assuming unilateral implementation of the original Montreal Protocol; through 2165	$1,373	$21	$1,352	65 : 1
For U.S. only; assuming broad implementation of the original Montreal Protocol; through 2165	$3,575	$21	$3,554	170 : 1
For European Union 15 plus Norway; for Montreal Protocol and all its adjustments and amendments through Copenhagen; through 2050	€ 12			
For world; for Montreal Protocol and all its adjustments and amendments through Copenhagen; through 2060	€ 2,220	€ 200	€ 2,020	11 : 1

Source: The U.S. estimates are from U.S. Environmental Protection Agency (1988); the estimates for northwest Europe are from Velders et al. (2000). The estimates for the world are also from Velders et al. (2000), drawing on the earlier work of ARC Research Consultants (1997).

Incentives

If any country were to reduce its use of CFCs, all countries would benefit, but not all would benefit by the same amount. The countries toward the higher latitudes would benefit most, because this is where the depletion is greatest. Countries with white-skinned populations would benefit more, because they would be more vulnerable to skin cancer. In absolute terms, the countries with larger populations would benefit more. Finally, the countries with higher incomes per capita would be willing to pay more to avoid the risk of ozone depletion. Taken together, all these considerations suggest that the country that would benefit the most from protection of the ozone layer is almost certainly the United States. No wonder, then, that the United States took significant action to cut its production and consumption unilaterally, beginning in the 1970s, even before the science of ozone depletion had been firmly established.

The first row of Table 3.2 shows that the United States had an incentive to cut back even more: the benefit it would receive by implementing Montreal, assuming that other countries did nothing, exceeds the cost by 65 to 1. This is an extraordinary return on investment.

Other countries also had an incentive to reduce their use of CFCs, and many did so. Belgium, Canada, Norway, and Sweden all banned the use of CFCs in aerosols at the same time as the United States.

So, was there really a need for a treaty? There was. The steps these countries took early on were easy and cheap. Doing more would be harder and costlier. As well, because only global releases of CFCs affect the ozone layer, these countries needed other countries to cut their releases. Finally, production restrictions by a small group of countries, acting unilaterally or minilaterally, would only create an incentive for CFCs to be produced elsewhere: a phenomenon known as "trade leakage." Indeed, India used the Montreal Protocol as an opportunity to expand production capacity, to serve the growing market for CFCs in developing countries. To make a significant and lasting difference, the Montreal Protocol needed to broaden participation even as it restricted production and consumption more and more. And to do this, it needed to create incentives. In particular, it needed to use a combination of carrots and sticks.

Carrots

Carrots were needed to encourage the participation of countries lacking a direct incentive to participate: the developing countries.

In the first renegotiation of the Montreal Protocol, held in London in 1990, the industrialized country parties agreed to pay for the "incremental costs" of implementation by developing countries. This meant that developing countries could not be made worse off by acceding to the agreement; they could only gain. They could not be made worse off because their costs were covered. And they would be made better off because they also benefited from ozone layer protection. They would not have benefited as much as the industrialized countries, but no country benefits from ozone depletion: black people are as vulnerable to cataracts and immune suppression as white people; agriculture, fisheries, and materials are vulnerable to radiation exposure everywhere.

If reducing releases of CFCs at home is a global public good, so is paying to reduce them (relative to a "business as usual" trajectory) elsewhere. The financial contributions to the Multilateral Fund thus supplied another global public good. The Montreal restrictions, coupled with the concept of "incremental costs," determined the financial cost of "buying" the participation of any developing country.[7] But how were these costs to be shared by the industrialized countries? A simple formula allocated this burden: each industrialized country party was to pay in proportion to its share, for this group of countries, of the assessments used to finance the United Nations.[8] In Chapter 4, I explain the logic of this financing arrangement.

Sticks

Ozone protection isn't like asteroid defense or smallpox eradication. Asteroid defense and smallpox eradication are all or nothing, but there can be more or less ozone protection.

As a country does more and more to protect the ozone layer, its costs go up and up, and a point can be reached where the costs of doing a little more exceed the benefits, to this country, of doing a little more. That is when the country wants to stop. Other countries, however, would like this country to keep going. They would benefit if this country did a little more, just as this country would benefit if others did more. When self-interest tells a country to stop, the collective interests of all countries urge it to keep going. This is the problem of collective action: how to get countries to keep going when self-interest tells them to stop.

How to change this incentive? One way is to make doing a little more conditional. Suppose all countries agree to do a little more if each does a little more. Then the incentive is different. If a country presses on, every country does more, and this country gets a lot more benefit for making a little extra effort. When actions are made conditional in this way, it pays every country to push on.

The incentive has to work in reverse as well. If a country does less, others have to do less. This is the stick that can enforce an agreement in which all countries pledge to do more.

This description of the problem makes enforcement seem easy. It isn't. The problem is that enforcing an agreement to cut back on CFCs is itself a collective action problem. Countries have incentives to free ride on enforcement, just as they have an incentive to free ride on the cutbacks themselves. The challenge is not just to devise big sticks—punishments that, when used, are hurtful to the target country. It is to make the threat to use the sticks *credible*. If a country reneges on its pledge to cut emissions, will it really pay all the other countries to increase their emissions? Doing so would punish the "cheater," but it would punish the countries using the stick even more. If these countries are worse off for using the stick, they will not use it, making the threat to use it incredible.

So, how were the Montreal cutbacks enforced? Instead of relying on conditionality, the agreement used a trade restriction. Under the agreement, trade was to be restricted between parties and non-parties both in substances controlled by the treaty (the CFCs themselves) and in products containing these substances (like refrigerators and air conditioners). The treaty also allowed parties to restrict trade with non-parties in products made using those substances (like computers), but this possibility was subsequently abandoned. Fortunately, it was not needed.

Whether trade restrictions will affect behavior depends on the participation level. If the participation level is low, non-participants will suffer very little from trade restrictions, and so will have little incentive to participate. Participants, by contrast, will be denied access to the largest markets, and so will have an incentive not to impose trade restrictions. If the participation level is high, these incentives will be reversed. Non-participating countries will suffer from the lack of market access, and so will have a strong incentive to participate. Participants, by contrast, will suffer little by imposing the trade restrictions. Indeed, they will positively gain by doing so if trade leakage is significant, for then the trade restrictions will prevent production from moving offshore. In theory, there should be a threshold level of participation that would cause the trade restrictions to tip behavior.

How can countries be assured that the treaty will exceed the threshold? This is easy. It is only necessary that the agreement enter into force (and so become legally binding on parties) after *enough* countries have ratified it. That critical level of participation identifies the tipping point. For the Montreal Protocol, the tipping point was the minimum participation level, defined by the agreement as representing two-thirds of global consumption. If participation were far below the two-thirds threshold, there would be nothing to lose by ratifying the agreement (since the agreement would not enter into force), whereas if participation exceeded the threshold, there would be a positive reason for ratifying it—the desire to avoid being the target of trade restrictions.

It is this combination of sticks and carrots, coupled with an extraordinary benefit–cost ratio that explains the treaty's great success. As of late 2006, there are only six non-participating countries: Andorra, Holy See, Iraq, San Marino, and Timor Leste.[9] This is not an agreement suffering from free riding.

Effectiveness

Has the Montreal Protocol succeeded? Has it been effective? According to the most recent scientific assessment, "The Montreal Protocol is working."[10] The abundance of ozone-destroying gases in the lower atmosphere has been declining. The abundance in the stratosphere is "now at or near a peak." Most importantly, "based on assumed compliance with the amended and adjusted Protocol by all nations, the Antarctic ozone 'hole,' which was first discerned in the early 1980s, is predicted to disappear by the middle of this century..."

Could more be done, even now? According to this same assessment, "A hypothetical elimination of all emissions derived from industrial production of all ozone depleting substances would advance the return of stratospheric loading to the pre-1980 values by about 10 years."[11] The gap between what is being done and the maximum possible effort is thus very, very small. By any standard, this is a remarkable achievement.

Unfortunately, the corresponding gap for global climate change could not be more different. I turn to this next.

Natural and human-induced climate change

Is the climate changing? Yes, certainly; but it has always changed. What is different today is that humans are causing it to change. This "human-induced climate change" is taking place against a background of "natural" climate change.

Two primary forces determine the climate: the amount of solar radiation that strikes the Earth and the amount of this radiation that is trapped by the atmosphere.

Solar radiation varies according to a cycle (of varying amplitude) of about 11 years, but the solar cycle is too weak to create a corresponding climate cycle. More important are the cycles that determine how solar radiation is *distributed*. Just as gravitational forces exerted by the Moon and Sun give us two high tides a day, so the gravitational pull of more distant objects like Jupiter cause the Earth's angle of tilt to change over a cycle of about 41,000 years, varying the amount of solar radiation that strikes the high latitudes. The Earth's orbit around the sun (its "eccentricity") also varies, bringing the Earth closer to the sun in cycles lasting about 100,000 years. Finally, the Earth's slow wobble (or "precession") causes another cycle lasting around 23,000 years. Together, these last three cycles (known as Milankovitch cycles) are powerful enough to explain the timing of the ice ages.

Gases in the atmosphere—primarily water vapor and carbon dioxide (CO_2), but also methane, nitrous oxide, and fluorocarbons (the same gases that deplete the ozone layer) absorb some of the heat that is re-radiated by the Earth. Most of these "greenhouse" gases exist naturally (fluorocarbons, the exception, are human made), warming the Earth by about $34°C$. Humans, however, have been adding these gases to the atmosphere (with CO_2 being the largest by far by volume). Since the beginning of the industrial era, concentrations have increased by about a third. Over the last century, mean global temperature has also increased (by about 0.6°C), and according to the Intergovernmental Panel on Climate Change, most of this warming "is attributable to human activities."[12] Temperature follows concentrations with a lag, however, and so the full effect of the increase in concentrations has yet to be felt. By 2100, mean global temperature is expected to increase by about 1.4 to 5.8°C.[13] Beyond 2100, temperature is expected to increase even more.

Climate complexities

If the climate were a simple, linear system, predicting future climate change would be easy. We would only need to know the dynamics of how concentrations affect temperature. The climate, however, is an enormously complex system. It cannot be explained by a single relationship.

Even the two primary forces of radiation and absorption interact. Solar radiation over the tropics drives the monsoons, which flood wetlands, which in turn release methane into the atmosphere. Warming over the Arctic has a similar effect: Arctic wetlands release methane in warmer periods.

Carbon dioxide concentrations also obey regularities that coincide with the 100,000, 41,000, and 23,000 year cycles noted earlier, though the reasons for this are not fully understood. At the minimum of these cycles, CO_2 concentrations are around 200 parts per million (ppm); at the peak, they are around 280–300 ppm.

According to climate scientist William Ruddiman, the history of the Earth's chemistry suggests that the concentration level at the start of the industrial revolution should have been around 240 ppm, when we know it was closer to 280 ppm.[14] Methane concentrations have also gone against trend; they increased over the last several millennia when the historical cycles suggest that they should have fallen. In his book, *Plows, Plagues, and Petroleum*, Ruddiman hypothesizes that both anomalies are due to earlier human activity, particularly the rise of agriculture. If he is right, human-induced climate change began around 8,000 years ago, not at the start of the industrial era. In Ruddiman's own words, the "Earth should have undergone a large natural cooling during the last several thousand years, and that at least a small glaciation would have begun several millennia ago had it not been for greenhouse-gas releases from early human activities."[15] In short, the stable climate experienced during the modern human era of the last few thousand years may have been unnatural.

This is a controversial hypothesis, and one that has been challenged by leading climatologists.[16] It may be false. It may be qualitatively correct (early humans did influence the climate) but quantitatively inaccurate (perhaps pre-industrial CO_2 would have been 270 ppm, rather than 240 ppm, were it not for human influence). Whatever the final verdict proves to be, Ruddiman's hypothesis provides a useful perspective. It forces us to ask the question, is human influence on the climate necessarily harmful?

If Ruddiman's calculations are correct, then human influence up to now would probably be viewed as being benign and perhaps even welcome because (ironically) it preserved stability. But does that mean that all human influence on the climate is to be welcomed? The evidence suggests that gradual and modest climate change will probably not be very disruptive. It may even promise some benefits (a higher mean global temperature coupled with higher CO_2 concentrations could be to the advantage of agriculture), though it may have worrying distributional effects (lowering agricultural productivity in some places, even as it increases productivity elsewhere). Abrupt climate change, however, would be a very different matter. Since the installed base of capital, including the stock of natural ecosystems, is tied to our present climate, change of any kind (warming or cooling) would be harmful overall if it occurred at a rate that exceeded the rate of capital turnover (about two human generations) and the rate of ecological adaptation (much longer than two human generations). Similarly, catastrophic change, such as would be caused by the melting of Greenland ice or the disintegration of the West Antarctic Ice Sheet, even if it occurred over a very long period of time, would be costly. These are the changes that should concern us most.

Abrupt and catastrophic climate change

The meridional overturning circulation carries warm, salty water from the tropics towards the North Atlantic where, upon encountering the frigid North Atlantic air, it cools and sinks.[17] The current then flows southward, where it mixes with the salt-laden Antarctic current, and is distributed to the Pacific and Indian Oceans. In these waters, the current warms again and, pushed by the winds, begins its northward journey to complete another lap.

Analysis of this system suggests that it is likely to be characterized by multiple equilibria, meaning that its strength can vary; the system could even collapse.[18] The record frozen in the ice covering Greenland shows that abrupt switches have occurred in the past, and human-induced climate change could cause more such switches in the future: a warming of the atmosphere over the North Atlantic combined with an infusion of fresh water from glacial melt, for example, would weaken the forces that now cause the current to sink. This in turn would cause the climate of northern Europe to cool (relative, that is, to a world already experiencing "global warming"). How serious is this prospect? At a meeting I recently attended, Earth scientist Richard Alley put it this way: 'In looking to the future, a wide range of evidence from models and the paleoclimatic record shows that a shutdown in the north Atlantic cannot trigger another ice age, stop all of the Gulf Stream (most of the flow is wind-driven), or extinguish humanity.'[19] So the downside risk may be limited, though there remain reasons for concern.

Sea level rise is another concern. 21,000 years ago, during the last glacial maximum, sea level was 120–135 meters lower than it is today—with all that "lost" water being stored in huge ice sheets.[20] As these great ice sheets retreated to their current positions, the meltwater refilled the oceans. Over the last century, sea level increased about one- to two-tenths of a meter; over the current century it is expected to rise another half a meter or so.[21] Part of this future increase will be due to the direct effect of temperature on water (water expands as it warms), but part will be due to the melting of water still frozen on land.

The latter effect depends on the fates of the Greenland and Antarctic ice sheets, which depend in turn on temperature increase and a number of other effects, including an increase in mass caused by greater snowfall.

The melting of the Greenland Ice Sheet is expected to exceed snow accumulation for warming over 3°C (and note that local warming over Greenland is likely to exceed global mean warming, possibly several times over), with sea level increasing perhaps seven meters over a thousand years. This change, however, may be accompanied by a negative feedback: the meltwater released could weaken the North Atlantic deepwater formation (fresh water is lighter than salt water), causing localized cooling and thus a slowing in the rate of melting.[22]

The East Antarctic Ice Sheet has thickened as a result of increased snowfall, but the West Antarctic Ice Sheet has been thinning, probably due to changes in the surrounding ocean. These changes may also trigger a feedback, but a positive one. In contrast to Greenland, the discharge of freshwater into the Southern Ocean may amplify the warming effect of the meridional overturning circulation.[23] Disintegration of West Antarctic ice sheet could add another five or six more meters to sea level. The prospects of this happening seem unlikely, but recent changes observed around the edges of both Greenland and Antarctica surprised ice scientists.[24] We may be in for more surprises.

So, this is what we know: the climate is a complex system. It has changed in the past; it will change in the future. The climate changes for natural reasons, but increasing concentrations of greenhouse gases, caused by human activities, will be a future cause of change, whether it has been so in the past or not. Climate science has progressed; it has resolved some uncertainties; but it has also discovered new ones that were previously hidden from view. In the future, science will show us even more. Predicting climate change, however, will remain difficult for the simple reason that we are conducting an experiment unlike any tried before. Just as the appearance of the "ozone hole" caught us unawares, so will climate change surprise us. We will not know the outcome of this experiment, at least in its details, until it is revealed to us, slowly, over the coming decades and centuries (our most advanced computer models can only guess at these futures).

Framework Convention

What should we do about climate change? The Framework Convention on Climate Change, adopted in 1992, says that we should aim to stabilize "greenhouse gas concentrations in the atmosphere at a level that would prevent dangerous anthropogenic interference with the climate system." This seems uncontroversial. Who could be in favor of dangerous interference with the Earth's only climate? No one, obviously; and that is one reason why almost every country has ratified this agreement.

And yet we do not know the concentration level needed to avoid dangerous interference. It has been widely suggested (by the European

Union among others) that global mean temperature should not be allowed to increase by more than 2°C. This may be right, or it may be too low or too high. Assume, however, that this is the ideal temperature change target. What concentration level should we then aim for?

That is difficult to say, because the relationship between concentrations and temperature is uncertain. At a concentration level of 550 parts per million (ppm) CO_2, mean global temperature could rise from 1.5° to 4.5°C (with small probability, it might even fall outside of this range). Put differently, to be confident (but not certain) of limiting temperature change to 2°C would require capping concentrations at a level far below 550 ppm—to a level more like 380 ppm.[25] This means limiting concentrations to the current level, and without major investment in technologies that can take carbon dioxide out of the air, that is essentially impossible.

In addition to climate sensitivity, we cannot be sure that a temperature change greater than 2°C is truly dangerous. Nor can we be sure that a smaller temperature change is really safe.[26] What we know is this: as concentration levels rise, the consequences of climate change will worsen (at least beyond some point), perhaps sharply (again, at least beyond some point). This means that we should be willing to make sacrifices to stay below a 2°C change but that we should not be willing to pay any price to avoid exceeding a 2°C change. Surpassing a 2°C increase is not equivalent to a ten kilometer wide asteroid slamming into the Earth.

Tradeoffs

Here is another fundamental point: Doing something about climate change also has consequences. Though climate change could be dangerous, preventing, slowing, or averting climate change could also be dangerous. For example, it is inconceivable that emissions will be reduced substantially over the next several decades without a massive expansion in nuclear power, posing problems for waste storage and proliferation.

The scale of the challenge is without precedent. According to climate scientist Ken Calderia and coauthors, "To achieve stabilization at a 2°C warming, we would need to install . . . the equivalent of a large carbon emissions-free power plant . . . somewhere in the world every day" for the next half century.[27] After that, the rate of installation in carbon-free electricity generation would have to increase even more.

More broadly, investing resources in climate mitigation has an opportunity cost—and one that we are morally obligated not to ignore. If we invest in reducing greenhouse gas emissions, that necessarily means not investing in something else.

Poor countries are especially vulnerable to climate change, partly because they are located near the equator, where temperatures are already high—higher than would be economically "optimal."[28] If there were a thermostat, people living in the low latitudes would probably choose to turn it down. From this perspective, climate change turns the thermostat in the "wrong" direction. As well, poor countries rely to a greater extent on the environment for their livelihood. Agriculture as a share of income is much higher in poor countries than in rich countries. Poor countries are thus relatively more vulnerable.

Poor countries also suffer from other problems. They lack the resources, institutions, and technologies that could shield them from the harmful consequences of climate change. For these same reasons, these countries are also the least able to adapt to climate change. And adaptation is going to be essential no matter how successful we are in limiting concentrations.

So, how should developing countries be helped? Would it be better for the industrialized countries to invest in limiting the increase in atmospheric concentrations? Or should they instead help to reduce the vulnerability of poorer countries to climate change? Of course, both actions are needed, but what is the right balance?

The answer isn't obvious. To take a concrete example, consider the possibility that climate change might increase the range of malaria, which already kills over a million people a year. Current research suggests that malaria might increase in areas of higher altitude, rather than in areas of higher or lower latitude, with perhaps a 5–7 percent increase in geographical exposure in Africa by 2100.[29] To limit this future risk, we could reduce atmospheric concentrations of greenhouse gases, so that climate change—and the attendant change in malaria prevalence—increased by less (relative to the "business as usual" increase) in the future. Alternatively, we could supply bed nets, carry out more environmental controls, prevent resistance to antimalarials, and invest in the research needed to develop a malaria vaccine. Reducing emissions would limit malaria's *increase* in some areas by a small amount decades from now. Spending directly on malaria control would reduce *total* malaria prevalence *everywhere* and perhaps much sooner. So, which approach to investment should we choose? Again, both approaches are needed, but the resources spent reducing greenhouse gas emissions cannot also be spent reducing malaria prevalence directly.[30] Choices really do have to be made.

To sum up, the problem is not only to limit concentrations to avoid dangerous interference; it is to reduce climate change risk: to make climate change, especially abrupt and catastrophic climate change, less likely; and to make the consequences of climate change less harmful (adaptation). It is also to recognize that the actions taken to mitigate or otherwise reduce climate change (including geoengineering, discussed in Chapter 1, this volume) entail costs and risks, and that what we do about climate change cannot be separated from the broader needs of sustainable development.

Kyoto Protocol

The Kyoto Protocol, adopted in 1997, was meant to initiate a sequence of emission reductions that would eventually fulfill the ambition of the Framework Convention. As the first step in that sequence, Kyoto only limits the emissions of a relatively small number of countries by just a little bit for only a short period of time. But as more steps were added, presumably in follow-on protocols, emissions were supposed to be cut more and more. Eventually, it was hoped, these emission reductions would allow concentrations to be stabilized—and at a level that would prevent "dangerous interference."

Will that hope be realized? With full participation, and assuming that the emission limits were extended indefinitely, or even reduced 1 percent per year, calculations by climatologist Tom Wigley show that, "the rate of slow-down in temperature rise [would be] small, with no sign of any approach to climate stabilization. The Protocol, therefore, even when extended as here, can be considered as only a first and relatively small step towards stabilizing the climate. The influence of the Protocol would, furthermore, be undetectable for many decades."[31]

To stabilize concentrations even at levels that, more likely than not, would allow temperature change to exceed 2°C, much, much more would have to be done. Stabilizing concentrations implies an atmospheric balance, with the quantity of molecules being added to the atmosphere equalling the quantity being subtracted. Not all of the gases put into the atmosphere stay there. A fraction of CO_2 is absorbed by the oceans and by biomass growth. As long as we emit more greenhouse gases (and do not reduce concentrations by "air capture"), however, concentrations will continue to rise. Limiting concentrations even to 550 ppm would require something like "50 years of flat emissions, followed by a linear decline of about two thirds in the following 50 years, and a very slow decline thereafter that matches the declining ocean sink."[32]

The emissions referred to here are *global* levels. Kyoto, as mentioned before, limits the emissions of only a relatively small number of countries. So, to have any chance of stabilizing concentrations, Kyoto would have to limit the emissions of many more countries. Current projections are that global emissions will more than double over the next 50 years.[33] This means that, just to stabilize CO_2 concentrations in the long run at a level like 550 ppm, global emissions would have to be cut by more than half by 2050, and by much more after this.

Contrast these numbers with what has been achieved so far. Global emissions have been rising ever since the Framework Convention was adopted in 1992. From Kyoto's 1990 base year through 2003 (the most recent year for which data are available), global CO_2 emissions have increased about 19 percent.[34]

Kyoto will not reverse this trend. Kyoto aims to cap the emissions of 38 industrialized countries, while imposing no limits on the world's more than 150 other countries, including large, fast-growing countries like China and India. Moreover, the limits for 13 of these 38 countries (all from Central and Eastern Europe and the former Soviet Union) far exceed their actual emissions (the difference is known to insiders as "hot air"). Finally, of the countries facing real limits, the largest, the United States, withdrew support for the treaty. So did Australia. This means that Kyoto really only constrains the emissions of about 23 countries. Even if Kyoto works as intended, global emissions will keep on rising.

Worse, compliance by the 23 emission-constrained countries is not assured. An official document of the Government of Canada says that Canada's emissions in 2010 will be at least 45 percent above its target.[35] For Canada to reduce emissions by that much, over such a short period of time (by 2012), would be very costly—and perhaps hard to justify given that Canada's big neighbor and main trading partner was doing nothing to limit its emissions. Canada could comply with the treaty by purchasing "hot air," but that would mean paying for compliance without the expenditure yielding any environmental benefit. What would be the point? Finally, Article 18 of the agreement says that, "any [compliance] procedures and mechanisms . . . entailing binding consequences shall be adopted by means of an amendment." As no such amendment has been agreed, Canada could not be punished for failing to comply. What then is its incentive to comply?

Of course, Canada is in a particularly sticky position. But if emissions are to be cut by the amounts needed to stabilize concentrations, even at a level that would make temperature change greater than $2°C$ more rather than less likely, the challenge facing Canada today will have to be addressed by *every* country. And then, after that is done, global emissions will have to be reduced by much more.

The problem with the Kyoto approach is not just that it aims to do too little. It is that it fails to provide a foundation upon which more could be achieved. Its success depends on effective enforcement—so that all essential countries are assured of participating, and all participating countries of complying. The approach is suited to domestic regulation (it bears a striking resemblance to the United States Clean Air Act amendments of 1990), but not to the international arena. Under the rules of international law, countries are free to participate in treaties or not as they please, and while there is a customary obligation for countries to comply, there is no world executive that can enforce compliance. The essential challenge of a treaty is to restructure incentives so that countries are better off participating than not participating, and better off complying than not complying. The Montreal Protocol did that. The Kyoto Protocol does not.

Kyoto reconsidered

What is Kyoto capable of? Many of the parties to this agreement have already instituted emission reduction programs, the most ambitious including the European Union's Emissions Trading Scheme and Sweden's carbon tax. These measures, however, are enforced internally. Where Kyoto overreaches is in relying on its own specific compliance mechanisms.[36] The problem is not only with Kyoto's design; it is with this design encountering the elemental forces of sovereignty.

The Stability and Growth Pact of the European Economic and Monetary Union also relied on its own mechanisms for enforcement—and collapsed when put to the test in 2003.[37]

Lack of an explicit enforcement mechanism need not undermine the agreement entirely. Declaring publicly an intention to do certain things or to achieve certain goals creates expectations that countries will at the very least make good faith efforts to fulfill their promises. And if these declarations are specific, as they are in Kyoto, then an opportunity is also created for progress to be monitored. Enforcement can then rely on domestic institutions, both formal and informal, and on the international sanction of "naming and shaming." Finally, when such declarations are made in an international setting, to address an issue of common concern, yardsticks are created against which the declarations of different countries can be compared.[38]

The problem with Kyoto is not that it will do nothing. It is that it cannot do enough.

Ozone versus climate

Why is climate change proving harder to address than ozone layer protection? The reason is that ozone depletion and climate change are very different problems. The economics of doing a lot are much more favorable to the global public good of ozone layer protection than to the global public good of climate mitigation.

Calculations by William Nordhaus and Joseph Boyer suggest that an "optimal" climate policy (meaning, basically, a policy that maximizes benefits minus costs for the world) would yield a benefit–cost ratio of about 3 : 1. This is an attractive ratio, even if it is less stunning than the estimates presented earlier for ozone protection. However, this "optimal" policy only reduces emissions by a small amount—by about 5 percent in 2015 and by 11 percent by 2100. These reductions would not stabilize concentrations. A policy of stabilizing carbon dioxide concentrations at 560 ppm, according to Nordhaus and Boyer, would yield a benefit–cost ratio of just 0.5. By their calculations, stabilizing concentrations at this level is not worth doing.

The numbers underlying this last ratio are revealing, particularly when compared with similar calculations for protecting the ozone layer; see Table 3.3. Care must be taken in comparing the estimates, but the qualitative image created by the comparison is valid. It is

Table 3.3. Comparison of the Economics of Ozone Protection and Climate Stabilization (Benefits and Costs in Billions)

	Benefit	Cost	B-C ratio
Protecting ozone layer	$2,775	$250	11 : 1
Stabilizing CO_2 concentrations	$681	$1,365	0.5 : 1

Sources: The values for ozone layer protection (converted from 1997 €) are taken from the last row of Table 4.2, multiplied by an exchange rate of $1.175/€, an approximation of the rate used by Velders et al. (2000) to convert 1997 U.S. dollar estimates from the ARC Research Consultants (1997) study into Euros. The values for stabilizing carbon dioxide concentrations, in 1990 U.S. dollars, are from Nordhaus and Boyer (2000: 130).

also striking. The benefits of ozone protection are a lot higher, and the costs of ozone protection a lot lower. The benefits are higher because, as explained before, ozone protection saves human lives (milder winters would offer a health benefit from climate change) and no country gains from ozone depletion (as noted previously, some countries may gain from climate change). The costs are lower because it is much easier to substitute for CFCs than fossil fuels. Note as well the contrasting scenarios being compared in Table 3.3. The estimates for protecting the ozone layer are for a policy that will restore the ozone layer. The climate policy shown in the table will not return CO_2 concentrations to their pre-industrial levels. It will instead allow them to double.

Commentary on the Stern review

Just as I was revising this book, the British Government published a new report on the economics of climate change. The review, undertaken by Sir Nicholas Stern, Head of the Government Economics Service, was headline news. London's *Independent* newspaper called its launch date, THE DAY THAT CHANGED THE CLIMATE. Why did Stern's review attract so much attention? It helped that the report was endorsed by the Prime Minister and the Chancellor of the Exchequer, but there was another reason. The Stern Review concluded that "the benefits of strong, early action considerably outweigh the costs;"[39] that atmospheric concentrations should be prevented from exceeding twice the pre-industrial level;[40] and that the benefit–cost ratio of doing so is about 10 : 1.[41] These conclusions contrast with the mainstream literature.[42] They differ from the results I have reported here.

Why the difference? Before answering this question, you might consider just how difficult it is to know what we should do about this problem. Economic analysis must obviously take into account uncertainties in the science, including the possibility of abrupt climate change. But it must also recognize other uncertainties. What new technologies will be available to us a century and more ahead? We do not know. How expensive will it be to reduce emissions substantially, over the long run, and on a global scale? Again, we do not know; the effort required is unprecedented. We are ultimately interested in the wellbeing of future generations, as well as of the current generation, but what will future generations care about? That we also do not know. As we peer further and further into the future, these uncertainties get larger and larger.

Another point: To know what we should do about this problem requires that we contemplate the ethics of making alternative choices. Economic analysis must also embrace ethical considerations. It must incorporate value judgments. A judgment has to be made about the criterion for evaluating our choices. A judgment also has to be made about particular values incorporated within the analysis. This is true of the study I cited earlier by Nordhaus and Boyer. It is also true of the Stern Review.

Two values are especially important in that they explain a large part of the difference between Stern's conclusions and those more typical of the "mainstream" literature.[43] Reducing emissions is an investment. We pay the cost in the near term. We reap the benefit in the future. The values that matter make these near term costs and future benefits comparable. They are incorporated within "the rate of discount," which puts a weight on the wellbeing of future generations relative to those of the current generation. In the Stern Review, these values appear in a technical appendix.

Though Stern recommends urgent action, he also says that, "Only a small portion of the cost of climate change between now and 2050 can be realistically avoided, because of inertia in the climate system."[44] The aim of acting urgently is thus to help future generations, and this is why discounting is so important.

The generations that will benefit the most from this urgent action will not be born for some time. Damages on a substantial scale that can be avoided do not arise until after around 2100 (according to

Stern, if nothing is done to curb emissions, "temperature increases may exceed 2–3°C by the end of this century").[45] They increase even more after that. According to Stern, "Preliminary estimates of average losses in global per-capita GDP in 2200 range from 5.3 to 13.8%, depending on the size of the climate-system feedbacks and what estimates of 'non-market impacts' are included."[46] These are substantial damages, but over the next 194 years more than the climate will change, and some of these other changes are also relevant to this analysis. One such change expected by Stern is a significant rise in per capita consumption. "In the baseline-climate scenario, 5°C warming is not predicted to occur until some time between 2100 and 2150. By then, growth in GDP will have made the world considerably richer than it is now."[47] So Stern's review urges the current generation to sacrifice for the future, even though the future will be better off (and better off, I should emphasize, by a measure that takes account of non-market impacts and the risk of catastrophic climate change).

That the world should be richer despite suffering substantial climate change damages may seem a contradiction. It need not be. Growth, compounded over many decades, can increase incomes substantially. Climate change may hit future generations hard in percentage terms, but many decades of growth may be more than able to absorb this loss. Even taking climate change into account, the future can be much better off than the present.

So the question is how much the current generation should assist the future, when the future is expected to be better off. This is where the values I mentioned before come in. With a near zero rate of discount, damages suffered a century or two from now are treated almost as if they were happening to us now. With a higher rate of discount, the future matters less to the present. Stern uses a lower rate of discount than Nordhaus and Boyer, and that is why his review recommends that we do more about climate change in the near term. It is also why his benefit–cost ratio is higher.

(The benefit–cost ratio for ozone layer protection summarized in Table 3.3 is calculated using a 5 percent rate of discount, which is much higher than the rate used by Stern. If ozone layer protection were analyzed in a manner consistent with Stern's analysis of climate change, ozone layer protection would appear much more attractive. The *contrast* between the economics of ozone layer protection and climate change mitigation would thus remain very striking.)

Where does the discount rate come from? It is not a number you can just look up in a book. It reflects value judgments—to be specific, it reflects two separate values.

The first is how we weight the wellbeing of a future generation relative to our own.[48] Is the future generation worth any less, simply because it exists in the future? Stern answers yes, because there is a small probability of extinction, and it would be a waste for the current generation to sacrifice for a future generation that may not even exist. Interestingly, Stern notes that extinction could occur from an asteroid impact or nuclear war or "a devastating outbreak of some disease."[49] All of these concerns, discussed elsewhere in this book, are important; but the probability of extinction is very, very low. Hence, Stern takes this value to be very low.

Other considerations may also deserve attention. Perhaps people have a preference for generations living sooner rather than later; perhaps they would rather help their grandchildren than their grandchildren's grandchildren. The point is that we can't determine this value simply by calculating the probability of the Earth being hit by a large asteroid. The weight we give to the future is a more fundamental social choice. As Thomas Schelling has put it, the problem is akin to "a foreign aid program, with some of the foreigners being our own descendants who live not on another continent but in another century."[50]

The second value is how we compare the wellbeing of societies having different per capita consumption levels. These include richer and poorer communities today, and richer and poorer generations. Stern also chooses a relatively low value for this parameter.[51] A higher value, reflecting a greater concern for equity, would have discounted the future more heavily simply because, in Stern's analysis, the future is expected to be better off.

Stern argues that rich countries should reduce their emissions today to help today's poor countries decades from now ("There is no single formula that captures all dimensions of equity, but calculations based on income, historic responsibility and per capita emissions all point to rich countries taking responsibility for emission reductions of 60–80% from 1990 levels by 2050"),[52] because poorer countries are more vulnerable to climate change ("The impacts of climate change are not evenly distributed—the poorest countries and people will suffer earliest and most.");[53] but he concludes that today's relatively poor generation should help richer generations living in the future. There seems to be an inconsistency here.

There need not be. Consider the question I asked before: Is it better to cut emissions today so as to reduce climate change damages experienced by poor countries in the future, or is it better to make other investments that can benefit poor countries today—and, in the bargain, help to insulate them from future climate change? Again, we need to do both, but how should we balance these allocations? A problem with the economic analyses of climate change is that they allow different societies, both within and between generations, to interact only in their choice of emission levels. Investment in, say, R&D for a malaria vaccine should be taken into account as well (Chapter 7). Such investments should be co-determined with the emissions path.

Stern also draws attention to the possibility of catastrophe (as do Nordhaus and Boyer in their analysis). What role does this play? Imagine that we knew there existed a threshold level of atmospheric concentrations beyond which catastrophe would be certain. Then it would obviously be imperative to avoid this threshold. Discounting would play a role, not in determining the threshold to be avoided, but in determining the path of emission reductions from today into the future. Low discount rates would shift the burden towards the present. High discount rates would move it to the future. Moving the burden to the future need not be unethical. Indeed, and as explained before, it would be commended if a dollar's sacrifice by the future were valued less than a dollar's sacrifice by the present (as would be the case if the future were richer and so had more dollars to play with). The point is that, under these assumptions, the discount rate would not affect the ultimate need to avoid crossing the catastrophic threshold.

To sum up, the Stern Review makes it seem as if the choices before us are simple and obvious. They are neither.[54] They depend on more than facts and science. They depend on value judgments. They also depend on the options for investment that are considered. Rather than choose particular values for the parameters noted here, it would be better to reveal the implications of choosing different values.[55] The implications of making alternative investments should also be revealed. Both will have profound social as well as environmental consequences.

Montreal versus Kyoto

From 1985 to 1999—a period of 14 years—international cooperation to protect the ozone layer achieved almost as much as was technically possible. From 1992 to 2006—another period of 14 years—international efforts to limit global climate change achieved almost nothing. Could the mechanisms that allow the Montreal Protocol to work effectively be used to make Kyoto work better? Could trade restrictions achieve the kind of enforcement that is needed?

The idea is seductive. It has been recommended by a Nobel Prize winning economist.[56] It has been proposed by the Prime Minister of France.[57] Indeed, it is hard to see how a treaty like Kyoto could be enforced by any other means. There may be a question as to whether trade restrictions would be legal, but at one level this may not matter. If the parties to the World Trade Organization wanted Kyoto to incorporate trade restrictions, they could change the multilateral trading rules. The Montreal Protocol trade restrictions probably violated the General Agreement on Tariffs and Trade when they were first adopted, and yet no party to this agreement ever challenged them.

The real problem with using trade restrictions is more fundamental. As noted before, to be effective a trade restriction has to be both severe and credible. As restrictions become more severe, however, they tend to become less credible. Trade restrictions applied against non-parties, including the United States, would harm the countries imposing them. They may also provoke countermeasures, making them even more damaging to the countries imposing them.

And if trade restrictions were incorporated in a new agreement, as they would need to be, then *all* of the treaty's provisions would be opened up for reconsideration. Since trade restrictions are only really credible when the participation level is high, a revised agreement might raise the minimum participation level for entry into force. This, however, would increase the chance of the treaty never entering into force. (In the limit, if all countries must participate for the agreement to enter into force, then every country has a veto.) Alternatively, to increase the participation rate, the obligations to reduce emissions might be weakened. But then the agreement would achieve very little, even if it were enforced using trade restrictions.

Use of trade restrictions also raises practical problems. Since the production of everything results in the emission of greenhouse gases, on what basis are trade restrictions to be applied? The Montreal Protocol trade restrictions were applied to CFCs and products containing CFCs. As noted before, the treaty suggested that parties might also restrict trade in products made using CFCs, but this provision was never exercised. That was for a simple reason: this last provision was thought to be impossible to implement.

There are probably good reasons why trade restrictions were not incorporated in the Kyoto Protocol from the beginning.

Conclusions

Global public goods requiring aggregate efforts are particularly susceptible to free riding. Not even the largest and most powerful country can supply them unilaterally, and every country's contribution to the overall effort is a perfect substitute for every other country's efforts. If one group of countries supplies more of a global public good requiring aggregate efforts, other countries will not have an incentive to step up their efforts. Indeed, they may have an incentive to pare back. This is particularly true when trade leakage exacerbates free rider incentives. Treaties can potentially restructure these incentives, but how?

Analysis of the Montreal Protocol on Substances that Deplete the Ozone Layer shows that a combination of carrots and sticks is needed—to make participation and compliance more attractive, even as the parties to a treaty step up their individual efforts at provision. The Kyoto Protocol was inspired by this earlier agreement and is in many respects even more ingenious. Its so-called "flexible mechanisms" are certainly a marvel, much more sophisticated than any to be found in the Montreal Protocol. But the Kyoto Protocol has had more difficulty in supporting enforcement, which is essential to the supply of this kind of global public good. That Kyoto has encountered such difficulties should not come as a surprise: the enforcement challenge for climate change mitigation is much greater than it was for protecting the ozone layer.

If mitigation fails, or if abrupt climate change should threaten us, there is another option available—one that is less vulnerable to free riding but that also poses different risks: geoengineering. I discussed this option in Chapter 1. It may also be possible to increase mitigation by relying on a radically different approach, by considering a different global public good dimension of the problem. I discuss this possibility in Chapter 6. Finally, it seems inevitable that at least some climate change will occur, making it necessary for countries to adapt. Adaptation will be harder for the poorer countries—one reason poorer countries are more vulnerable to climate change. I discuss this challenge in Chapter 7.

Another problem is the need to pay for the global public good of climate change mitigation. Paying for global public goods is the subject of the next chapter.

CHAPTER FOUR

Financing and burden sharing: paying for global public goods

> A newly prominent field of international economics has emerged during the last decade. It consists of programs...undertaken jointly by several countries and involving costs that have to be allocated among them...While there has been no coherent evolution of these cost-sharing schemes, some consensus on criteria does seem to be developing—criteria that are analogous to principles of international taxation or, perhaps more accurately, of intergovernmental taxation...The process seems likely to continue, for the present era of expensive international collaboration gives no evidence of being over.
>
> Thomas C. Schelling[1]

All the global public goods discussed thus far have to be paid for; they have to be financed. But since every country benefits from provision, which countries will pay? How will the costs of provision be shared? By what means will the costs be financed?

Financing arrangements inevitably reflect national interests. The amount of money raised depends on free rider incentives. Which countries pay the most depends on the distribution of benefits. Countries that benefit the most pay the most. When benefits are concentrated, free riding is less of a handicap; when benefits are diffused, it can be crippling.

Contributions can only be made "mandatory" in the sense that the amounts owed are explicit, and accompanied by a positive pledge or an implied obligation to pay. When a formula for cost sharing and an obligation to pay are both lacking, financing is more truly "voluntary." The differences between these approaches, however, are only a matter of degree. Both kinds of financing are vulnerable to free riding. In a world of sovereign states, they cannot be otherwise.

This chapter explains how global public goods are financed, and how the burden of paying for global public goods is shared.

Taxation and cost sharing

As noted in the introduction to this book, national public goods are typically financed out of general tax revenues—the public purse. The international system is different: there is no World Government, and there is no global tax. Indeed, it is striking that the European Union, which has achieved a remarkable degree of integration in a short period of time, does not (yet) have an EU-wide tax. Decisions about taxation within the EU require unanimity. Sovereignty still reigns in this critical area.

International coordination of taxes is possible. France recently proposed a "solidarity contribution levied on plane tickets...to combat hunger and poverty and finance global sustainable development."[2] The levy, supported also by Brazil, Chile, and Germany, would be collected by the airlines, and monitored and enforced nationally. Other proposals include a tax on carbon dioxide emissions or foreign currency transactions (the so-called "Tobin tax").

Tax coordination has advantages.[3] One of the reasons aviation fuel has gone untaxed for so long is the fear that, should any country adopt a tax unilaterally, the airlines would respond by refueling in a different jurisdiction.[4] Tax aviation fuel everywhere and at the same time and this incentive would disappear.

The motive of greed, however, would remain. As the number of countries adopting a new, coordinated tax increased, the temptation for other states not to adopt it, but to try to gain competitive advantage from the tax differential, or to free ride on the contributions made by others, would also increase.[5] In 1992, the European Community announced that it would adopt a harmonized carbon/energy tax (for the purpose of cutting emissions, not raising finance) provided other

OECD countries agreed to adopt the same tax. The other countries did not follow; Europe abandoned the tax.

The prevailing method of financing global public goods is to determine an overall budget, and then, somehow, to get countries to pay their share of the total. The contribution levels made by individual countries are then financed in the same way as national public goods—by each member country's tax system.

The size of the overall budget determines the amount of the global pubic good supplied. This was the subject of the previous three chapters. My focus here is on how the costs are divided, how the burden is shared.

Any number of cost sharing formulas can satisfy the algebra of adding up to the total required. But the decision to contribute is ultimately a voluntary one. Cost sharing arrangements must therefore take into account the possibility that countries may decline to contribute. Put differently, if these arrangements are to raise the monies needed, they must somehow make it in the interests of countries to contribute.

Unilateral versus multilateral funding

Some global public goods are self-financed—paid for entirely by the country providing them. Most small science research, for example, is financed in this way.[6]

Big science is different. It can be so expensive as to be beyond the reach of even the world's richest country. The United States once planned to build the world's largest particle accelerator, the Superconducting Super Collider, at a cost of $11 billion. When the U.S. failed to convince other countries to contribute to the project, it canceled construction—after having already sunk $2 billion into it. Apparently this project was too big even for the country likely to gain the most from it.

The United States later joined a similar project being built in Europe—the Large Hadron Collider, mentioned in Chapter 1. This project, which is also being financed by India, Japan, and Russia, was initiated by CERN (an organization known officially as the Conseil Européen pour la Recherche Nucléaire—in English, the European Organization for Nuclear Research—but almost always referred to simply as "CERN").

CERN is perhaps best known for inventing the World Wide Web (though readers of fiction may know it as the source of the antimatter stolen by a fictional secret society plotting to destroy the Vatican in Dan Brown's bestseller, *Angels and Demons*), but its main contribution to science has been in the field of high-energy particle physics. CERN was established in the 1950s by 12 states. Today it has 20 members.[7] CERN's web page explains why it exists:[8]

Countries spend some fraction of their gross national product on fundamental research but there are fields where the equipment needed is so expensive that it can be put together only with international efforts and collaboration. For particle physics, even the larger European countries could not afford to construct a laboratory as big as CERN, and the human resources to run it could not be found within a single nation.

Particle physics may seem detached from our everyday lives, but experiments at facilities like CERN have led to the development of a number of technologies that are in common use today. These include positron emission tomography (the PET scan), used for cancer diagnosis; lithography, used to make smaller and smaller computer chips—a reason the cost of computing has fallen so spectacularly; synchrotron radiation, used in the study of viruses; and mass spectrometry, used to detect very tiny objects, like dioxins in fish and steroids in athletes.

Who pays?

Who pays for a global public good? In the case of the fundamental knowledge produced at the facilities operated by CERN, it seems that none of the founding members had an incentive to finance the construction and operation unilaterally. For the members of CERN as a group, however, the *aggregate* benefits of supply exceeded the cost.

It is possible that participation by each of these 12 countries was critical—that is, were any member to drop out, no other country would step in, and the remaining members would have to cancel the project. It is more likely, however, that a different combination of countries would have been willing to finance CERN, or an organization much like it—a different dozen countries, perhaps, or more, or even fewer countries. The solution to the burden-sharing problem is generally likely to be more indeterminate than the solution to the problem of whether the global public good is supplied at all.

Why would more than the minimum required number of countries contribute? The reason is that it may be in their self-interest to do so.

Suppose that 11 countries were *willing* to pay for CERN. That is, suppose that their aggregate benefit from provision exceeded the cost. To be specific, let the country that benefits the most be labeled Country 1, the country that benefits second most be labeled Country 2, and so on. Denote Country 1's benefits by B_1, Country 2's by B_2, and so on again. These Bs represent values; they are expressed in amounts of money. Finally, let the cost of CERN be C—another value expressed as an amount of money. For 11 countries to be willing to finance CERN, their aggregate benefit must exceed the cost; formally, we must have $B_1 + B_2 + \ldots + B_{11} > C$.

To show that more countries might contribute, suppose that these 11 countries made a take it or leave it offer to Country 12. They would contribute an amount $\underline{C}$, but only if Country 12 paid the balance of the cost. If $B_{12} > C - \underline{C}$, then it would be in the interests of Country 12 to accept the offer, and a global public good that might have been supplied by 11 countries would instead be supplied by 12 countries. By the same logic, it should be easy to see that the number of countries contributing could be increased arbitrarily. While cost sharing implies a minimum participation level (provision is only in the collective interests of a group of countries when the aggregate benefit for the group exceeds the cost), it does not imply a maximum participation level.

Which countries will pay? The countries that benefit most from a global public good will not necessarily be the ones that contribute, but there will be a tendency for the major beneficiaries to contribute. Indeed, these countries are likely to contribute disproportionately to the effort.

Why is that? Consider a situation involving only two countries, with $B_1 > C \gg B_2$, where the "$\gg$" sign indicates that the cost of supplying the global public good is much greater than Country 2's benefit. In this situation, Country 1 (the "large" country) is in the weaker bargaining position. If it walks away from a negotiation over burden sharing, Country 2 (the "small" country) will not supply the global public good. By contrast, if Country 2 walks away, then Country 1 has an incentive to supply the good unilaterally. Being able to walk away from a negotiation is an indicator of bargaining strength. (You are always better off negotiating a higher salary when you have an attractive offer from another employer in hand.) Mancur

Olson called this phenomenon the " 'exploitation' of the great by the small."[9]

Another interesting situation is where more than one country has an incentive to supply a global public good unilaterally. Suppose $B_1 > B_2 > C$. In this case, it will pay Country 1 to supply the global public good if Country 2 does not supply it, but it will also pay Country 2 to supply the global public good if Country 1 does not supply it. Which country will supply the global public good? It is impossible to say. Either country might supply it. It is also possible, and perhaps even likely, that the two countries will share the cost.

All of this assumes that countries benefit only from the supply of the global public good. But countries may also benefit by participating in the effort to supply the global public good. Being a party to a big science project has its privileges. Members have a say in the experiments that are run; they gain access to new discoveries before the results are published; their scientists learn from interacting with colleagues from other countries.[10] Countries compete to host a project like CERN because of the associated benefits (the host country typically contributes more to the overall cost precisely for this reason). Not all of the benefits of CERN are purely public, at least not at the global level.

Countries may also contribute for reasons other than pure self-interest. They may want to show solidarity with a collective effort. They may feel a responsibility to contribute, particularly when it is known that they will benefit as much as the countries that are already contributing. They may feel an obligation to pay their "fair share." As we shall see later in this chapter, concerns for fairness quite deliberately enter into many burden-sharing arrangements.

Burden sharing in the Persian Gulf War

Hours after Iraq invaded its neighbor, Kuwait, on August 2, 1990, the United Nations Security Council passed Resolution 660, which condemned the invasion and demanded a withdrawal of Iraqi troops. A few days later, the Security Council imposed economic sanctions against Iraq; and soon after that, United States forces began massing in Saudi Arabia. In late November, the Security Council demanded that Iraq withdraw from Kuwait. A deadline was set—January 15, 1991— and Resolution 678 authorized the use of "all necessary means" to enforce Resolution 660. In the event, the threat had no effect; Iraq did not withdraw, and an attack was launched against Iraq on January 16, the day after the deadline. The war was quick; by late February it was over.

Restoring Kuwait's sovereignty was a global public good requiring a single best effort. It was a global public good because the liberation of Kuwait enforced, and so reaffirmed, the norm safeguarding a state's borders; it stabilized the global oil market (there was suspicion that, had Iraq not been confronted, it may have tried to take Saudi Arabia's oil fields); and it carried out the threat made in Resolution 678—an essential step to establishing the credibility of the Security Council: an investment in future global peace and security.

In all, the militaries of 33 countries joined the U.S. in helping to restore Kuwait's sovereignty. Estimates of the shares of the military contributions by the key coalition partners are shown in Figure 4.1.

Though the United States led the military effort to free Kuwait, the financial cost, as shown in Table 4.1, was borne mainly by other

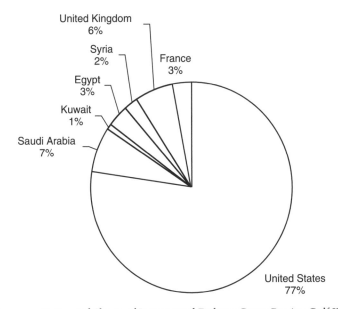

Figure 4.1. Estimated Shares of Incremental Defense Costs: Persian Gulf War

Source: Terasawa and Gates (1993: 15).

Table 4.1. Foreign Contributions Pledged in 1990–1991 to Offset U.S. Desert Shield/Storm Costs (Millions of U.S. Dollars)

Country	Commitments	Receipts			
		Cash	In-Kind	Total	Percent
Saudi Arabia	16,839	12,002	4,001	16,003	30.3
Kuwait	16,057	16,015	43	16,058	30.4
United Arab Emirates	4,088	3,870	218	4,088	7.7
Japan	10,012	9,437	571	10,008	19.1
Germany	6,572	5,772	683	6,455	12.2
Korea	355	150	101	251	0.5
Other	29	7	22	29	0.0
Total	53,952	47,254	5,639	52,893	100.0

Source: United States Department of Defense (1992: 725).

countries. These countries essentially compensated the United States for leading the effort to provide this global public good.

According to the U.S. Department of Defense report, the "incremental cost" of the Gulf War—that is, the cost over and above the expense needed to maintain the U.S. military in peacetime—was about $61 billion.[11] Based on this estimate and the figures shown in the table above, it seems that other countries paid about 87 percent of the costs incurred by the United States. Britain was also compensated partially for its sizable contribution to the military effort.[12]

Why did countries help to pay for these leading efforts? Why, in particular, did *these* countries help? They did so for the same reason that the countries in Figure 4.1 provided direct military assistance: they benefited from the action—more so than other states. Kuwait, of course, was the main beneficiary, but other states in the Gulf, including Saudi Arabia and the United Arab Emirates, were believed to be future targets for aggression. Japan and Germany, for reasons of history, domestic law, and politics, could not send troops. The best they could do was to send money.

How were their contributions arrived at? They reflected an allocation scheme proposed by the United States. According to a report prepared by the Congressional Research Service,

As projected US costs grew, the burdensharing issue became more heated, and it was a central matter of contention in the congressional debate over granting the President authority to use force against Iraq. In the wake of that debate, and following the start of hostilities, the Administration reportedly undertook negotiations to divide the financial burden of the military effort according to a formula that calls for Japan to provide 20% of the cost, the United States and other allies to provide 20%, and Kuwait and Saudi Arabia to provide 60%.[13]

As the numbers in Table 4.1 show, the actual contributions match these suggested levels almost to the dollar.

But why did these countries acquiesce? Why did they not free ride instead? According to one analysis, the reason is that the U.S. would not have intervened militarily without allied contributions: "It was precisely because the U.S. public was unwilling to act singly," these authors argue, "that other countries took seriously the risk of abandonment by the United States and avoided the temptation to ride free."[14] This implies that, if C were the cost of the war, and B_1 the benefit to the United States, then $C > B_1$. Other countries *had* to contribute in order to make it in the interests of the superpower to lead the effort.

Whether this is true or not, the United States benefited enormously by being part of a broad coalition. Of course, in exchange for the financial support it received, the U.S. also needed to share decision-making in the conduct of the war. But a collective response also confers legitimacy upon the decisions that are taken—an important consideration when the aim of the intervention is to reinforce international law.

The Iraq War

According to the estimates in Table 4.1, the Persian Gulf War, what is sometimes now called the *First* Gulf War, cost the United States just $7 billion. The current war in Iraq, the *Second* Gulf War, is proving much more costly.

Through 2005, the direct cost to the U.S. of the Iraq War topped $250 billion with coalition partners paying about $40 billion and Iraq itself bearing a cost of about $130 billion.[15] Since then, the costs have increased, with the costs to the U.S. alone exceeding $300 billion.[16] The final cost of the war cannot be calculated today— the war is still ongoing—but estimates range from $1 to $2 trillion.[17]

These estimates, I should add, omit vital if intangible costs, such as the loss of U.S. credibility, division among traditional allies, and the harm done to the United Nations. The second war could not have been more different from the first.

Why did the second war cost the U.S. so much more? One reason is that the different operations had different objectives: regime change versus the liberation of an invaded country; there was never going to be an insurgency movement in Kuwait. Another reason, of course, is that the First Persian Gulf War had the nearly universal support of other states. The invasion of Iraq lacked this support.

Writing before the Iraq War, Yale economist William Nordhaus asked, "Will other countries step up to pay the bills, as they did after the First Persian Gulf War? Probably not," he answered. "If the war is undertaken without UN sanction or broad international support, the US could be forced to pay the lion's share of the costs."[18] That, of course, is precisely what happened.

Benefits

What determines the benefits countries derive from a global public good? Benefits obviously vary according to the nature of the global public good. The eradication of smallpox, for example, yielded a greater benefit overall than would the successful eradication of poliomyelitis—for the simple reason that both diseases are about equally infectious, but smallpox killed around a third of infected persons, whereas polio causes paralysis in just one in two hundred cases, and kills only a small fraction of these victims.[19]

Benefits also vary among countries. The knowledge derived from the experiments conducted at CERN is of particular value to the most technologically advanced countries. Smallpox eradication benefited the endemic countries more than the countries that had sustained a high level of immunity. Ozone depletion is more damaging nearer the poles than the equator, making protection of the ozone layer more valuable to countries in the higher latitudes. Climate change is expected to increase temperatures by more in the higher latitudes, but these regions may benefit from a slight warming, as they are cold to begin with. Temperatures are expected to rise by less near the equator, but these regions may suffer the most, as their climate is already hot. Asteroids are more likely to crash into an ocean (since more than two-thirds of the Earth is covered by water), and the likelihood of a tsunami makes asteroid defense more valuable to coastal than to landlocked states. The Persian Gulf War benefited neighboring Gulf states more than states in other regions, oil-importing states more than oil exporters, and states needing to rely on international law for their security more than states with strong national defenses.

Holding everything else equal, however, two considerations are likely always to be relevant to the calculation of benefits: population and income per capita. This is because *people* benefit from the supply of global public goods, and their willingness to pay for provision—a measure of their benefit—while not determined by their income, will almost certainly increase in the level of their income.

Appendix Table 4.2A provides estimates of the population and income per capita of every member of the United Nations. (In the table, the members of the European Union are represented both as a group and as 25 independent states.[20] The EU has an established infrastructure for cooperation, but lacks both a common foreign policy and the authority to tax without the agreement of all its members, and so lies somewhere between being a single, federal state and a collection of truly independent states. In representing the EU as a single entity and its member states as independent units, I am following established treaty arrangements.)

The countries listed in the table are ranked according to the product of population and income per capita, or gross national income. The benefits of supplying global public goods will not be proportional to this measure (benefits may increase with income at a decreasing rate), but they will tend to be correlated with this measure. Bigger and richer countries usually benefit the most.[21]

United Nations scale of assessments

Do the amounts that countries *actually* pay for global public goods correlate with this crude indicator of benefits? The last column of Appendix Table 4.2A shows each country's actual share of financing the United Nations regular budget. All countries are members of the United Nations (well, nearly all), and all UN members help to finance the organization, which was established to contribute to the supply of global public goods such as peace and security generally.[22] The United

Nations is thus instrumentally important in supplying a general kind of global public good.

How is the UN financed? The regular budget (which, today, makes up only around one-tenth of total UN expenditure) is not financed voluntarily (at least not in the most narrow sense of that term; UN membership, of course, is voluntary, and as we shall see, states can influence their contributions both by their behavior and by their rhetoric); as I shall explain later in this chapter, a pure voluntary approach would be especially vulnerable to free riding. Nor is each country's share of the budget determined by direct bargaining; with more than 190 members, direct bargaining would be unwieldy. The arrangement instead is for assessments to be calculated by a committee—the Committee on Contributions, established by the members expressly for this purpose. The committee's recommendations are then approved by the General Assembly, almost always by consensus (unlike other resolutions, approval of the scale of assessments is binding on all members). The General Assembly also approves the organization's regular budget. The multiplication of these two numbers—a country's assessment (a percent or share) and the organization's budget (a value, measured in U.S. dollars)— determines each country's contribution.

The assessments are based loosely on a formula that reflects both population and income per capita, but not as a pure product. In its terms of reference, the Contributions Committee was asked "to follow the principle of 'capacity to pay,' and the suggestion was made to it that national income would be the 'fairest guide' to follow."[23] The Committee took this to mean that assessments should reflect the principle of "progressive taxation"—that countries should pay a progressively higher percentage of their national income, the higher was their income per capita. This made sense. This same principle, after all, is a common feature of most national tax systems, and the analogy between the assessments and taxes is hard to ignore.

The assessments are also subject to a ceiling and a floor. The maximum amount that any member must pay is limited to 22 percent. The minimum rate, set for the poorest countries, is 0.001 percent.

The principles upon which the assessments are based have remained largely intact since the Contributions Committee issued its first report in 1946. The values, however, have changed. I turn to these next.

The scale of assessments as a bargaining solution

The evolution of the ceiling is particularly interesting. The Contributions Committee originally proposed a ceiling of 49.86 percent (remember, the UN was founded in the aftermath of a war that had left much of the world, but not the United States, economically crippled), reflecting "the quite independent principle that the United States share should not exceed 50 percent."[24] At that time, the U.S. argued for a one-third share, but accepted 39.49 percent. Later, the ceiling was lowered to 33.33 percent. After that it was lowered to 25 percent. Today, as noted earlier, it stands at 22 percent.

The drop to 22 percent was agreed in 2000, following a period of gamesmanship in which the U.S. forced the hand of other states by withholding payment of past dues. The U.S. position was unpopular. (The assessments are a zero-sum game; if one country's assessment is lowered, the assessments of other countries must be increased; the total must always add to 100. However, the membership of the United Nations also increased over this time, making it easier to redistribute the burden.) The merits of the U.S. position were contested (Ambassador Richard Holbrooke explained that it reflected the twin criteria of "real ability to pay and real responsibility to contribute").[25] The manner in which it was expressed aroused strong feelings. But the assessments are not merely technical matters; they are the solution to a bargaining problem. However they may be determined, the assessments must ultimately be accepted by the membership.

As a comparison of the last two columns of Appendix Table 4.2A shows, the assessments are strongly correlated with a country's ranking as regards the product of income per capita and population. Although the assessments are calculated on the basis of capacity to pay, they also reflect—at least to some extent—willingness to pay, or the benefits countries derive from UN membership.[26]

This is the broad picture. There are also outliers. (The most striking outlier is Japan, discussed briefly below.)

One reason for the outliers is that the assessments are calculated using a different measure of income than are the data shown in the table (the table calculates income on the basis of purchasing power parity, which adjusts for the standard of living, whereas the assessments rely mainly on market exchange rates). The United States is currently arguing that the measure of income used to calculate the assessments ought to be changed.[27]

Another reason for the outliers is the progressive nature of the assessments. The simple product shown in the table increases linearly with income. If income per head doubles, and population is unchanged, the product of income and population precisely doubles. Under the progressive assessments formula, however, a country with twice the income per head, but the same population, pays a membership fee that is *more than* twice as large. (Costa Rica and New Zealand have the same population, but though New Zealand's income per capita is a little more than twice as large as Costa Rica's, its assessment is more than seven times as large.) As mentioned before, benefits are unlikely to increase linearly with income per capita. They might increase as a proportion of income, as income per head increases. But it seems unlikely that benefits would increase *this* strongly with income per capita.[28]

Although the assessments are derived from a principle of "capacity to pay," the discrepancies highlighted here may reflect a different consideration: not benefits, but bargaining power. As explained previously, there is a tendency for countries with a higher income per capita to bear a disproportionate share of the burden; there is a tendency for the "great" to be exploited by the "small."

Japan's assessment is the real standout, and consistent with the view that the assessments are a solution to a bargaining problem, it is Japan's assessment relative to those of other countries that is becoming the focus of negotiations today. Japan has argued not only that its assessment is too high. It has argued that the assessments of certain permanent members of the Security Council are too low.[29] The latter countries benefit disproportionately from membership, Japan argues, since their individual veto is decisive in the most crucial areas. To reflect this benefit, Japan believes that these countries should pay more. In particular, Japan has proposed that permanent members of the Security Council be subject to a floor of 3 or 5 percent. Japan also believes that the assessments need to be updated more regularly— a change that would increase the assessments of the fastest growing countries (such as China and India), relative to the slower growing, already rich countries. Such changes, if accepted, would increase the correlation between the product (of income per head and population) and the assessments. They would bring the assessments more in line with benefits.

Focal points

Because the UN scale of assessments provides a value for every country's relative contribution to the provision of a generic global public good—a value everyone knows and that everyone knows everyone knows—it serves as a *focal point* for other financing negotiations.[30] Indeed, the people who developed the scale were aware that it would play this role.[31]

How has the UN scale been used? In some cases, it has been applied directly. Most of the UN specialized agencies, such as the World Health Organization, are financed in this way.

In other cases, adjustments are made. For example, the Multilateral Fund established under the Montreal Protocol is financed on the basis of a single modification to the UN scale: developing countries that consume each year less than 0.3 kilograms per capita of ozone depleting chemicals pay nothing. These 143 countries instead receive assistance. The Ozone Fund (so far, totaling about $2 billion) is financed entirely by the other countries, with the relative contributions of individual countries determined by UN scale.

Probably the most well known financing arrangement to be based on the UN scale is for UN peacekeeping. I turn to this next.

Peacekeeping and humanitarian interventions

Peacekeeping is a means for supplying the essential global public good of world order.

Humanitarian missions serve a related purpose: in the words of Security Council Resolution 1674, they protect persons—civilians, especially—from the worst abuses of "genocide, war crimes, ethnic cleansing and crimes against humanity."

The global public good of world peace is akin to the others considered thus far. It affects what economists call "production relations:" it allows trade to flourish, it permits defense spending to be cut, it prevents disease from spreading. It also enables the supply of weakest link global public goods. Recall a lesson of Chapter 2: The success of the smallpox eradication effort depended on immunity being guaranteed within a country that later fell into the hands of warlords, forcing the withdrawal of UN peacekeepers. If Somalia had been as dysfunctional in the 1970s as it is today, we might still be vaccinating our children for smallpox, or watching them die from this disease.

The global public good of the protection of human rights is different. Our production relationships are not directly affected when people we do not know are raped, tortured, murdered, or otherwise brutalized, even on a massive scale. We do not experience their physical pain; our liberties are not infringed; our incomes do not fall. But are we emotionally harmed by these experiences, when they are brought to our attention? Do we feel shame when, having the wherewithal to intervene, we decline to do so? Would we prefer that there existed institutions that could be relied upon to protect people from such atrocities when their own governments fail to do so—or, perhaps worse, when their own governments instigate and perpetrate such deeds? Would we be willing to pay for such institutions? If the answer to these questions is yes, then our "utility" relations are affected when what we perceive as being the basic rights of *all* humans are denied to *some* humans, even people we do not know. The very term, a "crime against humanity," implies a universal injury, rather than one suffered only by those directly affected. In this sense, the safeguarding of human rights, and the prevention of atrocities, most especially genocide, is a global public good, perhaps the most fundamental global public good of all.

But are peacekeeping and conflict prevention operations *effective*? Not always. The UN's withdrawal from Somalia, noted in Chapter 2, is but one example of failure.

This is an important example, however, because the fresh memory of the UN's retreat from Somalia probably helped to precipitate the UN's greatest failure so far—the failure to prevent, and later to stop, the genocide in Rwanda. Of course, not every bad event can be prevented; and not every act of prevention should be undertaken, even when feasible. Interventions have consequences, too. But the tragedy of Rwanda, which killed about 800,000 people, cannot be justified by this kind of reasoning.

Protection of the Tutsi of Rwanda required the leadership of states with the capability to lead, just as the 1991 Gulf War required United States leadership. Unfortunately for the Tutsi, that leadership failed to materialize, and the reason is simple. As Samantha Power explains in her book, *A Problem from Hell*, the United States did not lead because "America's 'vital national interests' were not considered imperiled by mere genocide."[32] The real problem, Power explains, is that "no group or groups in the United States made Clinton administration decisionmakers feel or fear that they would pay a political price for doing nothing to save Rwandans."[33] The benefits of intervention to the U.S. were positive; they may even have been sizable; but they were widely diffused.[34] They lacked political bite.

While failures such as this one stand out to us, and for good reason, there have been successes. These include the implementation of a peace accord in El Salvador, the holding of elections in Cambodia, the demobilization of troops in Mozambique, and the establishment of a new and independent government of Namibia. Indeed, overall, the record suggests that UN peacekeeping has been effective. "UN peacekeeping is positively correlated with democratization processes after civil war, and multilateral enforcement operations are usually successful in ending the violence."[35] Remarkably, this is true even though UN peacekeeping missions are often under-funded.

Financing UN peacekeeping missions

Since 1948, the UN has led 60 peacekeeping operations. Today the UN runs 15 missions, using a total force of over 70,000 blue-helmeted personnel and a budget of around $5 billion. Some of these operations are long term—an example being the peacekeeping force in Cyprus, established in 1964. Others were authorized only recently. Four have been established since 2004 (in Côte d'Ivoire, Haiti, Burundi, and Sudan).

UN peacekeeping operations require the support of the 15-member Security Council: at least nine votes in favor, subject to none of the five permanent members voting against. The Secretary General makes recommendations for launching and carrying out operations, while the Department of Peacekeeping Operations directs operations in the field. Troops, equipment, and supplies are contributed by member states, for which the UN offers compensation at set rates.

These rates make it economically attractive for some countries to contribute troops, and economically unattractive for others to do so.[36] Currently, the main troop contributors are Bangladesh,

Pakistan, India, Jordan, Nepal, Ethiopia, Ghana, Uruguay, Nigeria, and South Africa. These countries pay their armies relatively low wages, and so their governments can actually gain financially by contributing troops. Countries with more expensive militaries, however, can also gain from this arrangement. Had the United States undertaken the peacekeeping operation in Haiti—a country that, by virtue of its location, was of vital interest to the U.S.—the cost would have been about twice as large as that of the United Nations mission.[37]

UN peacekeeping costs are shared according to an adjusted version of the UN scale—an arrangement first developed in 1975. Since the permanent members of the Security Council must approve UN peacekeeping missions, and since they are also responsible under the UN Charter for maintaining international peace and security, these states are required to pay proportionately more (relative to the standard assessments). Other industrialized countries pay according to the same rate as the standard UN assessments, while the remaining countries pay proportionately less. The arrangement for financing peacekeeping missions thus shifts the financial burden from the countries least able to contribute to the countries that make the decisions.

Actual contributions, however, often deviate from the assessments for three reasons.[38] First, not all countries pay their full assessments.[39] As of the end of 2005, $2.92 billion was outstanding.[40] Second, countries often make voluntary contributions.[41] Of the total $46 million budget for peacekeeping in Cyprus, for example, the government of Cyprus contributes one-third and Greece about one-seventh. These countries pay more because they have a direct interest in the success of this mission. Finally, countries can contribute towards the objective of a UN mission without channeling resources through the United Nations. Over the period 1996–2001, for example, the United States estimates that it made "indirect" contributions to UN peacekeeping missions of $24.2 billion, more than seven times the $3.2 billion that the U.S. contributed directly to the UN peacekeeping assessments.[42] These "indirect" contributions usually help provide a secure environment for peacekeeping, but can also contribute in other ways. $5 billion, for example, was spent by the U.S. to rebuild Kosovo and East Timor, providing not only security, but food and shelter for refugees, and assistance to "nation building."

All of these considerations are important because, though peace-keeping is a global public good, its benefits depend on more than a country's population and income per head. They also depend on the specifics of individual missions, such as a country's location in relation to a conflict. Econometric analysis by Paul Collier and Anke Hoeffler of Oxford University shows that the economies of countries in the neighborhood of a civil conflict grow significantly more slowly, losing around one percentage point off their "normal" growth rates.[43] The cumulative effect over time can be enormous. According to Collier and Hoeffler, the "typical" civil war costs neighboring countries around $23 billion.[44]

Regional organizations thus have a particular interest in peace-keeping. Unfortunately, such organizations, especially in the most conflict-prone regions, lack the capacity to be effective. (As I write, for example, the African Union's mission in Sudan's Darfur region has proved pitifully inadequate.) Rich countries, on the other hand, though able to finance peacekeeping missions, are reluctant to dispatch their own troops to distant trouble spots (not only have the people of Darfur been unguarded, but neighboring Chad and the Central African Republic have also been neglected). Recognizing these complementary capabilities, the UN Secretary General, Koffi Annan, proposed creating an "interlocking system of peacekeeping capacities," with the United Nations, "in very exceptional circumstances," being able "to use assessed contributions to finance regional operations authorized by the Security Council, or the participation of regional organizations in multipillar peace operations under the overall United Nations umbrella."[45] Annan has noted especially the need to invest in a decade-long plan to develop the capacity of the African Union.

Voluntary versus mandatory contributions

To finance a global public good, countries have to coordinate their contributions. Suppose that the cost of supplying a global public good is C (an amount of money) and that only two countries pay for the good. If Country 1 contributes an amount C_1, and Country 2 contributes C_2, the good will be supplied if the total of these contributions, $C_1 + C_2$, is at least as great as the overall cost, C; that is, the good will be supplied only if $C_1 + C_2 \geq C$. To know how much to contribute, each country plainly needs to have some idea of how much the other country will contribute. Lacking such knowledge, and remembering that each country would prefer to free ride, it is possible that both countries will under-contribute and that the public good will not be provided. Indeed, that outcome seems likely. In experiments, people supply a public good under these circumstances only about 20 percent of the time.[46] Most of the time, free riding prevents a public good from being supplied.

Can it help to make contributions "mandatory"? In international relations, contributions cannot be made mandatory in the same way as, say, paying taxes to the state is mandatory for individuals. If you fail to pay your taxes, you may be subject to fines and even imprisonment. If a government fails to pay its mandatory contribution to finance a global public good, it is subject to a much lighter punishment. For example, Article 19 of the UN Charter says that members of the United Nations that fail to pay their dues risk losing their right to vote in the General Assembly—a rather weak deterrent, since General Assembly decisions are non-binding.[47]

As noted in the Introduction, however, the enforcement powers of the state are also limited. In countries where people tend to pay their taxes (tax compliance varies widely among states), the reason is not only the prospect of detection, fines, and imprisonment. It is the belief that others are paying their taxes, reinforced by the belief that all taxpayers are obligated to pay their fair share (and that the revenues will be used for good purposes).

It is from this perspective that the "mandatory" nature of the UN assessments can help. The assessments are explicit; they are quantitative. Even when not backed by a punishment mechanism, they imply an obligation to contribute.

At a meeting of the parties of the Montreal Protocol, it was suggested that, because the treaty's financing arrangements were not backed by an explicit enforcement mechanism, contributions to the Multilateral Fund were voluntary. Other countries disagreed, expressing "surprise and serious concern that anyone could interpret [the financing provisions of the treaty as not containing] an obligation to contribute to the financial mechanism."[48] As one senior negotiator put it, in basing the ozone contributions on the United Nations scale of assessments, the treaty conveyed "the impression of at least a tacit commitment."[49] Experience supports this interpretation; compliance with the Montreal Protocol's financing arrangement has been very high.[50]

Compliance is helped when countries can verify which countries have paid their dues and which have not. Transparency allows the countries that have not complied to be named and shamed. It also allows the obligation to pay to be enforced by a strategy of reciprocity. If countries make their contributions contingent on other states contributing, each state has an incentive to contribute. However, should a state not contribute, then the other states would harm themselves by not contributing to the global public good. So the threat to punish non-payers may lack credibility. Intriguingly, experimental evidence suggests that people are willing to hold back their contributions to a public good if others do not pay their "fair share," even when doing so is self-harming.[51] This kind of behavior, though "irrational," helps to promote full financing.

Reinforcing these tendencies is the tradition that the UN assessments be approved by consensus. When countries approve an assessment scale and an associated budget, they essentially accept, individually, an obligation to pay. It is one thing not to pay an amount determined by others. It is quite another thing not to make a contribution that you have publicly declared you would pay.

So, making contributions "mandatory" may help. It remains, however, an imperfect arrangement. The experience of financing the smallpox eradication campaign illustrates why.

Financing smallpox eradication

In 1959, the Soviet representative to the World Health Assembly—a kind of General Assembly for the World Health Organization (WHO)—recommended that smallpox be eradicated. The resolution passed unanimously; every country wanted this global public good to be supplied.

At the time, smallpox was endemic in just 59 poor countries.[52] Achievement of the eradication goal thus depended on eliminating the disease in these 59 countries. The WHO estimated that this should cost about $98 million. Achievement of the goal to eradicate smallpox thus came down to raising the money.[53]

As noted in Chapter 2, smallpox eradication may have been the best social investment the world ever made. It also saved millions of lives. And yet, despite repeated requests by the WHO for financial assistance, between 1959 and 1966 only eight countries donated cash to the effort. The total contribution: just $27,345. This is an astonishing demonstration of free riding behavior. If a global public good of this extraordinary nature cannot be financed voluntarily, you have to wonder if any can be.

Why was financing so tightfisted? One reason is free riding, though the need to raise a fixed sum of money coupled with an attractive benefit–cost ratio should have made financing easier than it turned out to be. Another reason is that the prospects for success were less than perfect even given adequate funding. After all, the earlier effort to eradicate malaria failed. A final reason is the domestic political economy of financing smallpox eradication. Within donor countries, who benefited from smallpox eradication? Not a company. Nor even another kind of special interest group. Parents-to-be and future generations benefited the most—which is to say that the benefits were diffused. Though no party had reason to protest against the effort (the vaccine was not under patent), none had an incentive to push for it either.

So, how was the eradication effort ultimately financed? A break came in 1965, when the United States undertook to eliminate smallpox in 20 contiguous African countries. Though not really intended for this purpose, the U.S. effort changed the financing problem. It reduced the number of endemic countries still needing assistance and so reduced the amount of money needed to eradicate smallpox.

In 1966, the WHO revised its previous cost estimate. The organization now believed that eradication would cost $180 million. Though the revised budget was higher, under the WHO's plan, the remaining endemic countries would pay about 70 percent of the total required expenditure. "International assistance" needed only to pay the balance—$54 million. Essentially, under the WHO's new plan, the endemic countries would contribute their own vaccination staff, and the international community would supply the vaccine and technical expertise.

International financing was to come from three main sources: mandated contributions, agreed by a vote of the World Health Assembly, bilateral contributions (including the aid given by the U.S. to Africa), and voluntary contributions paid into a special account.

Small amounts were also contributed by UN agencies other than the WHO.

Like the regular WHO budget, the mandatory contributions to the smallpox eradication effort were based on the UN scale of assessments. But the contributions financed in this way covered only about a third of the amount needed ($2.415 million in 1967). Why request so little? One reason is that many of the same countries that voted in favor of eradication did not want to pay for it. Indeed, the resolution requesting this amount of money passed by a margin of just two votes—"the narrowest margin for the acceptance of a budget in the Organization's history."[54]

Like the earlier donation made by the United States, this additional financial commitment reduced the balance that needed to be contributed voluntarily (essentially, it lowered the value of C, the total cost of eradication, without reducing any of the Bs). And yet even after this, voluntary contributions only trickled in: from 1967 to 1973, cash donations totaled only $79,500.[55] Starting in 1974, however, voluntary contributions increased substantially. Indeed, the final stages of the eradication campaign were funded almost entirely by voluntary contributions. By the time victory was declared, $98 million in international assistance had been collected—the same amount that the WHO thought was needed in 1959.

Though the effort succeeded, financing was never easy; voluntary contributions remained miserly to the last; and the eradication effort almost failed because of a lack of money. As the WHO's smallpox eradication unit noted later, the

lack of resources constituted a serious, continuing problem and, even in the concluding years of the programme, those that were made available barely sufficed to sustain momentum. Donated vaccine, for example, was continually in short supply despite repeated appeals for assistance. The World Health Assembly was informed on a number of occasions of the need for additional funds, amounting to no more than a few million US dollars, and such funds were sought in correspondence and in meetings with potential donors, but the response was never adequate... Success was never a certainty even during the years immediately preceding the last known cases.[56]

The benefits of eradication would have been correlated with the scale of assessments, and the scale would also have acted as a focal point for financing the eradication effort. For both reasons, it is perhaps to be expected that voluntary contributions would be correlated with the UN scale. Statistical analysis shows that they were.[57] However, there were also noticeable outliers, the most striking of which was Sweden. Though the United States gave more than any country overall, Sweden gave more than any country relative to its assessment.

Sweden is famously generous, but in this case there were specific reasons why Sweden gave so much. Following an explosive epidemic that threatened to undermine India's effort to eliminate smallpox in 1974, the WHO approached "numerous governments for additional finances."[58] Few countries showed any interest in helping, "and no country indicated it was in a position to act quickly in answering an appeal."[59] As chance would have it, however, a WHO official learned "in a casual conversation" that Sweden was examining options for redirecting its assistance to India after canceling a development project.[60] The official contacted a senior representative of the Swedish embassy in New Delhi, who persuaded his superiors in Stockholm to fund the program. Within a few weeks, Sweden had given $2.8 million to support smallpox elimination in India—a sum later increased to $10 million. Overall, Sweden donated nearly $16 million (almost all of it in cash) to the voluntary fund.[61] The only country to contribute more was the United States (the U.S. paid $25 million, much of it in kind).[62]

The smallpox eradication effort demonstrates that simply making contributions "mandatory" does not guarantee financing. It also reveals that voluntary financing cannot be relied upon, even when the returns to supplying a global public good are overwhelming.

Financing polio eradication

The polio eradication initiative, which has cost over $4 billion through 2005, has been financed entirely by voluntary contributions—a remarkable, if less than fully successful, achievement.

Rotary International, a charity, has played a major role in the effort. It contributed $600 million through 2005, more than any donor except the United States government. A contribution this big reduces the need for international finance. Mathematically, it is equivalent to reducing C, the cost to countries of supplying the global public good by voluntary means. Rotary's contribution is thus somewhat akin to the unilateral contribution made by the United States and the mandatory contributions made by all countries to the smallpox eradication effort. It provided seed money for the initiative.

But Rotary's contribution has been even greater than this. Rotary provided the domestic political economy advocacy that was lacking in the smallpox eradication effort. It has urged governments to contribute. It calculated "fair shares" for individual states, based on the contributions they are required to make to finance the WHO's regular budget (as mentioned before, the WHO's assessments are based on the ordinary UN scale), and used these to create focal points to coordinate voluntary donations. The logic of doing this was impeccable: the countries that endorsed polio eradication (like the smallpox program, the polio eradication initiative was approved unanimously by the World Health Assembly) should be willing to pay for it; and since every country finances the WHO's regular budget (which they also approve) according to the UN scale of assessments, they should be willing to finance the polio eradication initiative in the same proportions.

Unfortunately, the effect has been mixed.[63]

... of the 22 WHO Member States who are members of the OECD's Development Assistance Committee that makes up the community of "traditional" ODA donors, only 16 have contributed to the eradication initiative. Of these, only 7 contributed the equivalent or more than their estimated "share," 6 are "free-riders" in that they made no financial contribution to eradication, while the remaining 9 contributed substantially less than their estimated "share" of the total budget of US $2,750 million dollars between 1985 and 2005.

Of course, and as explained in Chapter 2, polio eradication poses tremendous technical challenges. It may not succeed. Even if it did succeed in halting transmission of the wild viruses, rich countries may not benefit (they have vowed to continue using the inactivated vaccine, even if other countries stop using the live-attenuated vaccine). And yet the contrast between every country voting in favor of the resolution to eradicate polio and the uneven record of contributing financially towards achieving the goal betrays a fundamental challenge—a challenge common to the supply of many global public goods: the need to overcome free rider incentives.

Conclusions

Chapter 1 showed that international cooperation is needed even when countries are willing to finance the supply of a global public good unilaterally. This is because these decisions made unilaterally can have implications—and not all of them welcome—for other countries. Here we have seen that the countries willing to finance such an effort unilaterally also gain from international cooperation. They gain more than the approval of other states, and thus the stamp of legitimacy. They also gain from other states bearing some of the financial burden.

Financing is easiest when one country is willing to pay the full cost of supplying a global public good, even should other countries not contribute. However, even under these favorable circumstances full financing is not guaranteed. Though a state may be *willing* to pay for a global public good all by itself, it would *prefer* that others paid. Indeed, it may feel that others are *obligated* to pay. It is for this reason that discussions about financing are often conducted in the language of fairness.

Financial contributions by states cannot be made mandatory in the same way that tax payments by individuals are mandatory. Contributions can only be mandatory if states *agree* that they should be mandatory. But under these circumstances, the amounts raised are determined endogenously. Countries may agree to mandatory assessments only if the amounts raised by this means are small.

From this perspective, *all* international financing is really voluntary. Mandatory contributions simply put values on the amounts countries are expected to contribute. When backed by a country's explicit approval, mandatory contributions reinforce a state's obligation to pay a specific amount. Penalties for non-payment (such as a country losing its vote in the General Assembly) may also help, though to be effective such penalties must be credible, and substantial penalties often are not credible. Strategies for financing (such as the strategy of making an initial contribution, to reduce the final cost of supplying a global public good) may also help, but even they are not always enough. In some cases, as in the example of Sweden's contribution to the smallpox effort, full financing simply requires extraordinary generosity—and some good luck.

Appendix

Table 4.2A. Population, Income, and UN Assessment by Country, 2004

Country	Population (thousands)	Gross national income per capita (international dollars)	Product (millions of dollars)	Ranking	UN Assessment (percent)
European Union 25	458,534	26,352	12,083,268	1	36.525
United States	293,507	39,710	11,655,163	2	22.000
China	1,296,500	5,530	7,169,645	3	2.053
Japan	127,764	30,040	3,838,031	4	19.468
India	1,079,721	3,100	3,347,135	5	0.421
Germany*	82,631	27,950	2,309,536	6	8.662
United Kingdom*	59,405	31,460	1,868,881	7	6.127
France*	59,991	29,320	1,758,936	8	6.030
Italy*	57,573	27,860	1,603,984	9	4.885
Brazil	178,718	8,020	1,433,318	10	1.523
Russian Federation	142,814	9,620	1,373,871	11	1.100
Spain*	41,286	25,070	1,035,040	12	2.520
Mexico	103,795	9,590	995,394	13	1.883
Korea, Rep.	48,142	20,400	982,097	14	1.796
Canada	31,902	30,660	978,115	15	2.813
Indonesia	217,588	3,460	752,854	16	0.142
Australia	20,120	29,200	587,504	17	1.592
Turkey	71,727	7,870	564,491	18	0.372
Netherlands*	16,250	31,220	507,325	19	1.690
Iran	66,928	7,550	505,306	20	0.157
Thailand	62,387	8,020	500,344	21	0.209
South Africa	45,584	10,960	499,601	22	0.292
Poland*	38,160	12,640	482,342	23	0.461
Argentina	38,226	12,460	476,296	24	0.956
Philippines	82,987	4,890	405,806	25	0.095
Pakistan	152,061	2,160	328,452	26	0.055
Belgium*	10,405	31,360	326,301	27	1.069
Saudi Arabia	23,215	14,010	325,242	28	0.713
Colombia	45,300	6,820	308,946	29	0.155
Ukraine	48,008	6,250	300,050	30	0.039
Egypt	68,738	4,120	283,201	31	0.120
Bangladesh	140,494	1,980	278,178	32	0.010
Sweden*	8,985	29,770	267,483	33	0.998
Switzerland	7,382	35,370	261,101	34	1.197
Austria*	8,115	31,790	257,976	35	0.859
Greece*	11,075	22,000	243,650	36	0.530
Malaysia	25,209	9,630	242,763	37	0.203
Vietnam	82,162	2,700	221,837	38	0.021
Algeria	32,373	6,260	202,655	39	0.076
Portugal*	10,436	19,250	200,893	40	0.470
Czech Republic*	10,183	18,400	187,367	41	0.183
Romania	21,858	8,190	179,017	42	0.060
Norway	4,582	38,550	176,636	43	0.679
Denmark*	5,397	31,550	170,275	44	0.718
Chile	15,956	10,500	167,538	45	0.223
Israel	6,798	23,510	159,821	46	0.467
Hungary*	10,072	15,620	157,325	47	0.126

(cont.)

Table 4.2A. (*Continued*)

Country	Population (thousands)	Gross national income per capita (international dollars)	Product (millions of dollars)	Ranking	UN Assessment (percent)
Finland*	5,215	29,560	154,155	48	0.533
Venezuela	26,127	5,760	150,492	49	0.171
Peru	27,547	5,370	147,927	50	0.092
Ireland*	4,019	33,170	133,310	51	0.350
Nigeria	139,823	930	130,035	52	0.042
Morocco	30,586	4,100	125,403	53	0.003
Singapore	4,335	26,590	115,268	54	0.388
Kazakhstan	14,958	6,980	104,407	55	0.025
United Arab Emirates	4,284	21,000	89,964	56	0.235
New Zealand	4,061	22,130	89,870	57	0.221
Sri Lanka	19,444	4,000	77,776	58	0.017
Slovak Republic*	5,390	14,370	77,454	59	0.051
Tunisia	10,012	7,310	73,188	60	0.032
Belarus	9,832	6,900	67,841	61	0.018
Sudan	34,356	1,870	64,246	62	0.008
Syrian Arab Republic	17,783	3,550	63,130	63	0.038
Bulgaria	7,780	7,870	61,229	64	0.017
Dominican Republic	8,861	6,750	59,812	65	0.035
Ethiopia	69,961	810	56,668	66	0.004
Croatia	4,508	11,670	52,608	67	0.037
Guatemala	12,628	4,140	52,280	68	0.030
Ecuador	13,213	3,690	48,756	69	0.019
Uzbekistan	25,930	1,860	48,230	70	0.014
Ghana	21,053	2,280	48,001	71	0.004
Kuwait	2,460	19,510	47,995	72	0.162
Lithuania*	3,439	12,610	43,366	73	0.024
Slovenia*	1,995	20,730	41,356	74	0.082
Uganda	25,920	1,520	39,398	75	0.006
Costa Rica	4,061	9,530	38,701	76	0.030
Congo, Dem. Rep.	54,775	680	37,247	77	0.003
Nepal	25,190	1,470	37,029	78	0.004
Oman	2,659	13,250	35,232	79	0.070
Cameroon	16,400	2,090	34,276	80	0.008
Turkmenistan	4,931	6,910	34,073	81	0.005
Kenya	32,447	1,050	34,069	82	0.009
El Salvador	6,658	4,980	33,157	83	0.022
Azerbaijan	8,280	3,830	31,712	84	0.005
Uruguay	3,399	9,070	30,829	85	0.048
Cambodia	13,630	2,180	29,713	86	0.002
Zimbabwe	13,151	2,180	28,669	87	0.007
Bosnia & Herzegovina	3,836	7,430	28,501	88	0.003
Angola	13,963	2,030	28,345	89	0.001
Paraguay	5,782	4,870	28,158	90	0.012
Luxembourg*	450	61,220	27,549	91	0.077
Latvia*	2,303	11,850	27,291	92	0.015
Jordan	5,440	4,640	25,242	93	0.011
Lebanon	4,554	5,380	24,501	94	0.024
Tanzania	36,571	660	24,137	95	0.006
Côte d'Ivoire	17,142	1,390	23,827	96	0.010
Bolivia	8,986	2,590	23,274	97	0.009
Mozambique	19,129	1,160	22,190	98	0.001

Table 4.2A. (*Continued*)

Country	Population (*thousands*)	Gross national income per capita (*international dollars*)	Product (*millions of dollars*)	Ranking	UN Assessment (*percent*)
Panama	3,028	6,870	20,802	99	0.019
Honduras	7,141	2,710	19,352	100	0.005
Nicaragua	5,604	3,300	18,493	101	0.001
Senegal	10,455	1,720	17,983	102	0.005
Estonia*	1,345	13,190	17,741	103	0.012
Cyprus*	776	22,330	17,328	104	0.039
Guinea	8,073	2,130	17,195	105	0.003
Yemen	19,763	820	16,206	106	0.006
Albania	3,188	5,070	16,163	107	0.005
Botswana	1,727	8,920	15,405	108	0.012
Burkina Faso	12,387	1,220	15,112	109	0.002
Trinidad and Tobago	1,323	11,180	14,791	110	0.022
Mauritius	1,234	11,870	14,648	111	0.011
Haiti	8,592	1,680	14,435	112	0.003
Madagascar	17,332	830	14,386	113	0.003
Namibia	2,033	6,960	14,150	114	0.006
Macedonia, FYR	2,062	6,480	13,362	115	0.006
Georgia	4,521	2,930	13,247	116	0.003
Bahrain	725	18,070	13,101	117	0.030
Armenia	3,050	4,270	13,024	118	0.002
Papua New Guinea	5,625	2,300	12,938	119	0.003
Chad	8,823	1,420	12,529	120	0.001
Mali	11,937	980	11,698	121	0.002
Rwanda	8,412	1,300	10,936	122	0.001
Lao PDR	5,792	1,850	10,715	123	0.001
Niger	12,095	830	10,039	124	0.001
Jamaica	2,665	3,630	9,674	125	0.008
Zambia	10,547	890	9,387	126	0.002
Iceland	290	32,360	9,384	127	0.034
Kyrgiz Republic	5,099	1,840	9,382	128	0.001
Togo	4,966	1,690	8,393	129	0.001
Moldova	4,218	1,930	8,141	130	0.001
Benin	6,890	1,120	7,717	131	0.002
Gabon	1,374	5,600	7,694	132	0.009
Malta*	401	18,720	7,507	133	0.014
Tajikistan	6,430	1,150	7,395	134	0.001
Malawi	11,182	620	6,933	135	0.001
Mauritania	2,906	2,050	5,957	136	0.001
Lesotho	1,809	3,210	5,807	137	0.001
Swaziland	1,120	4,970	5,566	138	0.002
Bahamas	320	16,140	5,165	139	0.013
Mongolia	2,515	2,020	5,080	140	0.001
Fiji	848	5,770	4,893	141	0.004
Burundi	7,343	660	4,846	142	0.001
Eritrea	4,477	1,050	4,701	143	0.001
Central African Rep.	3,947	1,110	4,381	144	0.001
Sierra Leone	5,436	790	4,294	145	0.001
Barbados	272	15,060	4,096	146	0.010
Equatorial Guinea	506	7,400	3,744	147	0.002
Guyana	772	4,110	3,173	148	0.001

(*cont.*)

Table 4.2A. (*Continued*)

Country	Population (*thousands*)	Gross national income per capita (*international dollars*)	Product (*millions of dollars*)	Ranking	UN Assessment (*percent*)
Congo, Rep.	3,855	750	2,891	149	0.001
Gambia	1,449	1,900	2,753	150	0.001
Cape Verde	481	5,650	2,718	151	0.001
Belize	283	6,510	1,842	152	0.001
Djibouti	716	2,270	1,625	153	0.001
Seychelles	85	15,590	1,325	154	0.002
Comoros	614	1,840	1,130	155	0.001
Guinea-Bissau	1,533	690	1,058	156	0.001
Samoa	179	5,670	1,015	157	0.001
St. Lucia	164	5,560	912	158	0.002
Solomon Islands	471	1,760	829	159	0.001
Antigua and Barbuda	80	10,360	829	160	0.003
Grenada	106	7,000	742	161	0.001
Tonga	102	7,220	736	162	0.001
St Vincent & Grenadines	108	6,250	675	163	0.001
Vanuatu	215	2,790	600	164	0.001
St. Kitts and Nevis	47	11,190	526	165	0.001
Dominica	71	5,250	373	166	0.001
Myanmar	49,910	–	–	–	0.010
Iraq	25,261	–	–	–	0.016
Korea, Dem. Rep.	22,745	–	–	–	0.010
Cuba	11,365	–	–	–	0.043
Somalia	9,938	–	–	–	0.001
Serbia & Montenegro	8,152	–	–	–	0.019
Libya	5,674	–	–	–	0.132
Liberia	3,449	–	–	–	0.001
Timor-Leste	925	–	–	–	0.001
Bhutan	896	–	–	–	0.001
Qatar	637	–	–	–	0.064
Suriname	443	–	–	–	0.001
Brunei	361	–	–	–	0.034
Maldives	300	–	–	–	0.001
Sao Tome & Principe	161	–	–	–	0.001
Micronesia, Fed. Sts.	127	–	–	–	0.001
Kiribati	98	–	–	–	0.001
Andorra	66	–	–	–	0.005
Marshall Islands	60	–	–	–	0.001
Liechtenstein	34	–	–	–	0.005
Monaco	33	–	–	–	0.003
San Marino	28	–	–	–	0.003
Palau	20	–	–	–	0.001
Afghanistan	–	–	–	–	0.002
Nauru	–	–	–	–	0.001
Tuvalu	–	–	–	–	0.001
World Total	6,345,127	8,760	55,583,313	–	100.000

Notes and sources: Countries listed are the members of the United Nations; a * denotes European Union membership. Data on population and gross national income are from the World Bank Indicators database, World Bank, July 15, 2005. Estimates of income adjust for the purchasing power. The "product" multiplies population by income per capita. The ranking is for product. The UN scale of assessments is from General Assembly Resolution 58/1, March 3, 2004.

CHAPTER FIVE

Mutual restraint: agreeing what states ought not to do

> Question: Mr. President, after all of the years of failure in attempting to reach a nuclear test ban agreement at Geneva, and in view of the current stalemate at the Geneva conference, do you still really have any hope of arriving at a nuclear test ban agreement?
>
> The President: Well, my hopes are somewhat dimmed, but nevertheless, I still hope... [T]he reason why we keep moving and working on this question, taking up a good deal of energy and effort, is because personally I am haunted by the feeling that by 1970, unless we are successful, there may be 10 nuclear powers instead of four, and by 1975, 15 or 20...I regard that as the greatest possible danger and hazard.
>
> President John F. Kennedy, responding to a reporter's question at a news conference, March 21, 1963.[1]

Some global public goods, like some of the best things in life, are free. They do not need to be paid for because they do not require that something be done. Rather, they require that something *not* be done—an example being that more states not acquire nuclear weapons.

Though public goods of this kind do not require financing, they are still hampered by incentive problems. Even if other states do not possess nuclear weapons, some state will want to acquire them, probably especially because possession can deter an attack by conventional forces. However, as more states acquire nuclear weapons, the incentive for others to get hold of them increases, and proliferation makes every state more vulnerable. Each state can thus be made better off if every state agrees not to possess these weapons. The challenge is thus for states to agree to restrain their behavior, and to enforce this agreement. It is, as we shall see in this chapter, a formidable challenge—and one that applies to a variety of other global problems as well.

Nuclear non-proliferation

Fortunately, President Kennedy's famous prediction, given in this chapter's introductory quote, was never realized. In 1975, there were not 15 or 20 nuclear weapons states but seven (Britain, China, France, India, Israel, the Soviet Union, and the United States). The reason owes much to Kennedy's efforts, and to those of other leaders, who tried to contain the proliferation of this destructive technology. To be sure, their success was partial—there were, after all, only four nuclear weapons states on the day President Kennedy gave this press conference. But from the perspective of 1963, the containment of proliferation through 1975 has to be considered a remarkable achievement.[2] It supplied the global public good of a reduced threat of nuclear destruction.

Is the equilibrium stable? For a time, it appeared to be stable. From 1975 until 2005, only one state joined the nuclear club (Pakistan carried out its first test in 1998). Shortly before revising this book, however, North Korea carried out its first nuclear test, and Iran is suspected of seeking to develop a nuclear weapon today. We may be on the threshold of a new proliferation era.

There has been one exception to this trend. South Africa, which developed a small number of nuclear weapons in the early 1980s, gave up its arsenal—voluntarily and unilaterally—and joined the Nuclear Non-Proliferation Treaty in 1991. Why did it do this?

In an interview with *Newsweek* magazine, the president who took this decision, F. W. de Klerk, gave two reasons:[3]

First, after the fall of the Soviet Union, South Africa no longer faced an external threat. South Africa built the bomb, he said, "never to be used, but to have it as a deterrent."

Second, he "wanted South Africa to return as soon as possible to the international arena . . ." In releasing Nelson Mandela from prison, de Klerk knew that he had initiated a process that would lead to the collapse of the apartheid system. He hoped that this could be achieved peacefully, but he worried that his country might need "leading countries" to intervene, to prevent an outbreak of civil war; and he believed that they would not do this so long as the government's intentions were unclear. It was essential, he said, that the government, "convince the rest of the world that we really were not playing with words . . ." At that moment in history, the bomb, which had previously seemed so vital to the survival of the South African government, became, in de Klerk's words, "a millstone" around his country's neck; it threatened to deter the intervention that de Klerk feared his country might desperately need.

De Klerk strongly rejects a third reason: that he disarmed South Africa so that the Mandela-led African National Congress would not take possession of the bomb. "It's not true," he says. Scott Sagan disagrees, arguing that the de Klerk government's actions "spoke more loudly than its words."[4] Why else was South Africa's nuclear weapons program dismantled before international observers could verify the activities? Why else was all evidence relating to the program destroyed before the program was announced publicly?

South Africa's situation was obviously unique, but these three motives—security from external threats, a desire to integrate with the rest of the world, and domestic politics—lie at the heart of all proliferation decisions.

The nuclear taboo

That South Africa did not develop the bomb for the purpose of using it (except as a deterrent) is striking. It is a reminder that, though proliferation is an issue of vital importance, the disinclination to use such a weapon is more important still.

This disinclination or rather *inhibition* applies universally. In the words of Thomas Schelling, a co-recipient of the 2005 Nobel Prize in economics, "the most spectacular event of the past half century is one that did not occur." Not since Hiroshima and Nagasaki has a nuclear bomb been "exploded in anger."[5]

What makes this non-event spectacular is that there were numerous occasions when use of the bomb was contemplated and would have been of military advantage and *still* the bomb was not used. These were situations in which a nuclear power was at war with a non-nuclear state. It was not deterrence that prevented nuclear weapons from being used in these instances but something else: an informal institution, a prohibitive norm Schelling calls a "taboo." The taboo made using a nuclear weapon politically unattractive. Indeed, it made the use of nuclear weapons politically *unacceptable*.[6]

Why is that? To use a nuclear weapon today would be to risk two kinds of response, either complete alienation from the "international community," meaning a loss in sovereignty, or acceptance by other states of the legitimacy of the use of nuclear weapons. The former response would be devastating to the country that broke the taboo. The latter response would be harmful to all countries.[7] It could signal the end of the taboo.

The existence of the taboo was not inevitable. For a similar reason its continued hold on the nuclear powers is not assured.

A recent draft report by the Pentagon proposed changing the Doctrine for Joint Nuclear Operations to allow use of nuclear weapons against an enemy that is using or *"intending to use"* (emphasis added) weapons of mass destruction against U.S. or allied, multinational military forces or civilian populations.[8] Better to attack first than to wait and be attacked, the doctrine implies. If implemented, however, the policy would increase the likelihood that nuclear weapons will actually be used. It would therefore threaten the taboo.

Indeed, the policy may make the United States *more* vulnerable. If an enemy believes the U.S. will retaliate with full force should it be attacked first, but that the U.S. will not launch a first strike—such an enemy has every incentive to hold back. At the very least, it cannot lose by keeping its finger off the button for a little while longer—time enough, perhaps, for heads to cool in a crisis. But if the enemy believes the U.S. *will* strike first, then it has a very different incentive. The latter enemy is more likely to launch a first strike.[9]

It is not just policy that affects the stability of the taboo. Investments in technology can have a similar effect. Despite requests by President George W. Bush, the United States Congress has so far refused to fund development of a nuclear weapon that could destroy biological and chemical agents without dispersing them into the atmosphere. Such weapons would be of direct military utility. But for that reason they would make use of a nuclear weapon more likely, posing a threat to the taboo. Similarly, Congress has declined to fund research that would lead to the development of new "bunker busting" nuclear weapons. Once again, having such weapons would be useful. And that is precisely why their development would be dangerous. To sustain the taboo, the incentives to use nuclear weapons must remain unattractive.

Non-nuclear investments can also affect the stability of the taboo. A country possessing a substantial conventional force need not rely on nuclear weapons to respond to a non-nuclear attack. Having a robust conventional force thus makes other nuclear countries less fearful of a possible nuclear first strike, thereby reducing *their* incentive to launch a first strike. The United States ruled out the promise of "no first use" during the Cold War precisely because its conventional forces were weaker than those of the Warsaw Pact.[10] Today, of course, the conventional forces of the United States are without peer.

Preventing spread

If the inhibition to use nuclear weapons holds, why should we worry at the prospect that more countries will acquire the bomb? Spread increases the likelihood that these weapons will be exploded by accident, perhaps triggering a wider nuclear exchange. It increases the chance that the bomb will be possessed by an irrational leader, a paranoid who, believing that his country will be attacked in any event, chooses to strike first; a leader who misinterprets the intentions of his country's adversaries; or, conceivably but most unlikely, a leader who believes in the glory of his country's suicide. Spread also increases the probability that nuclear weapons will fall into the hands of an unstable government, making it easier for them to be acquired by terrorists.

And of course the taboo cannot be relied upon to hold indefinitely.

So long as the taboo continues to hold, however, a primary motive for acquiring the bomb is to deter an enemy attack. This means that, to prevent nuclear weapons from spreading, the security of non-nuclear states must somehow be assured.

Providing such an assurance was a primary aim of the North Atlantic Treaty Organization (NATO). Article 5 of the North Atlantic Treaty says that "an armed attack against one or more" of the NATO member countries "shall be considered an attack against them all." (The promise to come to the aid of a NATO ally was made credible by the stationing of U.S. forces in Europe.) Essentially, the treaty extended the nuclear deterrent even to countries that did not possess the bomb, making it inessential for them to acquire it. NATO thus helped to halt proliferation within Europe. Japan has enjoyed a similar measure of security assurance from the United States, and it has also forsworn development of the bomb.

Japan does, however, have the capability to produce and deploy a bomb fairly quickly (perhaps within a year). This capability is also a threat; and for that reason it is also a deterrent. Proliferation can be colored in grays and not only in black and white.

States lacking security guarantees feel a greater need to acquire their own deterrent. India was invaded by China in 1962, and became alarmed when China joined the nuclear club two years later. According to George Bunn and Roland Timerbaev,

in early 1968 the Indian government sent a high-level delegation to the capitals of [nuclear weapon states] to seek explicit positive security guarantees from them in case of a Chinese nuclear threat. The negative response by the [nuclear weapon states] was one of the reasons India chose not to sign the [Treaty on the Non-Proliferation of Nuclear Weapons].[11]

India subsequently acquired the bomb, but in making itself more secure, India made its neighbor and rival, Pakistan, less so, and that is why Pakistan responded by building its own bomb. This is the problem with nuclear weapons: as more states acquire them, still more want to acquire them.

Belarus, Kazakhstan, and Ukraine inherited a nuclear arsenal following the dissolution of the Soviet Union, and had to decide whether to keep them or to give them up. In the end, they decided to give them up, but only after receiving security assurances from Russia and the United States. All three of these countries later joined the Non-Proliferation Treaty.[12]

Although formally representing a bargain between the nuclear and non-nuclear weapon states, the Non-Proliferation Treaty also provides an implicit assurance as between the non-nuclear states. It reassures each of these states that it need not fear that its adversaries will acquire nuclear weapons. Moreover, the pledge has some credibility because withdrawal from the treaty by any non-nuclear party would send an alarming signal to other states, including the nuclear states, of an emerging nuclear threat. At one time, Argentina and Brazil both had active nuclear weapons research programs. Today, both countries are parties to the Non-Proliferation Treaty. The incentive for each to remain within the agreement is enhanced by the other's participation. Though the treaty has helped, its overall record is imperfect. North Korea used to be a member. But it cheated on the agreement, and then withdrew from the treaty in 2003. It conducted its first test in 2006. Iran remains a party to the Non-Proliferation Treaty, but it has also cheated on the agreement. Today, Iran is some years away from developing a bomb, but it seems determined to proceed with a program that could give it such a capability (Iran insists that its intentions are peaceful, but its covert nuclear program belies this claim). The risk in both of these cases is less that these countries will use nuclear weapons than that their possession of the bomb will embolden their governments, and so cause their respective rivals to acquire them.

If having a bomb is a deterrent, then seeking to develop a bomb is a threat to other states. Iran's suspected interest in building a bomb thus creates an incentive for the states most likely to be deterred by a nuclear-armed Iran to prevent Iran from succeeding. This makes Iran's nuclear policy a gamble. President Bush has said that, as regards his administration's policy towards Iran, "all options are on the table."[13] And according to one account, the Bush administration has considered a preventive nuclear strike.[14] Such a step would be risky for the United States, however, and it is perhaps for this reason that the Bush administration has hinted recently that it may be willing to talk to Iran after all.[15] The prospects for the future depend on the same three factors that shaped South Africa's earlier disarmament: Iran's perceptions of its security interests, its desire to integrate with the rest of the world, and its domestic politics.

Nuclear testing

On March 1, 1954, at 6.45 am precisely, the United States detonated a hydrogen bomb codenamed "BRAVO" on Bikini atoll (now part of the independent Marshall Islands) in the mid-Pacific. The explosion went off as planned, but the bomb's engineers miscalculated. The actual yield proved to be three times the expected value, a thousand times more power than the bomb dropped on Hiroshima. The government's meteorologists also erred. A sudden change in the winds caused fallout from the explosion to move to the northeast, outside the evacuation area.[16]

The BRAVO test was calamitous for the crew of the Japanese-registered *Lucky Dragon*, which happened to be fishing downwind of the blast. All the men on board became ill and developed skin burns soon after the explosion. They sailed immediately for home, and entered Yaizu Harbor on March 14. Upon arriving, the entire crew was hospitalized. One member later died from radiation exposure.

The incident sparked an outcry in Japan, and was soon followed by a panic over radiation-contaminated tuna. Then an American official, speaking at a press conference, claimed that the skin lesions on the *Lucky Dragon*'s crew were likely due not to radioactivity but to "the chemical activity of the converted coral material..." thrown up by the blast—a suggestion that made the Japanese public only angrier.[17] A joint U.S.–Japanese inquiry concluded that tuna and other seafood was safe to eat, but it also discovered that ocean currents transported radioactive waters from the Bikini lagoon all the way to Japan.[18] The public was not reassured.

More than 50 tests were conducted before BRAVO, and many times that number were conducted afterwards, but the incident of March 1, 1954, marked a turning point in the debate about nuclear testing. It demonstrated that a ban on atmospheric nuclear testing was a global public good.

Like the *Lucky Dragon*'s crew, the 64 residents of Rongelap, the atoll nearest the explosion, saw the flash first—one observer said it was "like the sun rising in the west."[19] Minutes later came the blast wave. Hours after that there followed a prolonged shower of radioactive snow-like flakes. Again, like the *Lucky Dragon*'s crew, the islanders had not been warned about the fallout, and so they took no precautions. Their skin burned, their eyes watered, their hair fell out. Some vomited. Many had diarrhea. It took two days before the U.S. military evacuated the atoll. The residents of Rongelap were not allowed home until 1957, but they were evacuated again in 1985 because of renewed health fears. A remediation and resettlement program financed by the United States began in 1998, but as of 2006 the Rongalapese have yet to be repatriated.

Of the four Rongelapese women who were pregnant at the time of the blast, one gave birth to a stillborn baby—though whether the baby's death was due to radiation exposure no one knows for sure. For a decade after the blast, an increasing number of pregnancies ended in miscarriages and stillbirths—though, again, whether these were due to radiation exposure was never proved. Other changes were clearer. The physical growth of children exposed to the fallout was stunted. Thyroid dysfunction became a common complaint. An infant exposed to the blast developed leukemia years later, probably as a result of radiation exposure.

Though people nearest to a test site are especially vulnerable to radiation fallout, the effects of atmospheric testing are global.

Radiation in the red bone marrow of Americans born between 1951 and 2000 has been found to be six times higher as a consequence of "global" as opposed to "domestic" testing at the Nevada Test Site. Radiation levels are particularly high among Americans living on the East Coast, especially in areas of high rainfall.[20] Evidence also suggests that fallout may have increased the risk of leukemia among young children in Britain, even though Britain's nuclear tests, like those of the United States, were carried out in the Pacific, on the other side of the world.[21] What are the overall risks from the fallout from nuclear testing? According to a U.S. study, "the population of 3.8 million people born in the United States in 1951 (the year the Nevada Test Site was established) will likely experience fewer than 1,000 fatal cancers as a result of fallout exposures, a lifetime risk of . . . about 1 in 3,800."[22] This is a significant risk.[23]

There are, however, other reasons for wanting to ban atmospheric testing: doing so would limit proliferation and reinforce the taboo against use. If weapons cannot be tested, their effectiveness (both if used and if serving as a deterrent) will remain in doubt, making the acquisition of weapons by non-nuclear states, and the development of new weapons by nuclear states, less attractive. A prohibition on testing would also deter countries from using weapons that may possibly fail—particularly in a first strike. Finally, a ban on testing would strengthen the normative appeal of the taboo (if testing were unacceptable, then use of a nuclear weapon must surely be intolerable).

The test ban treaties

The 1963 Limited Test Ban Treaty banned nuclear testing in the atmosphere, underwater, and in space—but not underground (though the treaty does require that the fallout from underground testing be contained within the country in which the test is conducted). Why limit testing in this way? Why not ban it altogether? One reason is that underground testing is more difficult to verify—a nuclear test

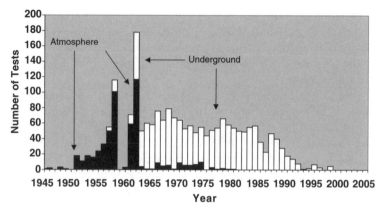

Figure 5.1. Nuclear Tests, 1945–2005

Source: Robert Norris and William Arkin. "Known Nuclear Test Worldwide 1945–1998" in *Bulletin of the Atomic Scientists*, v. 54, no. 6, 1998. Found at http://www.thebulletin. org/article_nn.php?art_ofn=nd98norris. Copyright © 1985 by *Bulletin of the Atomic Scientists*, Chicago, IL 60637. Reproduced by permission of *Bulletin of the Atomic Scientists: The Magazine of Global Security, Science, and Survival.*

might be confused with an earthquake. Another reason, however, is that the partial ban allowed the more technically advanced states that already possessed nuclear weapons to continue to test. The capability to test has improved even more since then, and a comprehensive nuclear test ban (to include underground testing) was negotiated in 1996. This new treaty, however, has not entered into force.

The data on testing, shown in Figure 5.1, reveal two patterns: first, a shift from atmospheric to underground testing; and, second, an increase and then decline in the total number of tests (North Korea conducted a nuclear test in 2006). The sharp drop in atmospheric testing occurred right after the first test ban treaty was adopted, and only a handful of tests have been carried out since the second treaty was adopted. Are the treaties responsible for these patterns?

Treaties are prone to selection bias. Countries often sign a treaty when they need not change their behavior to comply. Countries often decline to sign when their behavior would need to change. Participation in the first test ban treaty reflects these tendencies. The countries that ratified the agreement were the nuclear states that had already tested their weapons (the United States, the United Kingdom, and the Soviet Union), and the non-nuclear states that lacked nuclear aspirations. The countries that refused to ratify were the states with more nascent nuclear programs (China and France), and states that wanted to keep their nuclear options open.

And yet treaties can change behavior. Indeed, if they did not, there would be no purpose in negotiating them. In particular, a country may be willing to ratify a treaty that required it to change its own behavior if given an assurance that other states (sometimes particular other states) would be similarly constrained. For a treaty to work in this way, the restraints agreed must be *conditional*.

To enter into force, the Limited Test Ban Treaty had to be ratified by the United States, the United Kingdom, and the Soviet Union. It did not have to be ratified by France, which had already carried out several tests, or by China, which was about to carry out its first test (China tested its first bomb the year after the treaty was negotiated). The treaty might have required the participation of these countries before entering into force. But in that case the treaty may not have entered into force.

The Comprehensive Test Ban Treaty set the bar much higher. It will enter into force only after being ratified by all of the 44 "nuclear capable" states—that is, the states recognized (as of 1996) as having nuclear power or research reactors.

Unfortunately, and despite being negotiated a decade ago, the new treaty is some way from entering into force. As shown in Table 5.1, three nuclear weapons states have not even signed the treaty. Three other nuclear states and one country with nuclear aspirations have signed but not ratified the treaty.

Although ratification by all these states is necessary for the treaty to enter into force, the support of the United States is crucial (if less than sufficient). If the United States were to ratify the treaty, pressure would build for the others to do so.

Unfortunately, the United States Senate rejected the treaty in 1999, and the Bush administration does not support it. More provocatively, the administration indicated in its classified Nuclear Posture Review that it planned "to reduce the time between a decision to conduct a nuclear test and the test itself, is considering (among other options) modifying existing warheads for use against hard and deeply-buried targets, [and] has not ruled out resumed testing."[24]

Why has the U.S. not given the treaty more support? One reason given is the concern that, while participation in the treaty is conditional, verification of compliance will be imperfect, so that *compliance* could not be relied upon to be conditional. Seismologists, however, say that underground testing could only avoid detection if involving very small yields conducted in special geological formations—sites that are both rare and, being identifiable, more

Table 5.1. Status of Signature and Ratification: Comprehensive Nuclear Test Ban Treaty

Signed and ratified		Signed but not ratified	Neither signed nor ratified
Algeria	Mexico	China	North Korea
Argentina	Netherlands	Colombia	India
Australia	Norway	Egypt	Pakistan
Austria	Peru	Indonesia	
Bangladesh	Poland	Iran	
Belgium	South Korea	Israel	
Brazil	Romania	United States	
Bulgaria	Russian Federation		
Canada	Slovakia		
Chile	South Africa		
Dem. Rep. Congo	Spain		
Finland	Sweden		
France	Switzerland		
Germany	Turkey		
Hungary	Ukraine		
Italy	United Kingdom		
Japan	Vietnam		

Source: http://www.ctbto.org/s_r/sigrat.dhtml?wcstate=ANNEX&showing=YES&showrat=YES& region=ALL (The table is accurate as of December 2006).

easily inspected (the treaty establishes an international monitoring system for verification purposes).[25] Moreover, compliance need not be perfect for a treaty to be beneficial to a party. Usually compliance only needs to be good enough.

Characteristically, the Bush administration has also wanted to keep its options open. Doing so, however, comes at the price of helping other states to keep *their* options open (the U.S. would only be bound by the treaty if all other nuclear states also ratified it). Fundamentally, the choice facing the United States—and every other nuclear state— is between seeking to out-compete its rivals in a nuclear technology race and accepting an arrangement of mutual restraint.

Human cloning

On July 5, 1996, a sheep named Dolly was born at the Roslin Institute in Edinburgh. Dolly's birth marked an extraordinary leap in science, for Dolly was a clone. To create her, scientists transplanted DNA from a single adult sheep into an egg, the nucleus of which had previously been removed. Dolly had only one genetic parent.

Dolly was the creation of a technique called somatic cell nuclear transfer—more popularly known as "reproductive cloning." Another kind of cloning, "therapeutic cloning," is fundamentally different. It uses the stem cells of human embryos for research that may one day help in the treatment of diseases like Alzheimer's and Parkinson's disease. Opinions on the merits of therapeutic cloning vary. Some countries not only allow research cloning; they help to finance it. Others ban the practice altogether. By contrast, there seems to be a near universal antipathy to reproductive cloning. Banning it might therefore supply a global public good.[26]

Negotiations on a treaty banning reproductive cloning began in 2001 but later collapsed after some countries, including the United States, insisted that therapeutic cloning also be banned—a position that was never going to be acceptable to a large number of states. As a consequence of this interlinking of issues, *neither* form of cloning is prohibited by international law today. In March 2005, the General Assembly of the United Nations adopted a resolution approving the UN Declaration on Human Cloning, which calls upon member states "to prohibit all forms of human cloning inasmuch as they are incompatible with human dignity and the protection of human life."[27] However, the resolution (approved by a vote of 84 in favor and 34 against with 37 abstentions) is non-binding. It will have no effect.

This may not matter much. Indeed, it may be *because* this might not matter much that the issues were linked and the negotiations were allowed to collapse.

Reproductive cloning is difficult. The scientists who cloned Dolly failed in their previous 277 attempts to clone a lamb. Cloned animals are also prone to debilitating complications, some of which pose a risk to the gestational mother. Dolly was unusual for being free of noticeable birth defects, but later in life she developed lung cancer and arthritis and had to be put down by lethal injection. Dolly enjoyed only half the normal lifespan of a Finn Dorset sheep. Human cloning would be even riskier. It might impair intelligence and emotional development (what would it feel like to be the delayed twin, essentially, of one of one's parents?). And it would offer few benefits. It would enable "reproduction" in some cases where this is not possible by other means (a man who did not produce gametes and a woman who did not produce eggs could both pass on their genome). It would allow a child to be "produced" to supply bone marrow to a sick, older sibling. It would also permit a person to be "replicated." None of these purposes, however, would yield significant benefits—certainly not to society at large. No wonder the aversion to reproductive cloning has been nearly universal.

It thus appears that the failure to establish a treaty banning reproductive cloning may be of little if any consequence. A ban on reproductive cloning—if that were to be considered a global public good—may well be supplied by countries acting unilaterally.

Inheritable genetic modification

Controls on another biomedical intervention, inheritable genetic modification, may matter much more. This technique alters the genome that a person passes on to his or her offspring. It might someday prevent inherited diseases from being passed on to future generations. But it could also be used to "enhance" normal human characteristics, to "commodify human reproduction and foster attempts to have 'perfect' children by 'correcting' their genomes."[28] "Designer babies" might be made taller, perhaps, or more intelligent. And, much like the use of steroids in athletics, the incentive for more people to use this technology for enhancement would likely increase with the number of other people that used it for this purpose. Compared with reproductive cloning, the technology of inheritable genetic modification is more likely to have social consequences.

These consequences would be difficult to predict. The technology might "widen the gap between the 'haves' and the 'have nots' to an unprecedented extent," since the rich would be more able to afford the technique.[29] But as Francis Fukuyama has noticed, the technology might also inspire a democratic welfare state to "reenter the eugenics game, intervening this time not to prevent low-IQ people from breeding, but to help genetically disadvantaged people raise their IQs and the IQs of their offspring."[30]

Who should make these choices? Perhaps states should agree not to make these choices unilaterally. If policies were made independently, the safeguards adopted by some countries may only create incentives for the science to relocate—just as restrictions on stem cell research by some countries only shifted biomedical investment elsewhere, to countries with more liberal stem cell laws.[31]

The world might be better off if at least some uses of the technology of inheritable genetic modification were banned (according to Roberto Adorno, "what is at stake...is nothing less than the preservation of the identity of the human species").[32] A ban on using inheritable genetic modification for enhancement purposes seems especially compelling. It can be thought of as a global public good.[33]

But a global ban on inheritable genetic modifications would be difficult to initiate and sustain. The distinction between using inheritable genetic modifications for preventive and enhancement purposes can be blurred. Somehow, a line would have to be drawn, but countries may disagree on the kinds of genetic modification that should be prohibited.

Sustaining a ban would also be difficult. Even if all other countries could be relied upon to restrict use of this technology, the "last" country may not want to follow suit, just as an individual athlete may be tempted to use steroids even when assured that all others will not use them. It is for a similar reason that the dream of universal nuclear disarmament seems beyond our grasp.[34]

Francis Fukuyama has argued that international governance in this area "can come about through the effort of nation-states to harmonize their regulatory policies," much as countries have harmonized the drug approval process.[35] But the motivation for harmonizing the drug approval process is to lower transactions costs, not to restrict the use of a new technology. The challenge here is to prevent countries from establishing their regulatory policies independently in the first place.

The nature of this global public good requires very broad (though perhaps not universal) agreement. Countries are unlikely to agree to ban all forms of inheritable genetic modification. They may, however, be able to agree to ban *some* forms of intervention—a kind of ceiling on research and use—with the understanding that the parties to such an agreement would be free to establish more restrictive regulations on their own. The restrictions would need to be subject to future review. As the science evolved, the negotiated restrictions would need to be reconsidered.

Would such an agreement achieve anything? It might. If countries were assured that others would not carry out research in certain areas, then one rationale for doing so—the thinking that, if others are likely to work in this area, then your country might as well do so, too—would be removed. The normative power of the prohibition may also be influential. Finally, the treaty could reinforce these incentives, if the countries possessing biomedical knowledge in this area agreed to share it with other parties, and if all parties were prohibited from exporting their knowledge to non-parties (these features being common also to the nuclear non-proliferation regime). Even if a few "rogue states" remained outside of this arrangement, their influence might be contained.

Conclusions

What are the incentives for countries not to do something? Here is one way to think about this: imagine that all other countries are not doing something. Will the "last" country also want not to do that same thing?

The answer depends. In the case of *using* a nuclear weapon, the answer has been affirmative for more than 60 years, though as I have warned this fortunate situation cannot be relied upon to last indefinitely—not without constant nurturing and reinforcement. Reproductive cloning is more likely to be prohibited—if not everywhere, then nearly everywhere—but that is because the vast majority of countries oppose it and would not be inclined to allow it even if a few states did.

The acquisition of nuclear weapons is different. Some states will want these weapons even if other countries do not possess them. Worse, as more states acquire these weapons, the incentive for other states to acquire them only increases. This is why the non-proliferation regime asks countries without nuclear weapons not to acquire them and countries with nuclear weapons to disarm. It is also why those states that already possess nuclear weapons continue to keep them, and why preventing spread requires such great effort. Restrictions on the technique of inheritable genetic modification are associated with similar incentives. In these cases, agreed universal limits would have the character of a "lowest common denominator" agreement, but they would hold the line somewhere—and somewhere may be better than nowhere.

CHAPTER SIX

Coordination and global standards: agreeing what states ought to do

In my own profession, that of a seaman, the embarrassment arising from the many prime meridians now in use is very conspicuous, and in the valuable interchange of longitudes by passing ships at sea, often difficult and hurried, sometimes only possible by figures written on a black-board, much confusion arises, and at time grave danger. In the use of charts, too, this trouble is also annoying, and to us who live upon the sea a common prime meridian will be a great advantage.

> Admiral C. R. P. Rodgers, President of the International Conference for the Purpose of Fixing a Prime Meridian and a Universal Day, Washington, DC, October 1, 1884.[1]

In human interaction, coordination is often essential. When driving, for example, it helps if everyone going in the same direction drives on the same side of the road. It does not matter which side of the road people drive on; either the left or right will do. Nor does it matter if different countries drive on different sides of the road—unless there is an uninterrupted flow of cross-border, two-way traffic; then, a common standard is needed. As neighboring road networks have become more interconnected, standardization has become a necessity. The trend has been towards driving on the right. Britain, Ireland, Cyprus and Malta are the exceptions in Europe because they are all islands.

Standards are transnational public goods. (One country's use of a standard does not preclude others from using it, and no country can be excluded from using it.) But what makes a standard *global*?

Consider air travel, and the need for pilots and air traffic controllers to communicate with each other. For domestic flights, the local language can serve as the standard. For international travel, a global standard is needed. Under rules established by the International Civil Aviation Organization, a specialized agency of the United Nations, pilots flying international flights must be proficient *either* in the local language of all the countries to which they fly *or* in English. Air traffic controllers, by contrast, must be proficient in *both* the local language *and* English. These rules ensure that communication is always possible. They also make English the global standard.

This chapter considers the development of an even more universal global standard, one that connects everyone on Earth. This is the standard for determining the time. The challenge here is not in enforcing a standard but in *choosing* one. This situation is thus akin to the global public goods discussed in Chapter 1 but with the difference that standards can only be established when supported by a critical number of countries. In most cases, global standards cannot be established unilaterally or even minilaterally.

An attractive feature of standards is that, once they become established, they need not be enforced. You do not drive on the left in Britain because it is the law; you drive on the left because you cannot make progress, and risk a head-on collision, if you deviate from the local standard. This raises the intriguing question of whether global public goods that are vulnerable to free riding can be supplied more effectively in a roundabout way by creating a global standard. I consider this possibility later in this chapter. The focus in these sections is on international marine transportation—and on whether the approach used to reduce oil spills might also help to reduce greenhouse gas emissions.

Time and space

What time is it? The only correct answer is that the time is whatever people agree it is. The time your watch says right now is a human construct, not a phenomenon of nature. Of course, time has traditionally been measured by natural reckoners—most of all, by the rotation of the Earth. But that may be changing now.

Why do we care what time it is? We care because we use time to coordinate human activities. As David Landes writes in his *Revolution in Time*, "so long as there is only one time source, it does not have to be accurate; the hour is what the source says it is. But multiply the signals, and the hour becomes a matter of dispute and a source of misunderstanding."[2]

Earlier in history, a single clock in the city square would do. It wasn't essential for clocks in distant cities to be synchronized. Each city could set its own clock to its own true time, determined in relation to the sun (if every town set its clock to noon at the solar midday, noon would vary continuously with longitude). It wasn't even important that measurements coincide. Indeed, the starting point for the day varied from one locality to another. In Basel, for example, the day began at noon—but that hour was designated one o'clock rather than twelve. "Because all forms of communication were so slow, the co-existence of various methods of counting the hours were not a major annoyance—only travelers noted it with puzzlement."[3]

Speed changed this. Rail transportation required a timetable, so that passengers knew when a train was to depart and arrive. For the railway companies, this meant adopting a synchronized measure of time throughout their networks. At first, each railway developed its own "internal" time, usually set according to the time at the company's headquarters (and aided by the new technology of the telegraph, which allowed the "correct" time to be transmitted from the central office almost instantaneously). For the traveling public, "external" time schedules were displayed locally.[4] As long as the clocks were accurate, conversions would allow one measure of time to be translated into another. Convenience, however, favored a national time standard (with passengers traveling on multiple rail routes, there was at a minimum a need for the schedules of different railways to be coordinated, but passengers would also want to coordinate their travels with their other appointments). In Britain, the Great Western Railway began using Greenwich Mean Time for its schedules in 1840, and soon after that the other railways followed. By 1855, 98 percent of all public clocks in Britain were set according to Greenwich Mean Time.[5]

For countries spanning thousands of kilometers in longitude, a national standard, though desirable for coordination purposes, was problematic. (The metric system, of course, is another standard. Canada switched to the metric system in the 1970s. In the U.S., the continental span is still measured in miles rather than kilometers. It does not matter which system is used, so long as conversions are made correctly. As noted in Chapter 1, NASA's Mars Climate Orbiter was destroyed because of a conversion error.) It would mean that noon would bear little relation to the solar midday in much of the country (to this day, however, all clocks in China are set to the same time). Thus, the time zone was invented. At noon on November 18, 1883, the North American railway network established four time zones, each of 15 degrees longitude, calculated with reference to Greenwich. The 15-degree standard was a natural choice; it corresponded to a time difference of one hour. The time zones were labeled Eastern, Central, Mountain, and Pacific, and they were quickly adopted by most North American cities.[6] They remain the standard today.

Just as a national railway system connecting different cities and regions created the need for standardization within a country, so increased international traffic and the laying of the transatlantic telegraph cable created the need for international coordination of time measurement. But how would an international standard be chosen?

Choosing a prime meridian and universal day

In 1884, just a year after time zones were established in North America, an international conference was convened in Washington, "for the purpose of fixing a prime meridian and a universal day." The United States invited every country with which it had diplomatic relations. The countries attending, and voting, included 11 from Europe, 11 from the Americas, one from Africa (Liberia), and two from the Asia-Pacific region (Hawaii and Japan).

The conference first considered a resolution to adopt "a single prime meridian for all nations, in place of the multiplicity of initial meridians which now exist." The proposal was approved unanimously.[7] The desire for coordination, at least with respect to this group of countries, was universal.

Agreeing on the identity of the common meridian proved more difficult, however, as many countries had established their own meridian (Paris, Cadiz, Naples, Stockholm, etc.) National pride was at stake.

For various reasons, however, Greenwich had the edge. Most world shipping relied on the Greenwich meridian.[8] Navigators had set their chronometers to Greenwich Mean Time since the eighteenth century. As mentioned previously, the railways had already divided North America into time zones calculated relative to Greenwich. Finally, the host of the conference, the United States, proposed that Greenwich be chosen. Greenwich was thus the focal point for this negotiation.

Twenty-two countries approved the U.S. resolution. France, which had proposed a "neutral" meridian rather than Paris, and Brazil, which had its own meridian in Rio de Janeiro, abstained; only San Domingo—today, Haiti—a former French colony, voted against the resolution.

The vote was non-binding, but with the major maritime powers choosing Greenwich, use of a different meridian was inconvenient (and convenience, after all, was the reason for coordinating in the first place). France thus eventually adopted Greenwich Mean Time (to be precise, France adopted as its official time, "Paris mean time delayed by nine minutes and twenty-one seconds") in 1911.[9] The Netherlands, despite approving the resolution, waited until 1940 before adopting the standard of Greenwich Mean Time.[10]

The conference also established the standard for when the day should begin. As noted earlier, centuries before different cities established the beginning of the day at different times, such as sunrise and sunset as well as the solar midday. By the time the conference was held, two standards were common. Civil (or legal) days began at midnight. Astronomers and navigators started the day at noon. The conference decided that the universal day "is to be a mean solar day; is to begin for all the world at the moment of mean midnight of the initial meridian, coinciding with the beginning of the civil day and date of that meridian; and is to be counted from zero up to twenty-four hours." This resolution was approved by 15 of the 24 countries attending (of the other nine countries, two voted against and seven abstained).

Finally, the conference needed to establish an arbitrary longitude at which the date would change. If it is eight o'clock Monday morning in Greenwich, then it must be three o'clock in the morning in New York City—but is that three o'clock on Monday morning or on Tuesday morning? The conference determined that it was three o'clock on Monday morning.[11] But at what longitude should the adjustment be made? The conference chose 180 degrees, partly because that was exactly opposite Greenwich, and partly because this line of longitude coincided mostly with uninhabited ocean. The resolution establishing the degree of longitude we now call the International Date Line was approved by 14 countries (five countries voted nay and six abstained).[12]

All of these standards—dividing the Earth into 24 time zones, each of 15 degrees longitude; locating the prime meridian of zero degrees at Greenwich; establishing the International Date Line at 180 degrees; and declaring a universal day of 24 hours beginning at midnight at Greenwich—all of these standards were adhered to voluntarily and universally. There was no need for them to be enforced, because of the strong incentive to coordinate.

Globalization is a process; it did not appear suddenly, and it is thus incorrect to speak of a moment at which globalization began. But if a single moment were to be identified as a watershed, it would probably be this conference, convened in October 1884. That the conference was held in the first place reflected the desire already being expressed at that time for human interaction to be coordinated globally—an indication as powerful as any that the process of globalization was fully underway. The establishment of global standards for the time, however, enabled these desires to be fulfilled. It facilitated greater international integration. It put the process of globalization into a faster gear.

The 1884 conference also showed that the countries of the world could cooperate to define and shape the world.

Standards as global public goods

The standards established at this conference are global public goods. No country is excluded from using them, and one country's use of them does not impede the ability of others to use them. They are, to be sure, unlike the global public goods discussed in Chapters 1–4, because they do not cost anything to supply. They are also different from the global public goods discussed in Chapter 5, because their provision requires that countries agree what to do, rather than what not to do. Their provision may entail conflict, because different countries may prefer that different standards be chosen (a "neutral" meridian rather than Greenwich, for example). However, once a standard is chosen, and other countries adopt it, every country has an incentive to adopt it. Sustaining a standard is therefore easy. The international problem arises only in *choosing* the standard.

Countries choose standards all the time. Another important standard is being debated now. It is in many ways a continuation of the negotiations held in Washington in 1884. I turn to it next.

Time standards

What time is it? The 1884 conference established the universal day, but not the time. As noted earlier, true coordination is best achieved when there is a single clock. But is there a single clock for the world?

From the time of the 1884 conference, national time keeping organizations calculated the time according to the Earth's rotation using astronomical measurements. Clocks were essentially used to keep the time between astronomical readings. Astronomical measurements, however, were subject to error, as was the international transmission of particular readings via radio signals—a form of communication that emerged around 1910.[13] Time could be given a unique *definition* (based on the rotation of the Earth on its axis, nominally equivalent to the mean solar time at the Greenwich meridian, reckoned at midnight), but it had a multiple of *estimates*. Which estimate would serve as the global clock?

In 1911, the French government convened a conference to address this question. The conference established the Bureau International de l'Heure. Its purpose was to unify or coordinate world measurements of time, to create what became known as Universal Time. This time was determined not by a single country's reading but by the average of all the world's estimates of the same time scale.

In 1955, the world's first caesium atomic clock was developed at the National Physical Laboratory in the United Kingdom. Later, more atomic clocks were constructed, and the Bureau International de l'Heure developed an average of *these* estimates of time. This average became known as International Atomic Time.[14] By 1970, there thus existed two global standards (that is, two global averages of two fundamental measures) of time, one based on the Earth's rotation and the other based on the vibrations of an atom.

The two measures differ because the vibration of a caesium atom is nearly uniform (with an error of one second every 150,000 years),[15] while the Earth's rotation is subject to random and periodic fluctuations. It is also slowing down by the frictional effect of the tides. By studying the annual growth bands on fossil corals, scientists have deduced that about 370 million years ago there were between 385 and 410 days in a year.[16] The days were shorter back then because the Earth spun faster.

The world needs a single measure of civil time—coordination demands this. But which measure should be used, Universal Time or International Atomic Time? Rather than choose between these standards, countries agreed to adopt a new one. This is called Coordinated Universal Time.

Coordinated Universal Time is the time you and I rely on every day. It is essentially International Atomic Time, adjusted by the addition of "leap seconds," which reflect the lengthening of the day as determined by the Earth's rotation (negative leap seconds are possible but none has been needed thus far). Because variations in the Earth's rotation are irregular, leap seconds are added irregularly. Twenty-three have been added since 1972. The last one was added on December 31, 2005.

Over time, more leap seconds will have to be added; by 2100, roughly two leap seconds will have to be added each year.[17] The difference between Universal Time and International Atomic Time will thus widen over time. The gap could reach half an hour by the year 2700, a whole hour by around 3000.[18]

This would not matter except that an important new technology relies exclusively on International Atomic Time. Today, two standards of time are thus being used simultaneously. This cannot last. Coordination favors the use of a single standard. But which of the two existing standards will be chosen? Who will decide which standard is chosen?

Time for a new standard of time?

In late 2005, the United States made a proposal to the International Telecommunication Union, which is responsible for setting international time standards. The proposal was to change Coordinated Universal Time "due to some evidence of the difficulties experienced by communication, navigation and other electronic systems caused by leap seconds ... "[19] The United States wanted the world to stop adding leap seconds to Coordinated Universal Time from 2007 onwards. It proposed that leap *hours* be added as needed instead. Since the first leap hour would not be needed for many centuries, adoption of this proposal would essentially decouple time keeping from the Earth's rotation.

What "difficulties" would justify such a change? The most important relate to sophisticated telecommunications systems requiring precise time synchronization—no leap seconds. The Global Positioning System only incorporates leap seconds added *before* it began operating in 1980. The future Galileo system will also be leap-second-free.[20] As noted in Chapter 1, these two systems are to be made compatible with each other. But they will also need to interconnect with other systems. The concern is that, as the coordinated navigation systems depart more and more from civil time, coordination problems will arise as between these systems and the ones with which they interconnect, if the latter remain tied to Coordinated Universal Time.[21]

Adoption of a new standard of time free of leap seconds will, of course, impose switching costs on users of technologies, including astronomical and satellite systems, that currently rely on Coordinated Universal Time, leap seconds and all. Overall, it is unclear whether such a switch would constitute a positive sum, a zero sum, or a negative sum game. We only know that there would be winners and losers.

The more important issue concerns the process by which this decision will be made.

As explained by the Royal Astronomical Society in the United Kingdom, this issue, until very recently, "has been subject only to a specialist and rather closed debate. There is a clear need," the Society argues, "for broader debate that involves a wider range of those who will be affected by the proposed change. This should extend outside science and technology—for example, to consider whether civil/legal time should be based on precision time or mean solar time."[22] What the Royal Astronomical Society is suggesting is this: that the decision to change the standard is more than a technical and perhaps an economic matter; it is a question of whether the time that coordinates human interaction should be determined by the Earth's rotation, as it has since a human first put a stick in the ground and observed its shadow, or whether civil time should be determined by the needs of our new technologies.

The working party of the International Telecommunication Union responsible for reviewing the implications of the U.S. proposal has decided that more time is required to build a consensus. A decision does not appear imminent.

So, for the last time, what time is it? For the moment, it remains, for most of us, Coordinated Universal Time. Leap seconds and all.

Standards and coordination

As noted earlier, whether we drive on the left or the right does not matter. All that matters is that we coordinate. Whether pilots and air traffic controllers speak English or Esperanto also does not matter, so long as they speak the same language. Finally, apart from switching costs, and the deep historical ties of human time keeping to the Earth's rotation, it does not matter whether we use leap seconds or leap hours. Either will do. The important thing is that we all use the same standard.

The choice of some standards does matter. An example is the standard for the design of oil tankers.

Ocean dumping

When you think of oil pollution, you probably think of oil spills: major accidents like the *Torrey Canyon* and *Exxon Valdez*. Historically, however, much more oil was released into the sea routinely and deliberately. Most of these releases were caused by tankers filling their empty cargo tanks with ballast water, and then discharging the oily ballast into the sea before refilling the tanks with oil for the next delivery.

How to address this problem?[23] A first international conference, convened in 1926, decided that significant oil dumping (specifically, a limit of 500 parts per million or ppm) should be prohibited within 50 miles of shore. The agreement never entered into force.

Another round of negotiations, begun in 1935, endorsed the same 500 ppm limit, but extended the prohibition zone to 150 miles from shore. That agreement also never entered into force.

In 1954, yet another conference was convened. This time a tougher 100 ppm standard was established within the original 50-mile zone.

Unlike the earlier agreements, this one did enter into force. However, it provided neither the means nor the incentives for enforcement. It had no effect.

More negotiations were held in the 1960s, but they proved as ineffective as the earlier efforts.

In 1972 a new approach was tried. The United States passed a domestic law mandating certain technical standards for oil tankers. The U.S. hoped that these new standards would be adopted internationally, but the U.S. law required that they be adopted unilaterally by 1976, should international negotiations fail. Ships that violated the standards would be banned from U.S. waters.

International negotiations dragged, but in 1978 a new agreement was negotiated. Taking direction from the U.S. law, this new agreement required that oil tankers segregate their oil cargo and ballast water. The new standard thus prevented oil and water from mixing. (The new technical standard is compared with the previous one in Figure 6.1.) The agreement requiring separate tanks was called the International Convention for the Prevention of Marine Pollution from Ships. To insiders it became known as MARPOL 73/78.

The new agreement had a dramatic effect. In contrast to the earlier agreements, compliance was simple to verify—a quick, on-board inspection would suffice, and if the results of such inspections were shared with the other parties to the agreement, few inspections would be needed overall. The new approach was also easy to enforce—port states only needed to ban non-complying tankers from making deliveries in their waters, and they had an incentive to do this, for it was their own waters that they were seeking to protect in the first place. No wonder compliance with this agreement has been nearly perfect.[24]

The new agreement also promoted broad participation. The value of a tanker depends on the number of ports to which it has access. As more countries adopted the new standard, it thus became more attractive for tanker operators to meet the standard; and this in turn made it more attractive for yet more coastal states to adopt the standard. The adoption of the standard thus created a positive feedback, borne on the back of the incentives to coordinate. A threshold of adoption was probably needed to get the feedback going. But once the threshold participation level was passed, adoption of the standard would have been in nearly every country's interests; the standard would have tipped. MARPOL 73/78 (specifically, Annex I)

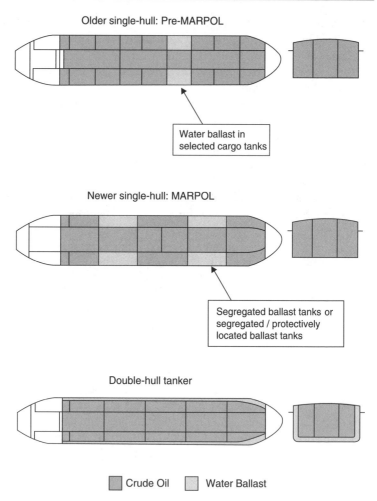

Figure 6.1. Basic Tanker Designs

Source: Reprinted with permission from (Double-Hull Tanker Legislation) © (1998) by the National Academy of Sciences, Courtesy of the National Academies Press, Washington, D.C.

has now been ratified by 138 countries, accounting for 98 percent of global shipping.[25] Participation in this agreement is thus nearly universal.

There is a lesson in this: what turned things around was a change in *perception*, not about the problem of ocean dumping itself but about the best way to restructure the incentives that were causing the problem. What turned things around was the decision to choose *technical* rather than *performance* standards.

Lock in

Though effective in the short run, would technical standards seem as attractive years later? From the perspective of 1978, it was not obvious that they would. There can be a tendency for standards to be "locked in."[26] Just as Greenwich became the meridian of choice because of its historical advantage, so a technology standard may be hard to displace once it has become established.

Recall that, historically, there were two major sources of oil pollution at sea. The first was deliberate dumping—a problem addressed by the new standard requiring segregated ballast tanks. The second was accidental oil spills, which would not have been helped by the new technical standard. The best way to reduce the environmental consequences of tanker accidents was to require that tankers be fitted with double hulls. This would require a new technical standard (see again Figure 6.1). But if standards were vulnerable to "lock in," might choice of the segregated ballast tanks standard have precluded subsequent adoption of double hulls?

Following the *Exxon Valdez* oil spill in 1989, the United States passed a law banning single hulled tankers from U.S. waters. This unilateral change led to MARPOL 73/78 being amended to include a new requirement for double hulls. After the breakup of the *Erika* off the coast of France in 1999, the European Union proposed accelerating the phase-out of single hull tankers agreed earlier. And then, after the sinking of the *Prestige* off of the coast of Spain in 2002, the European Union proposed accelerating the phase-out yet again. A 2003 amendment to the MARPOL 73/78, which came into force in 2005, made these new standards apply internationally. It also brought forward the date at which only double-hulled tankers will be allowed to transport oil at sea—to 2005 or (in the case of tankers fitted with segregated ballast tanks) 2010 at the latest. The earlier technical standard has thus been superseded by another, stricter one. Protection of the oceans has not been undermined by the earlier decision to establish a technical standard. In this case at least, lock in has not blocked progress.

Standards as strategies

Performance standards, such as the ones agreed in the 1920s, 1930s, and 1950s, have distinct advantages over technical standards. Indeed, that is why they were chosen in the first place. If compliance can be verified, and if the fines for non-compliance are big enough, performance standards will provide tanker operators with an incentive to discharge their ballast waters outside the prohibited zones. They would also provide an incentive for tanker operators to guard against accidental spills. Both of these incentives could in turn drive innovation, leading—possibly—to new ship designs. We will never know, but had it been possible to enforce an international agreement on performance standards, better approaches may have been developed and diffused than the technical standards mandated by MARPOL 73/78.

These technical standards, however, had one great advantage. They got around the enforcement problem by making compliance easy to verify. The reason for choosing technical standards was thus strategic. It was the effect these standards had on changing incentives that was paramount.

Standards for climate change mitigation

The emission limits in the Kyoto Protocol are akin to the performance standards in the earlier oil pollution agreements. Both approaches require enforcement. We now know that the earlier approach to protecting the oceans failed. We also know that the alternative of establishing technical standards worked. Might we look back on Kyoto someday and conclude that it failed for similar reasons as these earlier attempts to reduce oil dumping? Might a new approach to mitigating climate change—an approach relying on technical standards, as in MARPOL 73/78—work better?[27]

The answer depends on whether the incentives to coordinate choices of technologies can overpower the incentives to free ride.

What drives standardization? Cost is one consideration. Economies of scale drive unit costs down, making it cheaper to produce lots of the same thing rather than smaller quantities of different things. If economies of scale are strong enough, and variety is unimportant, a kind of standard will emerge. If there are economies of learning, so that costs fall over time as more units are produced, standardization is even more likely.

Network externalities—whether the technologies used by each country need to be compatible with the technologies used by other countries—are crucial. With driving, language, and time, compatibility is important if not essential. Also important are the local benefits of technology adoption. It was the incentive to protect the local environment that made port states want to enforce MARPOL 73/78. It just happened that, in seeking to protect their local environments, states succeeded in protecting the oceans everywhere.

Catalytic converters and their complement, unleaded gasoline, have become global standards for all of these reasons. Economies of scale favor the production of one kind of automobile and the refining of one kind of gasoline worldwide. Network externalities mean that, as people drive across international boundaries, a common fuel must be available, one that is compatible with the kind of car everyone is driving. Of course, local environmental benefits provide a further reason for countries to adopt the catalytic technology coupled with unleaded fuel—the reason these standards were developed in the first place. I suspect, however, that the commercial reasons for standardization dominate in some cases. That Sudan, a failed state, and the setting for both civil war and genocide—that even this country should have switched to unleaded gasoline is testimony to the power of commercial considerations in driving technology adoption worldwide.[28]

Trade restrictions can also help. The ability of port states to deny access to tankers that fail to comply with agreed standards helped propel the spread of these standards. Trade restrictions to enforce an agreement like Kyoto are problematic for the reasons mentioned in Chapter 3. But trade restrictions to enforce an agreement on technical standards are legal under the current trading rules and would be easy to enforce. Of course, trade restrictions do not always work, even when they are easily implemented. As explained in Chapter 3, they have largely failed to stop fishermen from re-registering their vessels, to avoid being subject to catch limits. But fishing is different from gasoline and ocean shipping. There are no network externalities in consuming blue fin tuna.

Currently, there do not exist, even on the drawing board, climate-friendly technologies that possess all of these desirable characteristics. The spread of a breakthrough automobile technology such as hydrogen is likely, especially because of the need to combine a new kind of automobile with a supporting energy infrastructure. But the hydrogen fuel needs to be produced (without releasing greenhouse gas emissions), and there are no sizable network externalities in hydrogen production.

Similarly, there do not exist network externalities in electricity generation. For example, though the light water standard dominates nuclear reactor design, nuclear power is not generally favored over alternative sources of generation.[29] There may exist other possibilities for this sector. Renewable energy, for example, would become more economically attractive if power could be distributed between continents and time zones.[30] New, high-temperature superconductor or carbon nanotube cables or even wireless power transmission may make creation of a global electricity grid feasible sometime in the future.[31] Currently, however, the technologies needed to promote spread are not being developed.

If the approach that worked for protecting the oceans is to work for mitigating global climate change, it will be necessary to develop new technologies that not only reduce greenhouse gas emissions substantially, but that have the characteristics that favor their diffusion worldwide.

Conclusions

Standards emerge whenever countries have strong incentives to coordinate. Global standards are much easier to supply than other global public goods. They do not need to be paid for, and they are easy to sustain once established. The problem with standards is *choosing* them.

Greenwich was a natural choice for the prime meridian because history had endowed Greenwich with advantages—not least the advantage of having been the meridian of choice for key states. Had the history leading up to 1884 been different, a different standard may have been chosen—and communications and navigation would have functioned just as efficiently. It was important that *a* common meridian be established. The choice of *which* meridian was less important.

Choice of a time standard is similar. The incentive to coordinate means that a single standard is needed for civil time, but whether that standard will need to change to suit the demands of certain emerging technologies or whether these technologies will need to be adapted to suit the current standard—well, time will tell.

Standards for the design of oil tankers are different. They matter a great deal. The new standards have substantially reduced ocean dumping.

These standards were chosen strategically. Might a similar approach help diffuse climate-friendly energy technologies? That would depend on whether the R&D efforts discussed in Chapter 3 succeed in identifying technologies that not only reduce emissions but that also possess the qualities needed to spur their diffusion.

CHAPTER SEVEN

Development: do global public goods help poor states?

Last year, 800,000 children in the world died of measles. Can you imagine dying of measles today in [the United States]?

> Melinda Gates, Co-Chair, Bill and
> Melinda Gates Foundation, 2000.[1]

At the hospital here in the troubled province of North Kivu near the Rwandan border, where villages have been ravaged by war, the burden on children is on grim, daily display. One 2-year-old boy, Amuri, struggled to breathe on a hospital bed while doctors and nurses went through the motions— attaching one of the hospital's scarce pulse-oximeters to his tiny index finger, placing an oxygen mask over his gasping mouth. But they knew it was too late...A few moments later, Amuri's eyes rolled back in his head, his chest stilled and he was dead...Amuri died of measles.

> *New York Times* correspondent Lydia Polgreen,
> reporting from Rutshuru, Congo, 2006.[2]

An estimated 1.4 billion people in the world are poor, and nearly half of these people—about one in eight people worldwide—are hungry.[3] Most of these people live in Sub-Saharan Africa, South Asia, and East Asia.

Does the provision of global public goods help these people? Not always. Prevention of a certain mega-asteroid strike would save everyone, including the destitute; but searching for an asteroid that might collide with the Earth centuries from now—to people who are hungry, that might seem a fanciful thing on which to spend money today. Experiments that test the standard model in physics, tanker designs that prevent oil spills, and security guarantees that limit nuclear proliferation—all of those things also may not matter much to people whose basic needs are not being met. Efforts to mitigate global climate change will matter to the descendants of these people, but the current generation of the poor and hungry might not choose even that to be a priority for spending today.

Other global public goods do touch the lives of the poorest people. Examples include the prevention of conflict, the knowledge of how to increase agricultural yields (a "green revolution" for Africa), and control of the spread of emerging diseases.

We should not be surprised that only *some* global public goods help the worst off people, for few if any are provided specifically for this purpose. As noted in the Introduction, global public goods are usually provided by and for the better off countries. But is there a relationship between the provision of global public goods and development? Are there some neglected global public goods that could improve the lives of the least well off people? Are there development policies that could ensure that the poorest people also benefit from the provision of global public goods?

The key to understanding these questions lies in a simple observation: global public goods are neither supplied nor enjoyed in a vacuum. Countries with the wherewithal to supply global public goods have other options. Faced with free riding incentives, they may choose to substitute national public goods for global public goods, leaving other countries to help themselves. Even when global public goods are supplied, the poorest people may not be able to benefit unless their own governments supply complementary national public goods. These connections between the national and global levels are thus crucial. They determine whether global public goods are supplied. They also determine whether their supply improves the wellbeing of the people most in need of help. They are the focus of this chapter.

Measles

I had measles as a child. Every child did in those days (measles is *very* infectious), unless you happened to grow up in an isolated community. My children have grown up in cities but they have not had measles and they will not get it. They were vaccinated for the disease.

The measles vaccine, first licensed in 1963, has been a lifesaver.[4] Measles is a highly contagious respiratory disease. It can also kill, but it rarely kills directly. Instead, it weakens the body's immune system, leaving its host vulnerable to other infections such as pneumonia and diarrhea. Malnourished children are especially defenseless to such infections.

In the United States, where I grew up, though nearly every child got measles, very few died from the disease. From 1958 to 1962, an average of around 500,000 children were infected with measles but fewer than 500 died each year from the disease.[5] It was in the poorest countries that measles was killing large numbers of children.

It still is. Today, around half a million children die every year of measles worldwide. The boy, Amuri, whose death is reported in the opening to this chapter, is just one such victim.

Thanks to improved immunization, however, the number of deaths attributed to measles is a lot smaller than it used to be. Over the five-year period 1999–2003 the number of measles deaths per year worldwide fell from 873,000 to 530,000.[6]

This decline is obviously to be cheered (though we should not assume that the decline can be sustained indefinitely), but over that same five-year period I have found evidence of only two measles deaths in the United States.[7] If the rest of the world had the same level of protection as the U.S., only around 40 people would have died from measles over that five-year period. As it is, around 3 million people died—nearly all of them young children.

This gap could be closed. All it would take is greater immunization. The cost per dose is about $0.30 if purchased through UNICEF. Saving these lives thus only costs money—and not very much of that.[8]

So, why isn't even more being done? A part of the reason is that the same vaccine that saves lives also separates communities epidemiologically. People who get the vaccine are made immune to measles, and so lose the incentive to care whether other people are protected. Measles elimination goes one step farther. It offers herd immunity locally even to the unvaccinated—a national public good. The provision of this national public good, however, creates an invisible barrier between this country and the rest of the world. A country like the United States that eliminates measles at home has little incentive to reduce measles prevalence abroad.

Measles is thus a killer globally partly because measles vaccination is *not* a global public good. If measles could be eradicated, then the rich countries might have a direct incentive to vaccinate children in poor countries. But because measles eradication is probably not achievable today, rich countries lack this incentive.[9] When they provide assistance to the United Nations' Measles Initiative, the main motivation is compassion, not self-interest.

Compassion is a virtue to be prized, but it cannot overcome this or the many other gaps in development—not on its own, anyway. As noted by Adel Mahmoud, the president of Merck, the company that first licensed the measles vaccine, "leadership and government commitment to closing the global vaccination gap have to come from the affected countries... Governments of these countries must place disease prevention above political conflict or weapons purchase."[10] The boy, Amuri, was as much a victim of war and official neglect as he was of measles.[11]

The knowledge of how to prevent a child from getting measles is a global public good, but whether its provision benefits people everywhere depends on whether complementary *national* public goods are also supplied. In particular, it depends on whether vaccination is undertaken at a rate sufficient to eliminate measles (and thus avoid nearly all measles deaths) within every country. That, however, can only be possible in areas that are free of conflict and administered by governments that are capable of, and have an interest in, delivering at least basic public services. For many years it has not been possible in countries like Amuri's. Congo is a failed state.

Turning round states like this will facilitate the supply of weakest link global public goods (as discussed in Chapter 2), which would benefit the great and middle powers. But doing this is itself a global public good—and one that, as explained in Chapter 4, is vulnerable to free riding. As also noted in Chapter 4, the countries likely to benefit most from peace- and state-building are the neighbors to a conflict. Reducing regional conflict is a regional public good. In this sense, it is a little like providing tsunami warnings.

Tsunami warnings

The tragedy of the Indian Ocean tsunami of December 2004 is not only that around a quarter of a million people died. It is that many of these deaths could have been avoided. Had the tsunami been noticed earlier (the earthquake that caused the tsunami was detected), and had vulnerable people been alerted in time, lives could have been saved. These steps were possible. Indeed, we know that these steps were possible because they were taken long ago in the Pacific.

Why was the regional public good of tsunami warning provided for one ocean but not for the other? One reason is that tsunamis are much more common in the Pacific—making warnings for that ocean much more valuable. Another reason, however, is that a Pacific tsunami warning system would protect rich nations like Australia, Japan, and the United States, whereas an Indian Ocean tsunami warning system would protect poorer states like India, Indonesia, Sri Lanka, and Thailand. In absolute terms, the Pacific states had more to lose economically from a tsunami. They therefore had a greater incentive to defend against such a loss.

Tsunamis are rare in the Indian Ocean (the last major one was caused by the eruption of Krakatau in 1883). But it is likely that a proposal to build a tsunami warning system there would have passed a benefit-cost test prior to the 2004 tsunami (from an *ex post* perspective, such a system was obviously to be desired).[12] To realize this benefit, however, would probably have required international cooperation.

Key ingredients of any tsunami early warning system are technologies that can detect ocean earthquakes and sudden changes in ocean pressure, including seismometers, tide gauges, and deep ocean assessment buoys. To provide a useful warning, such a system must be built to a sufficient scale, but only *one* such system is needed for any ocean: a single best effort.

What are the economics of providing this regional public good? In terms used previously in this book, let the country that benefits most from tsunami warnings be labeled Country *1*, the country that benefits second most be labeled Country *2*, and so on. Suppose that there are k countries in the region, and denote the benefits (measured in money terms) to each country by the letter B (Country *1* thus benefits by an amount B_1, Country 2 by B_2, and so on). Finally, let the cost of a tsunami warning system be denoted C. Very possibly, the economics of an Indian Ocean tsunami warning system might be summarized by the relationship, $B_1 + B_2 + \ldots + B_k > C > B_1 > B_2 > \ldots > B_k$. In words, all countries in the region would have been better off if the system had been provided, but it would not have paid any country in the region to supply it unilaterally.

Like disease surveillance, the value of having a tsunami warning system depends on the information obtained being shared. Distrust among countries creates blind spots, and India has refused to release seismic recordings in real-time, for fear that they would betray its nuclear testing. For this reason, additional seismometers are being added elsewhere—at additional cost—to provide the needed data to other countries. In contrast to the Pacific, there will not be a single, unified system for tsunami warning in the Indian Ocean, but a multiple of systems, linked by a number of bilateral, information-sharing agreements.[13] Still, a warning system is being assembled today, and one could have been in place in December 2004. What prevented cooperation from emerging earlier?

One reason might be the old age reason of governments not wanting to invest in projects that will only pay off in the distant future. In this case, however, there may have been another reason. To be of value, a tsunami warning system must be coupled with national systems of communications and emergency preparedness—systems capable of alerting people on the beach of the need to move to higher ground.[14] These national public goods are strong complements to the regional public good of an ocean-wide warning system. The experience of two African countries to the 2004 tsunami illustrates their value. "In Kenya, where radio and television stations had warned the population three hours in advance of the oncoming tsunami after discovering news reports on satellite television, there was only one loss of life. In neighbouring Somalia where no word was received of the approaching tsunami, 300 lives were lost eight hours after the earthquake."[15]

The complementary nature of these regional and national public goods may help to explain why neither was provided. The value of a tsunami warning system is higher when national emergency preparedness systems are in place, but these are only of value when accurate and timely tsunami warnings can be relied upon. Possibly, no country would have wanted to develop a regional warning system when each lacked a domestic preparedness and response system. Likewise, no country may have wanted to invest in national preparedness and response so long as warnings were unavailable. I have not done the calculations, but it is possible that the entire region lost out for having missed these connections.

River blindness vector control

The World Bank recognized the value of supplying another regional public good, river blindness vector control, over 30 years ago. Today, the river blindness program is considered a development success story.[16]

River blindness (*onchocerciasis*) is a parasitic disease transmitted to humans by the bite of the female black fly and prevalent mainly in tropical Africa.[17] Upon entering the body, the worms mature and reproduce, releasing millions of microfilariae into the host. It is these microscopic worms rather than the mature worms that cause illness. They migrate within the body, eventually reaching the skin or the eyes, where they trigger an immune response that causes intense itching. In some cases, the response causes blindness.

From the mid-1970s, the disease was controlled in seven contiguous West African countries by insecticide spraying. The target was the parasite's black fly vector.

Black flies are well adapted to their environment.[18] They are muscular, can store fat, and feed on plant nectar. They also live a long time for a fly—about 85 days. All of these attributes allow black flies to travel long distances. Savannah species can travel up to 500 kilometers when the monsoon winds are at their backs. On the migratory route of one species, from northern Sierra Leone to western Mali, black flies travel up to 20 kilometers a day. It was because of the black fly's peripatetic nature that the original river blindness control program had to be expanded from seven to 11 countries. When the program was limited to the original seven countries, black flies from outside the region re-colonized areas that had previously been cleared of the vector.

The benefits of the river blindness control program for development have been significant. In human terms, the program has prevented 600,000 cases of blindness. In development terms, it has opened up 25 million hectares of arable land to agricultural development—land that was abandoned to the black fly. In economic terms, it has earned a 20 percent return on the money invested.[19] All of this would not have been possible were only some states to control this disease. An international effort was required. The habits of the black fly vector made river blindness control a weakest link regional public good.

Though the control program has been successful, it appears that river blindness cannot be eradicated—at least not now, given current technologies.[20] Another regional disease, Guinea worm (*dracunculiasis*), can be eradicated; and yet, so far, attempts to eradicate this disease have failed. The reasons for this failure are interesting. They help to explain why other regional public goods have also been undersupplied.

Guinea worm eradication

Guinea worm is a parasitic disease transmitted to humans who drink water containing microscopic fleas bearing infective larvae. Once swallowed, the larvae develop within the human host. After about a year, the mature worms mate. The male worms die, but the females, each up to a meter long, migrate within the host, usually into the legs and feet. The worms then begin to emerge, forming blisters at the skin's surface. This causes an intense, burning pain, and sufferers seek cool, open water for relief. When the blisters rupture, the spaghetti-like worms emerge to release their larvae into the standing water. Fleas then eat the larvae, humans eat the fleas, and the worm's life cycle begins all over again.

The emerging worms cannot be pulled from the body all at once. Sufferers wrap them around a small stick, giving it a turn each day. It can take weeks for the worms to be fully extracted, and during this time the blister may become infected. The worms often emerge during the planting or harvesting season, and so, apart from the pain endured by the hosts, Guinea worm imposes an economic burden on affected communities.[21]

Guinea worm does not kill, and is confined to poor, rural areas. So the benefits of eradicating it are low compared to, say, smallpox. But Guinea worm is also cheap and easy to eradicate. To break the worm's life cycle, it is only essential to prevent people from drinking unfiltered, standing drinking water, and to stop sufferers from entering open water. Because of the parasite's life cycle, even these modest measures only need to be maintained for a few years at most.

A program to eradicate Guinea worm began in 1980. So far, the eradication effort—supported by the United States Centers for Disease Control, the Carter Center, the World Health Organization, and other organizations—has reduced the number of cases worldwide from around 3.5 million to fewer than 10,000 today.[22] It has also reduced the geographic range of the disease from 20 to nine countries. Guinea worm no longer exists in Asia; today, it lives only in Sub-Saharan Africa.

It is most prevalent today in Sudan—a country that has been caught in a civil war since 1983, home to the Darfur province, and the top ranked country in the Failed States Index. In 1995, to give the eradication effort a push, Jimmy Carter negotiated a four-month "Guinea worm cease-fire." His intervention helped, but as noted by Donald Hopkins and Craig Withers of the Carter Center, "dracunculiasis cannot be eradicated from Sudan until Sudan's civil war is ended."[23]

In the effort to supply the international public good of Guinea worm eradication, Sudan is the weakest link. Sudan also could have been the weakest link in the earlier effort to eradicate smallpox. It just happened that the smallpox campaign coincided with a rare break in Sudan's decades-long civil war. In the 1970s, we were lucky. Today, Sudan is preventing the rest of the region from enjoying the supply of another vital public good.

Sudan, however, is not the only weakest link. Indeed, the countries that most threaten the poorest Sub-Saharan African countries are located on different continents.

Preventing resistance

By most estimates, more than a million people die every year of malaria—almost all of them young children living in the tropical zones of Africa. Malaria also imposes a huge burden on development, possibly reducing income per capita by as much as half in the most malaria-ridden economies.[24]

Malaria treatment has relied for many years on an effective and inexpensive drug called chloroquine. Today, however, chloroquine has lost its powers in many regions of the world. Chloroquine-resistant strains of malaria first emerged independently in Columbia and on the Cambodia–Thailand border in the late 1950s. They then spread in the 1960s and 1970s throughout South America, Southeast Asia, and India, eventually reaching Africa in the late 1970s. They were first detected in Kenya and Tanzania, but later spread throughout the continent.[25]

Why would resistance develop in areas where malaria is *less* of a problem? The reason may be that, in low transmission areas, people take the drug only when they are sick, confronting the drug with large number of parasites, and so increasing the chance of a mutation emerging.[26] In high transmission areas, by contrast, people who survive to adulthood, and who continue to be exposed to the disease, develop immunity. Even if they take the drug (and many do), their low parasite count would be less likely to stimulate emergence. Young children in Africa lack immunity, but they have smaller blood volumes, and so sustain smaller parasite populations. Even if they are given the drug, they may not cause resistance to emerge.

New drugs are needed to replace chloroquine. Artemisinin-based drugs are the most promising, but if used in single drug form their potency will be short-lived. Two- or three-drug treatments, known as artemisinin combination therapy, can avoid, or at least dramatically delay, the emergence of resistance worldwide. But combination therapy costs about 30 percent more than monotherapy.[27] Given that preventing resistance offers essentially no benefit to the single user, monotherapy will be the treatment of choice to individuals. Indeed, it is already being used in Asia, which is also where, for the reasons already mentioned, resistance is most likely to emerge.

Unless use of this single drug treatment is stopped and replaced with artemisinin combination therapy, the effectiveness of artemisinin-based drugs as a whole will be compromised. All regions, especially tropical Africa, will then suffer. Lab tests have already discovered artemisinin-resistant malaria in areas where monotherapy is approved for use (Senegal) and where it is used but not approved (French Guiana). By contrast, tests have failed to discover resistance in areas where the use of artemisinin-based drugs is banned, suggesting that regulation can be effective. National regulation, however, cannot protect a country's population in the longer term. Regulation is really needed at the international level. The resistant malaria found in French Guiana, for example, were traced to drugs imported illegally from Southeast Asia.[28]

Unfortunately, international law does not prohibit the production or use of monotherapies, and the World Health Organization (WHO) lacks the authority to impose such a ban. It is characteristic of the international system that provision of this international public good is left to states to decide individually. The new director of the WHO's malaria program, Arata Kochi, has threatened to "name and shame" the drugs companies that are making and selling the monotherapies.[29] But will this be enough? Should stronger steps be taken? Should monotherapies be banned worldwide? These questions deserve immediate attention at the highest levels.[30]

Surveillance

There is some evidence that resistance to antimalarials can be suppressed even after it has emerged.[31] Resistant strains often bear an evolutionary disadvantage. They prosper when in the presence of the drug to which they are resistant. Remove the drug, however, and the original, drug-sensitive strains can overtake the resistant strains.

It may therefore be possible to *manage* emergence and spread. Doing so, however, will require effective surveillance. The resistant strains have to be identified at an early stage.

Identifying an emerging disease like a drug-resistant malaria parasite—a disease you are looking for—is relatively easy. Spotting a disease you do not know exists—that is much harder. But that is the kind of surveillance the world really needs.[32]

SARS, of course, was easily identified. As explained in Chapter 2, the bigger problem in this case was China's failure to report, not its surveillance capacity. But SARS was screaming to be noticed. An effective surveillance system needs also to be able to identify diseases that, when they first emerge, smolder rather than blaze. That is, it needs to pick up weak signals. It was only after the Centers for Disease Control noticed an unusual increase in the demand for pentamidine, a drug used to treat an extremely rare lung infection, that the HIV/AIDS epidemic was first identified in 1981 in the United States.[33] Now we know that the disease had been around for a long time before that, and that it first emerged on a different continent.

Pandemic HIV/AIDS

HIV/AIDS has killed about 25 million people since first being discovered in 1981. Today, it continues to devastate. In 2005, despite the availability of antiretroviral treatments, HIV/AIDS killed over three million people. About five million more people became infected in that same year. Around 40 million people in total are infected with HIV/AIDS today.[34]

The basic reproductive number for HIV is probably no greater than about five, but unlike influenza and SARS, HIV is transmitted mainly through sexual contact (also needle sharing and blood transfusions), and so transmission depends on human behavior.[35] If people everywhere were monogamous, the disease would never have spread. It spreads mostly within subgroups, such as networks of prostitutes, their customers, the partners of their customers, the children born to these partners, and so on. Transmission of HIV is also helped by an infectious period measured in years rather than days (although transmission is non-uniform and particularly likely during the advanced stage of the disease).

What were the origins of this disease? The earliest known case of HIV-1, the pandemic form of the virus, has been traced to a plasma sample taken from an adult Bantu male, living in Leopoldville, Belgian Congo (today, Kinshasa, Democratic Republic of Congo), in 1959.[36] But how did this person get the disease?

HIV is related to a simian immunodeficiency virus (SIV), found in non-human primates, and HIV-1—again, the pandemic form of the disease—is most closely related to a form of SIV found in chimpanzees. Viruses often jump the species barrier from simians to humans (an example being monkeypox, a relative of smallpox). Usually, however, these mutations prove to be dead ends (monkeypox is very difficult to transmit from human to human). HIV probably became a human disease on numerous occasions, but with most of these strains failing to catch on. Indeed, only one form of HIV has really taken off. This is the HIV-1 M group (M for "main") virus, the source of the global pandemic.

HIV mutates very readily, not only in the population but also within each infected individual. Indeed, this is what makes the disease so difficult to control.

Understanding how the disease evolves allows scientists to project backwards to the last common ancestor of the virus. Assuming that the most recent common ancestor of HIV-1 M group resided in a human host, research suggests that the disease passed from chimpanzees to humans around 1931.[37]

How might humans have contacted the disease initially? For many years, Beatrice Hahn of the University of Alabama has led a group of researchers looking for SIV in the wild. Her team first developed a method for detecting SIV in chimpanzee feces. She and her colleagues then collected samples from the forest floor in Africa. Upon analyzing the data, Hahn found that SIV prevalence was zero in some chimpanzee communities and as high as 35 percent in others. Of the areas her team has sampled, the populations with the highest prevalence were found in southeastern Cameroon. Her best guess of what happened is that the "virus was likely transmitted locally. From there it appears to have made its way via the Sangha River (or other tributaries) south to the Congo River and on to Kinshasa where the group M pandemic was likely spawned."[38] A single person may thus have become infected in a remote jungle area, traveled to a city with a high human population density, and thus planted the seed that sprouted the global pandemic. Other people may have been infected with different forms of HIV, but these either died out or have remained rare (HIV-1 group O) or geographically isolated (HIV-1 group N).

How might this first person have contracted HIV-1 M group? It is almost certain that he would have gotten the infection by hunting and butchering an SIV-infected chimpanzee for food—a practice that continues today.

And what created the conditions for all of this to happen? Anthropologists Amit Chitnis, Diana Rawls, and Jim Moore have speculated that opportunities for pathogen-exchange were enhanced in colonial French Equatorial Africa between 1890 and 1930—a period that overlaps with estimates of the date of infection of the index case (between around 1915 and 1941).[39] Rubber harvesting and infrastructure projects pushed people into remote forest areas where, armed with guns, and having little time to grow crops, laborers relied increasingly on bushmeat for food. This provided the spark for the human epidemic. The fuel source was the rising urban population, which created opportunities for human-to-human transmission (the population of Kinshasa increased ten-fold between 1905 and 1940, and ten-fold again between 1940 and 1961). Finally, the creation of labor camps, attracting the attentions of prostitutes, and the practice, in those days, of re-using needles for vaccination without sterilization, poured gasoline on the fire, so to speak, helping to amplify transmission (these practices would have substantially increased the basic reproductive rate for the virus).

Of course, that these circumstances would cause a disease like HIV/AIDS to emerge and spread could not have been foreseen at the time. But if this hypothesis is correct, it illustrates how the failures of development can spill over to harm other countries. Those same risks remain today.

Surveillance capacity

For poor countries to be able to identify a disease like pre-1981 HIV/AIDS—a disease that emerges slowly and quietly—basic surveillance capacity needs to be improved *worldwide*. The revised International Health Regulations, mentioned in Chapter 2, recognize this. They require that states "develop, strengthen and maintain...the capacity to detect, assess, notify and report..." Essentially, the revised regulations seek to establish minimum surveillance standards. Annex I of the revisions specify these. States must have the capacity, the Annex says, "to detect events involving disease or death above expected levels for the particular time and place in all areas..."

What level of capacity is required to meet the standard? And does this capacity already exist? The United States, where HIV/AIDS was first discovered, spent $5,711 per capita on health care in 2003; the Democratic Republic of Congo, where the disease may have incubated, spent $14.[40] Is $14 enough? And is it reasonable to expect that the Democratic Republic of Congo, the scene of a humanitarian crisis even greater than in Darfur, though one that lacks the moral clarity of genocide—is it reasonable to expect that this country will provide the facilities needed?

Apparently the international community's answer to both questions is yes, for the revisions say that parties "shall utilize *existing* national structures and resources to meet their core capacity requirements [emphasis added]." Elsewhere the revisions say that the "WHO shall assist States Parties, upon request, to develop, strengthen and maintain" surveillance capacity, but the revisions are silent about how much assistance will be given, and how it will be financed. In these respects, the International Health Regulations are reminiscent of Security Council Resolution 1540 (see Chapter 2).

Like Resolution 1540, the revised International Health Regulations are inadequate. As explained in a recent report by the United States Institute of Medicine,

Infectious diseases are a global threat and therefore require a global response...The United States' capacity to respond to microbial threats must therefore include a significant investment in the capacity of developing countries to monitor and address microbial threats as they arise.[41]

Of course, other prosperous countries should also contribute to this effort. The total of all such contributions would represent an aggregate effort to supply the global public good of infectious disease surveillance.[42]

Preventing spread

Every state has an incentive to control an outbreak, at its source as well as at home, and such measures will also help to inhibit spread, offering a measure of protection to the rest of the world. But the balance of effort can be distorted when the same resources are needed to control a disease and to limit its spread and supplies are limited. With SARS, resource constraints were not a problem. The crude methods of quarantine and contact tracing proved effective. The control of other diseases, like pandemic influenza, may be different.

A number of rich countries are now building stockpiles of antivirals, in the hope that they will provide protection should a new influenza pandemic emerge. Is the investment worthwhile? Probably. According to one study, if the antivirals were given to infected persons within a day of symptoms showing, and if there were enough drugs for half the population of a country, the number of clinical cases might be cut by as much as half.[43]

But suppose a dangerous influenza strain emerged in a country that lacked stockpiles. Should the countries with abundant supplies and few if any cases of infection make their drugs available to this country?

To do so would be to supply a global public good, for the prophylactic use of such drugs at the start of an epidemic might reduce the risk of a full-blown pandemic, or at least reduce its rate of spread, and so provide an opportunity to develop, produce, and distribute a vaccine that would offer protection from the new strain. But, though a country that gives up its supplies to prevent global spread will benefit (as will, of course, the countries that do not donate their drugs), when stockpiles are low and need to be rationed, such an intervention would leave the donor country's population vulnerable. To give up a nation's stockpile under such circumstances would be a difficult political decision.[44]

It would be better to prepare in advance of the eventuality, by building up a global stockpile that could be dispatched to the source of an outbreak, to prevent global spread, even should the disease emerge in a country where a domestic stockpile was lacking.

As it happens, the World Health Organization does possess a stockpile of the antiviral drug Tamiflu (donated by the Swiss pharmaceutical manufacturer, Roche, not by WHO member states). However, the stockpile is small; it can only treat three million persons. It is not obvious that it could stop or slow the spread of a deadly pandemic influenza strain that emerged in, say, Indonesia, where bird flu has already killed dozens of people, and where 242 million people live in close proximity to about 1.3 billion birds.[45] By contrast, the United Kingdom, with a population of only 60 million people, is building a stockpile of almost 15 million doses. If 15 million doses is the right stockpile for the UK, how could three million doses suffice for the entire developing world? The global allocation of antivirals is plainly lop-sided. It is tilted in the direction of national rather than global protection—that is, towards the provision of national rather than global public goods.

Vaccines, even if of low efficacy, can also help to halt or disrupt spread, provided they are stockpiled in advance of an outbreak and can be distributed quickly.[46] Better vaccines, however, can be developed *after* a dangerous pandemic strain first emerged. (Before that, vaccine development is all guess work.) Indeed, one of the benefits of using antivirals and other measures to limit spread is to buy the time needed to develop and produce an improved vaccine. The richest countries can be relied upon to supply the single best effort global public good of the knowledge of how to stimulate immunity to a new virus. But once a vaccine is developed, the bottleneck becomes production capacity. Current capacity can supply only 14 percent of the world's population.[47]

With capacity being constrained, which countries should get this vaccine? And which should *decide* which countries get it? According to Michael Osterholm,

In the event of an influenza pandemic, [the countries with production facilities] would probably nationalize their domestic production facilities, as occurred in 1976, when the United States, anticipating a pandemic of swine influenza (H1N1), refused to share its vaccine.[48]

Nationalization may make sense from the perspective of the country that possesses the capacity, but infectious disease control is not a zero sum game. If vaccines were distributed for the purpose of reducing global spread, rather than immunizing a privileged country, more lives could be saved overall. Osterholm offers a suggestion for how this gap could be closed. "What if the pandemic were 10 years away and we embarked today on a worldwide influenza Manhattan Project aimed at producing and delivering a pandemic vaccine for everyone in the world soon after the onset of sustained human-to-human transmission?" he asks. "In this scenario," he judges, "we just might make a real difference."[49] Of course, the *next* influenza pandemic is *always* some years away, so the challenge posed by Osterholm remains. Current efforts fall far short of this ambition.[50]

River blindness treatment

An interesting feature of Table 1.2 is that, while many states undertake small science research, none from tropical Africa does so. Does that mean that research that would *uniquely* benefit these countries is not being done? There is evidence to support this hypothesis. Of the 1,233 drugs licensed worldwide between 1975 and 1997, only 13 were for tropical diseases like malaria, leishmaniasis, lymphatic filariasis, shistosomiasis, Chagas' disease, and African trypanosomiasis.[51] Global agricultural research also neglects the tropics.[52] Public spending on agricultural research as a share of agricultural output is many times lower for tropical than for temperate zone agriculture.[53]

As noted before, river blindness was controlled from the mid-1970s by aerial spraying of the black fly breeding areas. Unfortunately, because of differences in foliage cover and terrain, spraying proved ineffective in Eastern and Central Africa. It also failed to help people who were already infected (the mature worms can live 20 years in the human body). To fill both of these gaps, a new drug was needed.

Clinical trials at the University of Dakar in Senegal in 1981 demonstrated that a drug called ivermectin was effective in relieving symptoms of river blindness for a year. This was an important finding, but "the scientists who discovered ivermectin...did not set out to develop a pharmaceutical that would prevent river blindness."[54] These researchers, working at Merck, the pharmaceutical company, were instead searching for an anti-helminthic drug to treat *animals*. Indeed, ivermectin became the world's most profitable veterinary drug. It was only after the drug had been developed for animals that its efficacy in humans was explored. And this only happened at the insistence of a researcher working at Merck—Dr. Mohammed Aziz, a Bangladeshi national, who had previously worked for the World Health Organization and had seen river blindness while stationed in Sub-Saharan Africa.[55] It was Aziz who carried out the pilot study in Senegal.

The delay in testing the efficacy of the drugs in humans was for a good commercial reason: the people most in need of the drug could not pay the price that would make its development and manufacture profitable. Merck asked governments like the United States if they would pay for the drug, but none agreed to do so. Compassion, at least at this official level, was wanting.

The company decided to donate the human form of the drug, known by the brand name Mectizan®, for free, and it is to be applauded for doing so. But drugs that must be given away for free are not profitable for companies to discover and develop in the first place.[56] It is by understanding why this drug was developed that we can understand why so few others like it are.

Essential medicines

The reason half a million children die every year of measles is not because the price of the vaccine is too high. As already explained, the vaccine is inexpensive and cost-effective. Other reasons explain this sad statistic.

Many vaccines and drugs, however, *are* priced too high (relative, that is, to marginal production costs). In these cases, people in need are denied the benefit of the knowledge embodied in these products.

Combination antiretroviral therapy for HIV/AIDS initially cost over $10,000 for a year's treatment, but competition by generics producers in developing countries forced the price down to about $140 per patient per year.[57] The difference between these prices is an indication of the markup that restricted, temporarily, access to this life-preserving drug worldwide. The markup is possible because of the monopoly given to the patent holder.

There are two main ways to finance supply of the public good of new knowledge. The first is by government expenditure. The second is by the patent system. In the former case, taxpayers finance supply.

In the latter case, consumers pay for it. Medical R&D is typically financed by a combination of the two approaches, with the balance between them being a social choice.[58]

If the patent were eliminated, the price gap for antiretroviral therapy would disappear. Doing so would also ensure the efficient distribution of the knowledge embodied in these drugs. Given that this knowledge has already been produced, efficiency from today's perspective demands that it be distributed freely (that is, that drugs prices reflect production costs and not the costs of the R&D already spent). So, why not do away with patents? The reason, of course, is that doing so would kill the incentive for companies to produce *new* knowledge. The financing of new knowledge would have to come from another source—either that or we would have to accept a future of diminished R&D. In essence, the patent system creates a conflict between intra- and inter-generational equity.

However, even as regards intra-generational equity, patents are not the real problem. If patent holders could discriminate in setting prices—if they could sell their product at high prices to the people willing to pay high prices and at low prices to the people willing to pay only low prices—then their profits would actually rise even as allocative efficiency was improved. Under this arrangement, people willing and able to pay $140 or more for the antiretroviral therapy would be able to get it—but only if people willing to pay much more had to pay a higher price. It is the promise of being able to charge a markup to these latter consumers that creates the incentive for future discoveries.

To price in this manner, markets must be separated and arbitrage between them prevented. Unfortunately, the Agreement on Trade-Related Aspects of Intellectual Property Rights (incorporated within the World Trade Organization), by seeking to harmonize the intellectual property rules, helped to create a more unified global market—just the opposite of what was needed to improve the distribution of drugs already under patent.

This has now changed.[59] The agreement now allows market segmentation for essential medicines. States may order compulsory licensing of drugs under patent (a benefit to the large developing countries). They may also import cheap generics made by foreign manufacturers under compulsory licensing arrangements (a benefit to smaller developing countries). Both measures allow antiretroviral therapy to be sold at high prices in industrialized countries (creating an incentive for the production of new knowledge) and at low prices in developing countries (ensuring a more efficient allocation of existing knowledge). Merck, of course, settled on this same formula when it chose to give the drug ivermectin away for free to sufferers of river blindness, while continuing to charge a high price for the same drug sold for veterinary purposes in industrialized countries.

Is the current arrangement sustainable? Can it, in particular, be counted on to stimulate continued innovation in medicines that would benefit large numbers of people in both rich and poor countries?

The difficulty is political.[60] For the arrangement to work, consumers in rich countries must be willing to pay a premium to cover R&D costs. Consumers in the United States already pay more for drugs than do consumers in other rich countries—a difference that has caused many U.S. consumers to buy direct from countries like Canada. The contrast in pricing as between industrialized and developing countries would be even greater. If consumers and voters are unwilling to tolerate such differences, there will be consequences. Either the burden for financing R&D will need to change (perhaps being shifted from consumers to taxpayers or being shared more widely among the industrialized countries) or R&D will decline overall.

A malaria vaccine?

Antiretroviral therapy for HIV/AIDS and ivermectin are examples of medicines that were developed to satisfy markets in rich countries but that happen also to benefit people living in poor countries. Addressing the discovery, development, and distribution of these kinds of medicines is important, but doing so would still leave a gap. What about drugs and vaccines that would be valued *uniquely* by the poorer and weaker states? How can an incentive be created for *these* medicines to be supplied? How, in particular, could incentives be created to stimulate discovery of a malaria vaccine?

Calculations by Ernst Berndt and his colleagues provide a rough idea.[61] Their approach is to ask how much revenue pharmaceutical companies would need, as a lump sum reward—you can think of it as a "prize"—to make them willing to invest in the R&D needed to develop a malaria vaccine. The authors assume that investment in this area would have to promise the same expected return as these companies could earn by investing their R&D in other areas. Their calculations show that companies should be willing to invest in malaria vaccine R&D for the revenue equivalent of a prize worth just over $3 billion.

Would a malaria vaccine be worth buying at this price? Berndt and his coauthors do not calculate the benefits of a malaria vaccine. Instead, they calculate whether the cost of improving health by this means would compare favorably with alternative interventions.[62] They find that it does: a malaria vaccine would be as cost-effective as residual spraying of the mosquito vector, more cost-effective than treated bed nets, and much more cost-effective than antiretroviral therapy for AIDS, even at today's low prices.[63]

So the economics of developing a malaria vaccine appear very favorable. And yet little money is being spent on malaria vaccine R&D today.[64] Why is that? One reason is that the big, rich, and powerful countries—the countries that take the lead in supplying global public goods—do not have the incentive to undertake this effort on their own; they are not (directly) affected by malaria; they eliminated malaria within their own borders decades ago.[65] Price discrimination will not help supply a malaria vaccine.[66]

Another reason is that the countries that would benefit the most from a malaria vaccine may not benefit enough individually to justify paying the full $3 billion. In keeping with the notation used previously to examine the economics of tsunami warnings, suppose that n countries in total could use the vaccine, that Country 1 benefits the most, Country 2 the next most, and so on, with Country n benefiting the least, and with the benefits to Country i being denoted B_i. Then, it may be the case that $B_1 + B_2 + \ldots + B_n > C > B_1 > B_2 > \ldots > B_n$, where C might be $3 billion. There are 54 countries in Africa, many of them very small. This fragmentation makes unilateral provision unattractive.

Of course, under these circumstances, *cooperation* by all these countries is attractive. But can we expect it to materialize? These countries lack a history of cooperating on this kind of scale. Many of these countries also do not have the wherewithal to cooperate, or have governments that care little for their own publics. Many, of course, are failed states.[67] Recall the measles vaccine gap noted earlier. It is not enough for a vaccine to exist. To benefit humanity, the vaccine must be *distributed*. If states will not distribute a vaccine that already exists and that we know is cost-effective, they certainly will not finance the

R&D needed to develop a new vaccine that would help these same people. Greater compassion by industrialized states could help narrow both of these gaps—the gap in financing vaccine R&D and the gap in procurement—and a number of proposals have been developed to show how this could be done.[68] There may, however, be an additional rationale for financing these efforts. I turn to it next.

Climate change adaptation

Global climate change on some kind of scale seems unavoidable, and its effects will only be amplified if our efforts to supply the global public good of mitigation continue to falter. As I have explained before, R&D into new energy technologies should be a priority, but funding in this area will be limited by expectations about the future prospects for mitigation. Geoengineering could potentially help, particularly should climate change prove abrupt. But this technology introduces new risks and is likely to be controlled by big, rich, and powerful states. What will happen if the poorest and weakest states are the most affected by climate change? Will geoengineering be used to help *them*? Should it be?

A comprehensive climate change policy has to consider another dimension of the problem: the need to *adapt* to climate change. Adaptation is normally taken to be a *response* to change—an example being replacing the Thames Barrier with a new structure to protect London from ever-rising sea levels. Adaptation of this kind (a local public good) will be undertaken unilaterally. Even the most frail of states will adapt a little on their own (their farmers, for example, may plant different crops, or change the timing of planting). But for all of the reasons noted previously in this chapter, the poorest and weakest states are unlikely to invest enough in adaptation. It is the big, rich, and powerful states that can substitute local and national public goods most easily for the global public good of climate change mitigation.

So the poor and weak states would seem especially vulnerable. Should they be helped? This situation is novel, because most of the greenhouse gases in the atmosphere were put there, and continue to be put there, by the big, rich, and powerful states. This adds a different moral dimension to the calculus of offering assistance.[69]

Moreover, and as noted in Chapter 3, money spent on mitigation has an opportunity cost. It cannot be spent on other good causes, one of these being investments that reduce the vulnerability of poor countries to climate change.[70] From this perspective, climate change is a development challenge and not only an environmental challenge. How to incorporate this idea in a climate treaty? Adaptation means expenditure that reduces climate change damages (as opposed to climate change itself). Such investments can be made in response to climate change (a beefed up Thames Barrier). But many investments will reduce climate change damages and offer other benefits besides when made in *advance* of climate change. These investments should be made now. I noted in Chapter 3 that investment in reducing malaria prevalence across-the-board could yield a much higher return than investment in mitigation, which would only reduce the spread of malaria into new areas in the distant future. This is an example of the kind of investment that should be a part of a broader international approach to climate change.

Investments in R&D that could yield a malaria vaccine, or a similarly beneficial innovation, bear a likeness to investments in R&D that could lead to new, carbon-saving technologies. They both offer the promise of a welcome and discrete change. Returns on the latter investments, as I noted in previous chapters, depend on the prospects of new technologies, once developed, being diffused. They thus depend on overcoming free rider incentives in supplying a global public good requiring an aggregate effort. Returns on a malaria vaccine, as I have explained in this chapter, depend on governments, including today's failed states, supplying the national public good of malaria control. These are the two greatest obstacles to progress today—free riding by the big, rich, and powerful states and failed governance by the poorest and weakest states. Addressing both of these obstacles will be difficult, but this is what we must do. An understanding of global public goods shows us that.

Conclusions

The supply of global public goods relies on the leadership of the big, rich, and powerful states. When their efforts succeed, the poorest states benefit. Smallpox eradication benefited every state, but as I showed in Chapter 2, it benefited the weakest and poorest states the most. It is often referred to as the greatest achievement in global public health. It might also be considered the greatest achievement in international development.

National public goods sometimes substitute for global public goods. Smallpox *elimination* at the national level, for example, was a substitute for smallpox *eradication* at the global level. Because big, rich, and powerful states are efficient suppliers of national public goods (like elimination), their incentive to supply global public goods (like eradication) can be dampened. When it is, the poor and weak states suffer especially, for they are typically unable or unwilling to supply the national public goods that can compensate for this loss. It is really for this reason that the poor and weak states benefited so much from smallpox eradication.

Some global public goods have the opposite property, being complements to national public goods. Many of the poor and weak states lack these national public goods. They therefore benefit little from the supply of many global public goods. A new vaccine will not improve the lives of the citizens of a state that is unwilling to procure it, even when doing so promises a benefit far in excess of the cost.

Big, rich, and powerful states lack an incentive to supply international or regional public goods that would benefit only developing countries. To supply these, either the leadership must come from the poor and weak states themselves or the motivation for intervention by the big, rich, and powerful states must change—to reflect compassion rather than self-interest. Unfortunately, compassion, even when abundant, rarely suffices. Official support is also needed from the states that would benefit the most from provision.

It is perhaps ironic that what prevents global public goods from being supplied, or the benefits of their supply from being distributed widely, is not only the constraint of sovereignty, as noted in the introduction to this book, but the failures of sovereigns to manage their own affairs in the interests of their own peoples. International cooperation is in every state's interests—that has been the theme of this book. But to be effective, international cooperation needs to be joined with improvements in national governance. The challenges are local and not only global.

Conclusions: institutions for the supply of global public goods

When the world succeeds in supplying global public goods, people everywhere benefit. Our international institutions, however, are clumsily suited to this task. As explained in the introduction to this book, they lack the coercive powers that every state uses to supply national public goods. Why not give international institutions these powers? Why not create a world government? As also explained in the Introduction, the reason is that the citizens of every state would then have to be bound by the decisions made by other peoples (a global majority, say), who may have very different values. Sovereignty, for all its faults, offers protections to individual societies and their governments. If the supply of global public goods is diminished as a consequence—well, that may be the price we have to pay for this freedom.

Of course, the institutions of the state are also imperfect. The power to coerce creates opportunities for corruption and rent seeking. Checks on that power are therefore essential. But those checks, including the restraining influence of democratic accountability, introduce other inefficiencies.[1] For both these reasons, national and local public goods may also be inappropriately supplied.

The real problem, as discussed in Chapter 7, lies with those states that lack a capable government. These are the weak, fragile, failed, and destroyed states. These states are unable to supply even the most basic of public goods such as personal security to their own publics. They can also serve as a territory from which non-state belligerents, including terrorists, can threaten others. The international system, tied as it is to the principle of sovereignty, is defective for the reasons I explained in the Introduction. But the system can become dangerous when states are unable to exercise sovereignty over their own territories. In a way, having too little sovereignty can be worse than having too much (by which I mean states having full sovereignty in the usual sense of that term but declining to cooperate by mutual agreement, for mutual benefit). As explained in Chapter 2, it is the states that lack sovereignty that are the most likely to block the provision of weakest link global public goods.

Indeed, it is against this background of domestic institutional failure that the successes of international cooperation really stand out. By working together, the world has done as much to protect the ozone layer as any domestic environmental regulation has ever done to supply, say, the national public good of cleaner air. Few public health measures have saved as many lives, directly or indirectly, as the eradication of smallpox—an effort that depended on the assistance of the world's worst governed states. And which has provided states with more security, possession of the nuclear deterrent or the taboo against first use of a nuclear weapon? For all of the problems with the international system, we cannot say that it never works. We should rather marvel at how well it has worked.

Overall, however, the record is spotty. For every success there has been at least one failure, probably more. Almost nothing has been done to reduce greenhouse gas emissions, despite an unprecedented amount of attention being given to this issue. Nuclear proliferation may now be on the edge of a new cascade, as the acquisition of nuclear weapons by one or two more countries causes others to contemplate acquiring them. As I write these words, little is being done to stop the genocide in the Darfur region of Sudan.

Reciting these and other failures, it is easy to be disillusioned with our international institutions. What good is the treaty instrument if it cannot even make a start in reducing greenhouse gas emissions? What benefit is the United Nations Security Council if its members are unwilling to enforce their own resolutions, or if some of its members can act without the backing of the others? What is the value of the current proliferation regime if it allows parties (North Korea) to cheat and withdraw, with few consequences to pay? What is its value if a long-standing non-party (India) is granted privileges by a leading party (the United States) that were previously reserved only for other treaty members? How hollow are the words, "never again," when the United

Nations stands by as hundreds of thousands of Darfurians are raped, tortured, disfigured, and killed?

These failures, however, though disturbing, comprise fragments of a bigger image. They are specific instances of failure, not indicators of a general malfunction.

It is a mistake to condemn the treaty instrument in general terms, when it has had successes like the Montreal Protocol. The climate change treaties have been disappointing, but so was the regime for ocean dumping before countries discovered a different approach that worked better. Rather than turn away from the treaty approach, we need to learn from past mistakes and devise a treaty system that can address the fundamental challenge of global climate change. As I explained in Chapter 3, there is no other way in which global emissions can be scaled back. The incentives to free ride must be met head on; and then they must be defeated.

The non-proliferation regime, though imperfect, has worked. Like all institutions, however, it will continue to be effective only if it is used. International regimes, like all institutions, need to be nurtured. If neglected, they can wither and die. The foundation of the non-proliferation regime is mutual restraint: the non-nuclear states agreed not to arm; the nuclear states agreed progressively to disarm. To provide further comfort to non-nuclear states, the nuclear powers offered positive and negative assurances: they agreed both to assist any non-nuclear state threatened by nuclear attack and not to use nuclear weapons against the non-nuclear parties to the Non-Proliferation Treaty. The nuclear-capable states also offered assurances. In exchange for the right to develop nuclear programs for peaceful purposes, they agreed to safeguards, making it possible for other countries—nuclear and non-nuclear alike—to verify that they were fulfilling their pledge not to acquire nuclear weapons. All of these provisions form a system of interlocking incentives. Should any one be diminished, the others lose their grip. This is the current problem: as different countries have sought to release themselves from the restraints of this arrangement, covertly or openly, the effectiveness of the regime overall has been compromised.

The Security Council achieved relatively little during the Cold War. With a few exceptions, it has achieved relatively little since. But is it reasonable to expect more of this body? Previously, it was deadlocked by opposing superpowers. More recently it has been bypassed by the only remaining superpower.[2] In between it had a brief period of success, particularly the liberation of Kuwait (1991). The overall record—both the failures and the successes—has been determined less by the institution itself than by the interests and capabilities of its permanent members, and by how these five states have chosen to use their authority.

In his 2003 State of the Union address, President George W. Bush asserted that, "the course of this nation does not depend on the decisions of others."[3] He meant, of course, that the Security Council could not hold down the United States—and, indeed, the United States was not restrained; the U.S., with Britain and a small "coalition of the willing," invaded Iraq without Security Council approval. The United States did this partly because it *could* do this. But what were the consequences? A lesson of the Iraq War is a theme that runs through this book: in an interdependent world, the set of outcomes that every state is capable of realizing depends on the decisions of others. Moreover, the course set by every state helps to shape the decisions that others will make. By acting minilaterally, the United States and its "coalition of the willing" sacrificed the benefits of broader international support. This not only cost the U.S. and its coalition allies resources. It endangered the mission. It also created the conditions for threats to emerge elsewhere.

Should military actions always require Security Council approval? In 1998, conflict erupted between the Serbian army and Kosovar Albanian forces. By 1999, thousands of Kosovar Albanians had been killed and more than nine out of ten ethnic Albanians had been displaced from their homes—many expelled at gunpoint. To allow this "ethnic cleansing" to stand would be to put peoples everywhere at risk (enforcing a prohibition, such as the norm establishing the "responsibility to protect," deters future norm violations). It might also cause violence to spill into neighboring countries. Intervening would thus supply a global public good, with countries in the region perhaps benefiting the most. The Security Council, however, declined to act (China and Russia both opposed a military intervention). Instead, another group of countries stepped in. On March 24, 1999, NATO launched air strikes against Yugoslavia. After 77 days, Yugoslav forces began withdrawing from Kosovo, and the air strikes were suspended. The United Nations Security Council then authorized the establishment of an international Peace Implementation Force in Kosovo. It remains there today.

Though the NATO air strikes were not authorized by the Security Council, is the world better off for this action having been taken? The air strikes had the unanimous support of the NATO members. A Security Council resolution condemning the bombing, though approved by China and Russia and one other member, Namibia, was rejected by 12 other voting countries, seven of which were non-members of NATO. An Independent International commission on Kosovo, established by the government of Sweden, concluded that, "the NATO military intervention was illegal but legitimate."[4]

So, which is more important, legality or legitimacy? The answer is complicated because the Security Council as a body lacks legitimacy today, due to its membership and the power of the veto.[5] With a different membership and voting system, a resolution authorizing the use of force in Kosovo might have been approved.

The High Level Panel on Threats, Challenges and Change, established by the Secretary General of the United Nations, Kofi Annan, and comprising a distinguished membership, including senior representatives from each of the five permanent members of the Security Council, made a number of recommendations for reform.[6] Two are important to this discussion. The first is to endorse

the emerging norm that there is a collective international responsibility to protect, exercisable by the Security Council authorizing military intervention as a last resort, in the event of genocide and other large-scale killing, ethnic cleansing or serious violations of international humanitarian law which sovereign Governments have proved powerless or unwilling to prevent.[7]

The second is to recommend changes to the membership of the Security Council. The Panel was realistic. It noted that there existed "no practical way of changing the existing members' veto powers."[8] But it went on to say that,

as a whole the institution of the veto has an anachronistic character that is unsuitable for the institution in an increasingly democratic age and we would urge that its use be limited to matters where vital interests are genuinely at stake. We also ask the permanent members, in their individual capacities, to pledge themselves to refrain from the use of the veto in cases of genocide and large-scale human rights abuses.[9]

The conflict between legality and legitimacy is evident in these recommendations. According to the High Level Panel, an intervention intending to meet the responsibility to protect requires Security Council approval (legality), but the Security Council members are to refrain from using the veto in cases where a resolution authorizing such an intervention is most needed (legitimacy). The question is: Can we rely on the Security Council members to refrain from using the veto when it is in their interests to use it? The situation is akin to one I noted in the Introduction. To repeat Franklin Roosevelt's words, "In a democratic world, as in a democratic nation, power must be linked with responsibility, and obliged to defend and justify itself within the framework of the general good." The legitimacy of the Security Council depends not only on the existence of the veto and the rules for membership. It depends also on how the power it gives is exercised. Informally agreed restraints on the use of power are often needed to ensure that an institution is able to meet its basic responsibilities—and thereby secure its legitimacy by its results.[10]

Deviating from established law can also be a means for changing the law—a step that may be necessary to improve the supply of global public goods. Customary international law is made when countries violate established law—and those violations are perceived by other states as being legitimate. During the Cod Wars between Iceland and Britain, Iceland extended its maritime jurisdiction: from three to four miles in 1952; from four to 12 miles in 1958; from 12 to 50 miles in 1972; and from 50 to 200 miles in 1975. These were unilateral actions. They were condemned by the British government, which dispatched the Royal Navy to the seas around Iceland, to enforce the existing legal limits. In the end, however, the Icelandic action was accepted, by Britain and the world. Indeed, the 200-mile Exclusive Economic Zone became a model for maritime law, and was later codified in the Law of the Sea. The evolution of customary law in this case was a response to the inability of existing institutions to halt over-fishing. I think it is likely that the failure of states to protect stocks of highly migratory and high seas fisheries will necessitate a similar change in international law in the future. So far, states have relied exclusively on treaties to restrain states from over-fishing. But as explained in Chapter 2 the treaty instrument is poorly suited to this purpose. A new approach is needed.

Not only are violations of the law sometimes welcomed; mere obedience to the law can also be perceived as being unacceptable. Under international law, China was not required to warn the world about the SARS outbreak. Like all countries, China was only required to notify the World Health Organization of outbreaks of three diseases—cholera, plague, and yellow fever. Though China did not violate the law, its actions endangered other states. To prevent this from happening again, the law on reporting was changed. When the revised International Health Regulations enter into force in 2007, states will be required by law to report outbreaks of all diseases of "international concern," including diseases like SARS. This again is an example of an international institution evolving to increase the supply of a global public good.

Why has the Security Council not protected Darfurians from the Janjaweed militias? In August 2006, the Security Council adopted Resolution 1706 (China, Russia, and Qatar abstained), which authorized the sending of up to 17,300 peacekeepers, at a cost of about $1.6 billion, "to protect civilians under threat of physical violence." However, the resolution also reaffirmed the Security Council's "strong commitment to the sovereignty, unity, independence, and territorial integrity" of Sudan. The Security Council was offering to dispatch personnel to Darfur, but only with the consent of the Khartoum government, for which the Janjaweed are acting as agents.

In a resolution adopted only months earlier (Resolution 1674), the Security Council reaffirmed "the provisions of paragraphs 138 and 139 of the 2005 World Summit Outcome Document regarding the responsibility to protect populations from genocide, war crimes, ethnic cleansing and crimes against humanity."[11] These paragraphs say that the international community, through the United Nations, is

prepared to take collective action, in a timely and decisive manner, through the Security Council, in accordance with the Charter, including Chapter VII, *on a case-by-case basis* [emphasis added] and in cooperation with relevant regional organizations as appropriate, should peaceful means be inadequate and national authorities are manifestly failing to protect their populations from genocide, war crimes, ethnic cleansing and crimes against humanity.[12]

Why should humanitarian decisions be made on a case-by-case basis? (Are not human rights universal?) The reason is that interventions also have consequences, and states with the capability to intervene will insist that doing so be in their interests. So far, the United Nations has declined to intervene in Darfur. In contrast to Kosovo, NATO also has not intervened. The African Union continues to maintain a minor presence in Darfur, but it lacks the capability as well as a mandate to protect civilians. So the genocide continues. The world, it seems, is not prepared to supply the global public good of humanitarian protection—not yet, anyway.

If the Earth were about to be hit by a colossal asteroid, we can be pretty sure that the world's nearly 200 countries would be united in their efforts to deflect it. The scenario is hypothetical, but it serves as a useful metaphor. It reminds us that the world is capable of cooperating. The problem, of course, is that our real challenges are not at all like this. They are much harder.

What makes them harder is that in most cases incentives conflict. States have incentives to act unilaterally, even when doing so injures other states, but they also have incentives to cooperate, for the benefit of all states. Successful international institutions (like the Montreal Protocol) restructure these incentives; they change the rules of the game so that the incentives to cooperate dominate the incentives to act unilaterally. Unfortunately, many of our international institutions are poorly designed. Worse, in some cases even well designed institutions are unable to change how states behave. It is in these situations that the world pays the full price for sovereignty. As just noted, it is for this reason that the people of Darfur are not being helped today.

The tripartite treaty signed by Nazi Germany, Fascist Italy, and Imperial Japan in 1940 (with Bulgaria, Hungary, and Romania joining later) was a minilateral agreement with a malign purpose: to "establish and maintain a new order of things calculated to promote the mutual prosperity and welfare of the peoples concerned [meaning the favored peoples of the axis powers]."[13] Speaking of the implications of this treaty for the Pacific region, United States Secretary of State Cordell Hull said that the term, "new order," means,

politically, domination by one country. It means, economically, employment of the resources of the area concerned for the benefit of that country and to the ultimate impoverishment of other parts of the area and exclusion of the interests of other countries. It means, socially, the destruction of personal liberties and the reduction of the conquered peoples to the role of inferiors.

The axis posed a grave threat to the rest of the world.

The 26 parties to the Declaration by United Nations, a military alliance adopted in 1942, cooperated to meet this challenge, being convinced that complete victory over their enemies is essential to defend life, liberty, independence and religious freedom, and to preserve human rights and justice in their own lands as well as in other lands, and that they are now engaged in a common struggle against savage and brutal forces seeking to subjugate the world.

This multilateralism served a high purpose: to secure the freedoms of people everywhere (that is, people in the lands of the cooperating countries *as well as in other lands*) and to engage in a *common* (that is to say, universal) struggle. The efforts of these countries served to supply the most fundamental global public good: world peace. As President Harry S. Truman said in his address at the closing session of the United Nations Conference in 1945, "We have tested the principle of cooperation in this war and have found that it works."[14] It was as if the world were threatened by a huge asteroid, and cooperated to punch it into a different orbit.

The enduring legacy of that effort derives less from the military triumph itself than from the institutions that were created even before total victory was declared. The United Nations Charter, as Truman said, provided "a great instrument of peace and security and human progress in the world," but one that would only help if it were *used*. "If we fail to use it," Truman said, "we shall betray all those who have died in order that we might meet here in freedom and safety to create it. If we seek to use it selfishly—for the advantage of any one nation or any small group of nations—we shall be equally guilty of that betrayal." The same might also be said of all international institutions. What they are able to achieve depends on them being used. It depends also on how they are used. It depends perhaps most of all on the major countries—the countries most able to act—fulfilling their responsibilities to the world, successfully defending and justifying their exercise of power "within the framework of the general good."

The institutions created towards the end of the Second World War were imperfect. They remain imperfect today. But was there a better alternative then? Is there a better one today? In recent years, the United States has pulled away from these institutions, seeking to impose a new world order. That experiment has failed. The future supply of global public goods depends on unity being restored. It depends, as it always has done, on cooperation succeeding.

Endnotes

PREFACE AND ACKNOWLEDGEMENT

1. The Task Force report, *Meeting Global Challenges: International Cooperation in the National Interest*, was published in September 2006; see International Task Force on Global Public Goods (2006).
2. There are several excellent texts containing more formal treatments of the subject. These include three by Todd Sandler (1992, 1997, 2004); three edited volumes produced by the United Nations Development Programme under the direction of Inge Kaul (Kaul et al. 1999; Kaul et al. 2003; and Kaul and Conceição 2006); an edited volume produced in association with the World Bank (Ferroni and Mody 2002); a volume of papers on regional public goods published jointly by the Inter-American Development Bank and the Asian Development Bank (Estevadeordal et al. 2004); and a book of papers in the area of global health, published in association with the World Health Organization (Smith et al. 2003).
3. The Task Force was co-chaired by Tidjane Thiam and Ernesto Zedillo; its other members were K. Y. Amoako, Gun-Britt Andersson, Fred Bergsten, Kemal Dervis, Mohammed El-Ashry, Gareth Evans, Enrique Iglesias, Inge Kaul, Lydia Makhubu, Trevor Manuel, Hisashi Owanda, Nafis Sadik, Brigita Schmögnerová, Yves-Thibault de Silguy, and M. S. Swaminathan.

INTRODUCTION

1. For a comprehensive analysis of these effects, see Toon et al. (1997).
2. In the literature, this is usually referred to as a "best-shot" public good. However, supply of a best-shot public good is normally taken to equal the largest effort by an individual country. By my interpretation, supply of a "single best effort" global public good is determined by the best effort, whether undertaken individually or collectively. As we shall see, many single best efforts involve and may even require collective action.
3. As I shall explain later, the younger generations are unfortunate in one respect: having not been vaccinated previously, they are more vulnerable to a new smallpox outbreak. The people who were previously vaccinated

are also vulnerable, however, because the immune response stimulated by the vaccine diminishes over time.

4. Technically speaking, this makes eradication a coordination game. It is possible, though perhaps unlikely, that eradication could require enforcement; see Barrett (2003).

5. James Lovelock ("James Lovelock: The Earth is About to Catch a Morbid Fever that May Last as Long as 100,000 Years," *The Independent,* January 16, 2006; http://comment.independent.co.uk/commentators/article338830.ece) predicts that, "before this century is over billions of us will die and the few breeding pairs of people that survive will be in the Arctic where the climate remains tolerable." His prediction is not contingent. My own interpretation of the evidence draws from the reports of the Intergovernmental Panel on Climate Change and peer-reviewed scientific papers.

6. All these points are discussed in more detail in Chapter 3.

7. See Barrett (2006d).

8. From this perspective, financing is akin to a global public good requiring an aggregate effort; see Barrett (2006a: 365).

9. The global public good of the standard for determining the time is similar to smallpox eradication. The supply of both requires coordination. One difference is that smallpox eradication required financing. Another difference is that it is only essential for *"enough"* countries to switch to a new standard for determining the time for it to be in the interests of other countries to switch. For smallpox, it may only pay a country to eliminate the disease at home if *all* other countries eliminate it.

10. Hirshleifer (1983) was the first to point this out. Samuelson (1954) developed the seminal analysis of public goods requiring aggregate efforts.

11. My colleague, Michael Mandelbaum, explains the role played by the United States in supplying global public goods; see Mandelbaum (2005).

12. http://www.presidency.ucsb.edu/ws/print.php?pid=16595

13. For evidence of the latter effect, see Scholz and Lubell (1998).

14. Dohrn-van Rossum (1996: 154–155).

15. Cooperation at the local level can succeed; see Ostrom (1990); and Baland and Platteau (1996). However, in these situations, the state has the potential to intervene, and local communities are different from the "international community." Care must be taken in extrapolating from the local to the global level. See Barrett (2005: 16–17).

16. Glynn and Glynn (2004: 153).

17. Glynn and Glynn (2004: 163).

18. This point, of course, is fundamental to Nozick's (1974) advocacy of the minimal state.

19. Offit (2005: 24 and 54).

20. Offit (2005: 178–179).

21. I am drawing here from North (1990: 3).

22. If the marginal damage of climate change were increasing in the level of emissions, then as some countries cut their emissions, the incentive for other countries to do so would fall. This is the free rider effect. If reductions in emissions raised production costs, comparative advantage in the emission-intensive industries would shift to other countries. This is the international trade (leakage) effect. See Barrett (2005).

23. Interestingly, Collier and Hoeffler (1998) find that highly fractionalized societies are no more prone to civil war than homogeneous ones. Intermediate cases are the more problematic. For an alternative view, see Fearon and Laitin (2003).

24. See Alesina et al. (1999).

25. For a perspective on the number and size of states, see Alesina and Spolaore (1997).

26. "Coalitions of the willing" involve no legal obligations, and apply only to the countries that give their consent. They are an expression of like-mindedness rather than a form of multilateralism. Examples include the multinational force operating in Iraq and the Proliferation Security Initiative, which imposes no obligations on its members to provide operation support for interdiction of suspected shipments of weapons of mass destruction, and which relies on reciprocal ship-boarding agreements for inspections, rather than a more universal restriction on freedom at sea.

27. Madrian and Shea (2001).

28. High Level Panel on Threats, Challenges, and Change (2004: 52).

CHAPTER 1

1. Tedeschi and Teller (1994: 183).

2. Edit Staff, "Why a Large Hadron Collider?" *seedmagazine.com*, July 6, 2006; http://www.seedmagazine.com/news/2006/07/why_a_large_hadron _collider.php

3. Stuart Dye, "World Abuzz Over Space Invater," *The New Zealand Herald*, June 14, 2004.

4. Toon et al. (1997: 48).

5. See Milani (2003).

6. It is also a possibility that has attracted much attention. See Rees (2003) and Posner (2004).

7. Of course, it may be that, in developing the capability to deflect smaller asteroids, we can also deflect mega-asteroids. The point is that the smaller asteroids are the greater risk.

8. Viscusi (2006).

9. Viscusi and Aldy (2003). Note that, if net benefits for a society are maximized, the value of a statistical life saved should equal the opportunity cost of a statistical life saved.
10. Viscusi and Aldy (2003).
11. Bowland and Beghin (2001).
12. Schweickart et al. (2003).
13. The estimate of 1,000 lives per year is from Milani (2003).
14. For explanations of the reasons for and implications of discounting, see the papers in Portney and Weyant (1999).
15. See Morrison (2005: 101, footnote 21).
16. The United States is not alone in searching for near Earth objects. The international network includes Sweden, Italy, Germany, and the Czech Republic.
17. Near-Earth Object Science Definition Team (2003: iii).
18. Task Force on Potentially Hazardous Near Earth Objects (2000: 24).
19. Posner (2004: 129)
20. See, for example, Schweickart (2003).
21. Sagan and Ostro (1994: 501).
22. Morton (2002).
23. Lembke (2001: 21).
24. Rees (2003: 121).
25. Blaizot et al. (2003: iii).
26. See Fenner et al. (1988: 1097–1098).
27. See Tucker (2001: 126–132).
28. See Committee on the Assessment of Future Scientific Needs for Live Variola Virus (1999).
29. All of this is explained in detail in Tucker (2001).
30. Tedeschi and Teller (1994: 183).
31. Schweickart (2003: 5).
32. In October 2005, the Disarmament Committee of the United Nations General Assembly voted on a draft resolution on the prevention of an arms race in outer space. 160 states voted in favor, one state (Israel) abstained, and one (the United States) voted against. See http://www.un.org/News/Press/docs/2005/gadis3310.doc.htm
33. See also Barrett (2006b).
34. Geoengineering was also proposed to mitigate stratospheric ozone depletion, but the energy requirements in this case were prohibitive (Solomon 1999: 280).
35. So may jet aircraft contrails. After the terrorist attacks of September 11, 2001, commercial aircraft in the United States were grounded for three days, and there is some evidence that, during this time, the daily temperature range (the difference between the daytime maximum and the nighttime minimum) increased. See Travis et al. (2002).

36. Crutzen (2006).
37. Teller et al. (2003: 5). Nordhaus and Boyer's analysis of the economics of climate change policies assumes that geoengineering would be costless (Nordhaus and Boyer 2000: 127). Crutzen (2006) cites a higher cost, but one that is still low compared with the mitigation alternatives.
38. Crutzen (2006).
39. For comparison, the Stern Review on the Economics of Climate Change estimates, perhaps optimistically, that carbon dioxide concentrations could be stabilized at a level of around 500 ppm by 2050 at an annual cost of around $1 trillion in that year. See Stern (2006: 234).
40. The significance of this will become clearer upon reading my discussion of the Stern Review in Chapter 4, this volume.
41. Schelling (2006: 48).
42. Nordhaus and Boyer (2000: 131).
43. Consider a rough calculation. Suppose the U.S. could make an annual payment to avoid climate change indefinitely. How much would it be willing to pay? As noted before, the benefit of avoiding climate change in present value terms might be around $82 billion. The constant annualized benefit, using a discount rate of 3 percent, would be just under $2.5 billion (0.03 × $82 billion = $2.5), or more than twice the estimated annual cost of geoengineering.
44. Teller et al. (2003: 5–6).
45. Crutzen (2006).
46. See Schneider (2001) for a critique of this approach.
47. See Robock (2002).
48. Crutzen (2006).
49. See Govindasamy and Caldeira (2000) and Govindasamy et al. (2003).
50. See the report on ocean acidification by the Royal Society (2005).
51. Nordhaus and Boyer (2000: 131) estimate that Russia, China, and Canada would all gain.
52. See also Bodansky (1996) and Schneider (2001) on the risks of using geo-engineering.
53. I once heard someone suggest that research on geoengineering should be done covertly.
54. For a preliminary study of detection, see Baehr, Keller, and Marotzke (forthcoming).
55. I have sketched a proposal for such a multi-track climate treaty system; see Barrett (forthcoming).
56. See Hoffert et al. (2002).
57. How much R&D funding is required? This is a hard question to answer, not least because an assumption needs to be made about how R&D expenditure translates into technological success. Popp (2005) has made a first attempt to estimate this value. With a focus only on gradual climate

change, he finds that, today, a little over $13 billion (in 1990 dollars) should be spent on R&D that improves energy efficiency generally, and just over $1 billion on R&D that lowers the cost of developing a zero emission ("backstop") technology. (For comparison, the ITER's construction is expected to cost $5 billion.) These investments would help climate mitigation, but his estimate of the desired additional level of spending on climate change R&D is low—about $200 million per year. A concern about avoiding abrupt and catastrophic climate change would warrant greater investment.

58. Before India joined, the other parties agreed to finance the project in the following proportions: the European Union would pay half of the cost, and the other five parties 10 percent each. When India joined, these shares were reduced to 45.45 and 9.09 percent respectively, with India also paying 9.09 percent. See Clery and Normile (2005); see also http://www.iter.org/sharing.htm.

59. Barrett (2006c).

60. OECD Consultative Group on High-Energy Physics (2002: 2).

61. The table aggregates research, and so conceals contributions in particular fields. Though China ranks ninth in terms of total publications (counting the 15 members of the European Union as a bloc), a recent analysis using similar data ranked China second in the world in nanotechnology research. See Zhou and Leydesdorff (2006).

62. Oshinksy (2005: 161).

63. Oshinksy (2005: 215).

64. Skarbinski et al. (2006).

65. http://www.rbm.who.int/wmr2005/html/1-2.htm

66. Kremer and Glennerster (2004: 26).

67. There does exist a customary principle that states should not harm others, but this obligation is tied to the right of states to act. See Barrett (2005: 121–124).

CHAPTER 2

1. Fenner et al. (1988: 1064).

2. Deria et al. (1980: 283).

3. Deria et al. (1980: 282).

4. See Barrett (2004) and Barrett and Hoel (fothcoming).

5. The estimates for India were prorated according to the estimated number of deaths from smallpox worldwide—almost all of these, as explained below, in developing countries. The estimates for the United States were prorated across other industrialized countries according to population. See Fenner et al. (1988: 1364–1365).

6. Fenner et al. (1988) refer to this as the "loss from diminished economic productivity." The benefit is taken by Fenner et al. to be about $825 (in

1967 U.S. dollars) per avoided death. Very roughly, this is an estimate of the net lifetime earnings of a typical victim. As noted in Chapter 2, the value of a life lost should reflect the actual choices people make in their own lives to reduce risks, and these values are typically a multiple of lifetime net income.

7. Working Group 2 of the Commission on Macroeconomics and Health (2002: 52).

8. Fenner et al. (1988: 332).

9. See Tucker (2001: 51).

10. Fenner et al. (1988: 327).

11. Fenner et al. (1988: 1363).

12. Fenner et al. (1988: 1043).

13. Fenner et al. (1988: 1032).

14. Fenner et al. (1988: 1047).

15. UNICEF press release, March 28, 2004; http://www.unicef.org/media/media_20190.html

16. UNICEF press release, March 28, 2004; http://www.unicef.org/media/media_20190.html

17. http://www.who.int/csr/don/2005_09_13/en/index.html

18. Centers for Disease Control and Prevention (2006).

19. To earn a high ranking, a country's government must have weak control of its territory, lack domestic legitimacy, fail to provide domestic security and basic public services, and face domestic rivals in the use of force.

20. See Miller et al. (2006); see also Arita (2006) and Roberts (2006).

21. Centers for Disease Control and Prevention (2005).

22. Gani and Leach (2001).

23. Such persons, if at serious risk of becoming infected, can be given vaccinia immune globulin (if the supplies are available) along with the vaccine.

24. Fenner et al. (1988: 1341).

25. It is sometimes noted that steps such as these serve to deter a terrorist attack. This is unclear, but to the extent that a smallpox attack is deterred, the effect may only be to cause terrorists to shift to another mode of attack; see Sandler (2005).

26. See Barrett (2006d).

27. Fallows (2005: 9).

28. United States GAO (2002a).

29. Abt Associates, Inc. (2003).

30. Allison (2004: 1).

31. http://www.nti.org/h_learnmore/nuctutorial/chapter03_04.html

32. I am referring here to the same index as used in Table 3.2. This is the index developed by The Fund for Peace and *Foreign Policy* magazine; see http://www.fundforpeace.org/programs/fsi/fsindex2006.php

33. The Convention has 118 parties (non-parties include North Korea and Iran; and many parties, including Pakistan and Russia, have exempted

themselves from the dispute resolution procedure). The amendment will become binding upon being ratified by at least two-thirds of the parties to the original agreement, but like all amendments, it would then only be binding on the countries that ratified it.

34. A number of states have provided assistance in securing "loose nukes," primarily in Russia. These include the G8 members, sponsors of the Global Partnership Against the Spread of Weapons of Mass Destruction. However, the sum of all these measures has been inadequate. See the comprehensive analysis by Bunn and Weir (2005).

35. See Fidler (2005) for a discussion of the revisions and Fidler (1999) for a description of the earlier International Health Regulations, and of the history of international cooperation in this area.

36. The WHO Constitution also allows members to make reservations, essentially contracting out of individual provisions. These, however, are subject to the approval of the World Health Assembly. See Fidler (1999: 59–60).

37. This was as of 1997; see Fidler (1999: 60, footnote 16). Fidler also notes that only three countries (Egypt, India, and Pakistan) had made reservations to the earlier regulations.

38. The epidemiology of this disease is summarized in SARS Epidemiology Working Group (2003). See also Longini et al. (2004) and Mahmoud and Lemon (2004).

39. See Appendix II of United States GAO (2003).

40. Wong and Hui (2004: 339).

41. WHO (2003: 74–75).

42. See the overview of the SARS case in WHO (2003, chapter 5). Note that the consequences of an emerging infectious disease epidemic can also be counted in dollars. SARS is estimated to have cost around $40–$54 billion in 2003 (Lee and McKibbin 2004). This cost includes more than the direct costs associated with illness, death, and quarantine. It reflects also the changes in behavior associated with the epidemic, including (in the higher estimate) the effect on investor confidence.

43. See Anderson et al. (2004).

44. Anderson and May (1991: 70).

45. Chowell et al. (2004).

46. Preston (1994: 367).

47. For a detailed analysis of the SARS outbreak and the effect this had on the International Health Regulations, see David Fidler's *SARS, Governance and the Globalization of Disease* (Fidler 2004).

48. Phillips and Killingray (2003: 5–6).

49. See Barry (2005), Phillips and Killingray (2003), and Johnson and Mueller (2002).

50. Marshall (2005: 325).

51. See Enserink (2004: 2025) and Taubenberger and Morens (2006: 21). The costs of pandemic influenza can also be measured in economic terms. Meltzer et al. (2005) prepared estimates for the U.S. alone. They estimate that the next influenza pandemic could result in 89,000–207,000 deaths, many more hospitalizations, and millions more additional illnesses, with an economic impact of perhaps $71–$166 billion. A more recent analysis by the World Bank (2005), but one that extrapolates from other previous research, calculates that a pandemic influenza might cost high-income countries $550 billion. (Strangely, the World Bank, to my knowledge, has not produced an estimate of the cost to developing countries.)

52. Mills et al. (2004: 905).

53. Mills et al. (2004).

54. Chowell et al. (2004).

55. Ferguson et al. (2006).

56. Fraser et al. (2004).

57. See Taubenberger and Morens (2006).

58. For an overview, see Knobler et al. (2005).

59. Lydia Polgreen, "Nigeria Tries TV Jingles, Anything to Chip Away at Ignorance of Spreading Bird Flu." *New York Times*, February 26, 2006, p. 6.

60. Developing countries are not the only weak links. Industrialized countries may also create the conditions for emergence, particularly by the introduction of new technologies and industrial processes. BSE emerged in the United Kingdom because of the practice of rendering cattle offal, including brain and spinal cord, to feed other cattle. Were it not for this rendering process, the original prion mutation would not have spread so widely. See http://www.defra.gov.uk/animalh/bse/controls-eradication/causes.html

61. See Alan Sipress, "Bird Flu Drug Rendered Useless: Chinese Chickens Given Medication Made for Humans." *The Washington Post*, June 18, 2005, p. A1.

62. Fisheries and public goods are different in another respect also. Consumption of a public good by one party does not diminish the quantity available to others, whereas fishing involves tremendous rivalry; if one fisherman catches more fish, fewer fish are left for others to catch.

63. Over 40 such agreements are listed in Barrett (2005).

64. Food and Agriculture Organization (2004: 32).

65. Swan (2002: 3).

CHAPTER 3

1. Secretary General of the United Nations (2000: 56).

2. "French Plan Would Tax Imports from Non-Signers of Kyoto Pact." *New York Times*, November 14, 2006, p. A6.

3. This is for CFC-11; CFC 115 has a lifetime of about 500 years. See Solomon (1999: 279).

4. The process of ozone depletion and the history of its discovery are beautifully told by Irwin (2002).

5. Editorial in *The New York Times*, May 31, 1987.

6. Richard Benedick, the chief United States negotiator at the Montreal Protocol talks, has written a remarkable first-hand account of these important negotiations (see Benedick 1998).

7. For a formal, game-theoretic analysis of this problem, see Barrett (2001).

8. As explained in Chapter 4, this is the natural focal point, the basis for cost sharing in many other treaties.

9. See http://ozone.unep.org/Treaties_and_Ratification/2Ci_states_not_ratificatified_treaties.asp

10. World Meteorological Organization (2002: 12).

11. World Meteorological Organization (2002: 13).

12. Intergovernmental Panel on Climate Change (2001: 5). I am referring here to the IPCC's third assessment report. After this book was written, a summary of the IPCC's fourth assessment was published. The estimates reported here changed very little in this updated assessment.

13. Intergovernmental Panel on Climate Change (2001: 8).

14. Ruddiman (2005: 87).

15. Ruddiman (2005: 105).

16. See Mason (2004); and Broecker and Stocker (2006).

17. See Broecker (1997).

18. Clark et al. (2002).

19. This quote is from notes Professor Alley prepared to accompany his presentation. Richard B. Alley, "Abrupt Climate Change—An Update," handout prepared for the NBER-Yale Center for Global Change Workshop on Abrupt and Catastrophic Climate Change, Snowmass, Colorado, July 31–August 1, 2006, p. 4.

20. Clark and Mix (2002).

21. Intergovernmental Panel on Climate Change (2001: 9).

22. Alley et al. (2005a: 460).

23. For a discussion of the relationship between the ice sheets and the North Atlantic circulation, see Alley et al. (2005b).

24. For an assessment of the probability of the West Antarctic Ice Sheet disintegrating, see Vaughan and Spouge (2002).

25. Caldeira et al. (2003: 2052). If climate sensitivity is 1.5°C, then the 2°C increase could be achieved at a concentration level of 700 ppm.

26. See Intergovernmental Panel on Climate Change (2001). O'Neill and Oppenheimer (2002) try to make the case for stabilizing concentrations at 450 ppm.

27. Caldeira et al. (2003: 2053).

28. See Mendelsohn et al. (2006).
29. The estimate is from Tanser et al. (2003). Patz et al. (2005) provide a broader review of the evidence linking climate change and human health.
30. See Schelling (2002).
31. Wigley (1998: 2287–2288).
32. Pacala and Socolow (2004: 968).
33. Pacala and Socolow (2004).
34. These data are from http://cdiac.ornl.gov/ftp/ndp030/global.1751_2003. ems
35. Government of Canada (2005).
36. Under an agreement reached after Kyoto was negotiated, countries exceeding their allowed level of emissions would be required to make up for this non-compliance by reducing their emissions in the next commitment period (presumably 2013–2017) by the amount of the excess plus 30 percent (the latter being a penalty). As I have explained elsewhere, this mechanism, should it ever be applied, would have no effect (Barrett 2005: 385–386). As matters now stand, however, the mechanism has not been incorporated into an amendment, and so cannot be binding in any event.
37. See the afterword in Barrett (2005).
38. Levy (1993), in his analysis of the acid rain treaties, calls this "tote board diplomacy."
39. Stern (2006: ii).
40. In particular, Stern recommends that we stabilize atmospheric concentrations at a level not greater than 550 ppm CO_2e (a target expressed in terms of the concentration of *all* greenhouse gases and not only carbon dioxide. Today's level is about 430 ppm CO_2e; as mentioned before, CO_2 concentrations are around 380 ppm today.) This level mirrors the European Union's own recommendation for a target intended to limit temperature rise to 2°C; see Commission of the European Communities (2005).
41. Stern (2006: 285).
42. Stern's conclusions are, however, similar to those obtained by Cline (1992).
43. My discussion here has benefited from discussions with both Partha Dasgupta and William Nordhaus. See Dasgupta (2006) and Nordhaus (2006).
44. Stern (2006: 156).
45. Stern (2006: 143).
46. Stern (2006: 155).
47. Stern (2006: 158).
48. This is known as the pure rate of time discount; see the appendix to chapter 2 of Stern (2006).
49. Stern (2006: 47).
50. Schelling (1995: 397).
51. This is the elasticity of the marginal utility of consumption, which Stern takes to be 1.0. This is the same value used by HM Treasury today, but

the Treasury had previously used a higher value of 1.5, and Evans (2005) shows that the larger value is more consistent with social preferences for equity as reflected in the income tax schedules of OECD countries. What is the effect of this assumption? As shown in the appendix to chapter 2 of the Stern Review, the social rate of discount is equal to the pure rate of discount (which Stern takes to be 0.1) plus the product of the elasticity (which Stern takes to equal 1.0) and the rate of growth in per capita consumption (which Stern takes to equal 1.3; see Stern 2006: 162). This yields a discount rate of 1.4 percent. Using an elasticity of 1.5, the discount rate would equal 1.95. To see the difference, discount $1 million in damages to be incurred 194 years from now—that is, in 2200. How much would that be worth in today's value? Using Stern's assumptions, it would be worth $66,139. Using the elasticity of 1.5, it would be worth $22,754, or a third as much.

52. Stern (2006: xxiii).
53. Stern (2006: vii).
54. Contrast Stern's approach with the analysis of the "social cost of carbon" by Pearce (2005).
55. Nicholas Stern subsequently added a postscript to his original analysis, which includes a sensitivity analysis—a welcome change. The postscript shows that increasing the elasticity of the marginal utility of consumption from 1 to 1.5 lowers the cost of climate change by about 40 percent.
56. See, for example, Stiglitz (2006).
57. "French Plan Would Tax Imports from Non-Signers of Kyoto Pact." *New York Times*, November 14, 2006, p. A6.

CHAPTER 4

1. Schelling (1955: 1).
2. Berlin Declaration, June 2005; http://www.diplomatie.gouv.fr/en/france-priorities_1/development_2108/innovative-ways-to-fund-development_2109/colonne-droite_2110/key-documents_3016/berlin-declaration-by-algeria-brazil-chile-france-germany-and-spain-pdf-141-ko_3589.html
3. In addition to the advantage discussed in this paragraph, the tax proposals mentioned can reduce the "externalities" of air travel, excessively volatile currency markets, and global climate change. Note, however, that taxes that are very effective at changing behavior are less effective at raising revenue. For a recent, comprehensive treatment of international taxation, see the collection of essays in Atkinson (2005).
4. At least for low tax rates, worries about "leakage" may be overblown. According to Keen and Strand (2005: 29–30), "In Norway . . . when an avia-tion fuel tax at a rate of 16 US cents per gallon was first proposed . . . major

airlines threatened to purchase substantial excess aviation fuels abroad. Such a fuel tax was enacted in 1999, and has since been increased moderately, to about 18 US cents per gallon. In fact little or no such excess fueling has taken place."

5. This makes the coordination of taxes very unlike the coordination problems discussed in Chapter 6.

6. Small science research is sometimes undertaken and financed collectively. An example is internationally collaborative research supported by the International Institute of Applied Systems Analysis.

7. The current organization was created by the Convention for the Establishment of a European Organization for Nuclear Research. The original parties included the Federal Republic of Germany, Belgium, Denmark, France, Greece, Italy, Norway, the Netherlands, United Kingdom, Sweden, Switzerland, and Yugoslavia. Yugoslavia later withdrew, but nine other states (Austria, Bulgaria, Czech Republic, Finland, Hungary, Poland, Portugal, Slovak Republic, and Spain) subsequently joined, bringing the total to 20.

8. http://www.cern.ch.

9. Olson (1965: 29). Olson and Zeckhauser (1966) provided the first confirmation of this theory—the case of NATO financing. For a recent survey of the subject, see Sandler and Hartley (2001).

10. In the jargon of economics, supply is a "joint product," yielding both global and nation-specific benefits. See Sandler (1992) and Cornes and Sandler (1996).

11. U.S. Department of Defense (1992).

12. Bennett et al. (1994).

13. Daggett and Pagliano (1991: 10).

14. Bennett et al. (1994: 74).

15. Wallsten and Kosec (2005).

16. J. Weisman, "Projected Iraq Costs Soar: Total Spending is Likely to More than Double, Analysis Finds." *Washington Post*, April 27, 2006, p. A16.

17. According to Wallsten and Kosec (2005), the present value of direct costs for the conflict extending through to 2015 would be about $1 trillion, of which about $600 billion would be borne by the U.S., $95 billion by coalition partners, and over $300 billion by Iraq. This same paper also attempts to calculate the costs avoided by the war. It does not, however, provide a complete cost–benefit analysis. The larger estimate given here is from Bilmes and Stiglitz (2006). Of course, the merits of the war need to be considered from other perspectives. First, had there been no war, the existing policy of containment would have needed to be sustained, and this also would have been costly. Davis et al. (2003) believe that continued containment would have cost about $300 billion. These authors also note

that Iraqis would have suffered under this scenario as well as under the present one.

18. Nordhaus (2002: 25).

19. In saying that the diseases were about equally infectious, I mean that they have about the same "basic reproductive number." See Chapter 2.

20. Bulgaria and Romania joined the EU in 2007, raising membership to 27 countries.

21. That is, they usually benefit the most in *absolute* terms. In relative terms, poor countries may benefit more. Benefits—the Bs—are expressed in absolute (money) terms.

22. Non-members today include the Holy See and Taiwan. Article I of the UN Charter says that the organization's purposes are, first, to

> maintain international peace and security . . . ; [second,] to develop friendly relations among nations . . . ; [third,] to achieve international cooperation in solving international problems of an economic, social, cultural, or humanitarian character, and in promoting and encouraging respect for human rights and for fundamental freedoms for all without distinction as to race, sex, language, or religion; and [finally] to be a centre for harmonizing the actions of nations in the attainment of these common ends.

23. Schelling (1955: 1).

24. Schelling (1955: 2).

25. Statement by Ambassador Richard C. Holbrooke, United States Permanent Representative to the United Nations, on the Scale of Assessments for the Apportionment of Expenses of the United Nations, in the Fifth Committee of the General Assembly, October 2, 2000; http://www.un.int/usa/00_131.htm

26. Lawrence Officer (1994: 419) claims that, "Under a crude application of the benefit principle, smaller and developing countries—with less ability to defend themselves—benefit more than large and developed countries from the UN role in fostering world peace and international cooperation." This, in my view, gets things exactly wrong. The more the UN succeeds in promoting peace and security overall, the less every country needs to spend on its own defense. The countries that benefit the most (in absolute terms) are the countries that spend the most on their own defense. National defense and overall security are substitutes.

27. According to an article appearing in *The New York Times* (Warren Hoge, "Bolton Presses for New Method of Calculating Dues at the UN," March 29, 2006), the change in calculation would reorder the ranking in terms of income noticeably in some cases. The income measure used for calculating the assessments rank China's gross income 7th, India's 12th, and Russia's 16th. In Appendix Table 4.2A, all these countries are ranked higher.

28. If the global public goods supplied by the UN were "normal goods," and not "luxury goods," then benefits would increase with income per capita at a *decreasing* rate.

29. "Submission of Japan's Proposal on the Methodology for the UN Scale of Assessments for the Next Three Year Term," Ministry of Foreign Affairs of Japan, March 10, 2006; http://www.mofa.go.jp/announce/announce/2006/3/0310.html

30. See Schelling (1960) for the seminal treatment of the concept.

31. Schelling (1955: 4).

32. Power (2002: 504).

33. Power (2002: 373–374).

34. The financing of the smallpox eradication campaign was hampered by similar considerations—by the earlier failure of the malaria eradication effort and by the lack of a domestic political constituency for financing eradication. It was really only after smallpox was eradicated that its benefits were celebrated, just as it was only after the genocide in Rwanda had ended that the world's collective failure to act was regretted. See Barrett (2006d).

35. Doyle and Sambanis (2000: 779).

36. Shimizu and Sandler (2002: 654).

37. United States GAO (2006).

38. For analyses of the economics of financing peacekeeping, see Khanna et al. (1998) and Bobrow and Boyer (2005).

39. See Bobrow and Boyer (2005: 258).

40. http://www.un.org/Depts/dpko/dpko/faq/q9.htm

41. Indeed, the costs for disarming, demobilizing, and resettling forces—an essential element of peacebuilding—are currently financed entirely by voluntary contributions.

42. United States GAO (2002b: 2).

43. Collier and Hoeffler (2004).

44. This is in present value terms.

45. Secretary General of the United Nations (2005: 31 and 52).

46. Cadsby and Maynes (1999).

47. As of the end of March 2006, 12 member states fell in this category, though the General Assembly has extended permission for them to vote in all but one case (the Dominican Republic). Most of the countries substantially behind in their payments have been experiencing trauma. These include Liberia, Niger, and Somalia.

48. Anderson and Sarma (2002: 133).

49. Benedick (1998: 187).

50. Non-payment has really only been a problem for the former Soviet bloc countries, but their circumstances were special. When the Montreal Protocol and London Amendment were negotiated, the Soviet Union and its

satellites were treated the same as other industrialized countries. Their status, however, changed dramatically after the Soviet Union collapsed. Recognizing that the former communist states of Eastern and Central Europe were unable to fulfill the commitments they had entered into previously, a companion arrangement was developed whereby the other industrialized country parties offered financial assistance to these transition economies, to aid their compliance with the Montreal Protocol.

51. Fehr and Gächter (2000).
52. Fenner et al. (1988: 393–394).
53. My analysis here draws from Barrett (2006d).
54. Fenner et al. (1988: 416).
55. Henderson (1999).
56. Fenner et al. (1988: 423).
57. See Barrett (2006d).
58. Fenner et al. (1988: 768).
59. Fenner et al. (1988: 768).
60. Fenner et al. (1988: 768).
61. Self-interest may also have been a motivation. Sweden eliminated small-pox in 1895—the first country in the world to do so—and yet, like all other countries in Europe, remained vulnerable to imports. In 1963, a Swedish seaman, returning home from the Pacific, unwittingly imported the disease, and infected 24 others, of whom four died (Hopkins and Millar 1996). About 2,500 persons exposed to the disease had to be quarantined (Sencer and Axnick 1973). And of the 300,000 residents of Stockholm who were vaccinated in the wake of the epidemic (Hopkins and Millar 1996), about 200 had reactions requiring hospitalization (Sencer and Axnick 1973). For Sweden, the memory of this outbreak may have made the benefits of eradication especially palpable.
62. See Fenner et al. (1988, table 10.6, p. 464).
63. Aylward et al. (2003: 48).

CHAPTER 5

1. http://www.jfklibrary.org/Historical+Resources/Archives/Reference+Desk/Press+Conferences/003POFO5Pressconference52_03211963.htm
2. My concern here is with horizontal non-proliferation. Vertical non-proliferation, or arms control, is also important, and also requires mutual restraint.
3. See http://www.msnbc.msn.com/id/12758097/site/newsweek/
4. Sagan (1996: 70).
5. Thomas C. Schelling, "The Nuclear Taboo," *The Wall Street Journal*, October 24, 2005, p. A14.

6. Schelling (2006: 313–325).

7. The situation is akin to the Bush administration's efforts, underway as I write this, to "clarify"—that is, to deviate from—Article 3 of the Geneva Convention relative to the Treatment of Prisoners of War. Such a move may invite other countries to set *their* own rules for the treatment of prisoners.

8. Walter Pincus, "Pentagon Revises Nuclear Strike Plan," *Washington Post*, September 11, 2005, p. A1.

9. Schelling (1966: 227–232).

10. Lieber and Press (2006: 52–53).

11. Bunn and Timerbaev (1993: 12).

12. The treaty generalizes and improves on the United States "Atoms for Peace" program, which offered nuclear reactor technology on a bilateral basis to countries willing to forswear weapons development and commit to "safeguards" (accounting and inspection standards). The treaty codifies a bargain in which the five nuclear powers of the time agreed to provide access to peaceful nuclear technology to non-nuclear states in exchange for a commitment not to develop weapons and to abide by a safeguards regime to be managed by the International Atomic Energy Agency. The bargain also involves a commitment by the five nuclear weapons states to pursue in good faith negotiations for complete nuclear disarmament (Article VI).

13. http://www.whitehouse.gov/news/releases/2006/04/20060418-1.html

14. Seymour M. Hersh, "The Iran Plans." *The New Yorker*, April 17, 2006.

15. Zbigniew Brzezinski, "Do Not Attack Iran." *International Herald Tribune*, April 26, 2006; http://www.iht.com/bin/print_ipub.phb?file=/articles/2006/04/25/opinion/edzbig.phg

16. According to Simon (1997: 9), there is evidence that "the wind was blowing... dangerously close to the direction of the inhabited atolls, at the time of the detonation."

17. Quoted in Simon (1997: 8).

18. The episode is summarized by Simon (1997).

19. Cronkite et al. (1997: 177).

20. Department of Health and Human Services, Centers for Disease Control and Prevention, and the National Cancer Institute (2005).

21. Haynes and Bentham (1995).

22. Department of Health and Human Services, Centers for Disease Control and Prevention, and the National Cancer Institute (2005: 4).

23. This risk is greater than the risk of radation exposure from building materials, industrial emissions, and the like (that is, exposure excluding medical, background, and indoor radon). It is about the same as the risk of hazardous toxic air pollutants or pesticides on food. For estimates of these risks, see Gough (1990).

24. Medalia (2002: Summary).
25. See Richards and Kim (1997) and Davis and Sykes (1999).
26. As Annas et al. (2002: 153) put it, "Altering the human species is an issue that directly concerns all of us and should only be decided democratically, by a body that is representative of everyone on the planet. It is the most important decision we will ever make."
27. Resolution 59/280, adopted on March 8, 2005, can be found at http://www.un.org/law/cloning/
28. Frankel and Chapman (2000: 8).
29. Frankel and Chapman (2000: 8).
30. Fukuyama (2002: 81).
31. Annas et al. (2002: 169).
32. Andorno (2002: 960).
33. The logic is similar to the idea of a "frame of reference" being a public good. See Frank (1997).
34. As noted before, it is the capability to produce a nuclear bomb that really matters, and this particular genie cannot be put back into his bottle.
35. Fukuyama (2002: 194).

CHAPTER 6

1. http://72.14.205.104/search?q=cache:yNep7ckoGzgJ:www.clintonglobal-initiative.org/pdf/transcripts/plenary/cgi_09_15_05_plenary_1.pdf+tony+blair+climate+change+clinton&hl=en&gl=us&ct=clnk&cd=10
2. Landes (2000: 76).
3. Dohrn-van Rossum (1996: 117).
4. Dohrn-van Rossum (1996: 348).
5. Zerubavel (1982: 7).
6. Zerubavel (1982: 10).
7. International Conference (1884: 199).
8. International Conference (1884: 77).
9. Audoin and Guinot (2001: 42).
10. Zerubavel (1982: 16–17).
11. Start at Greenwich at eight o'clock Monday morning and move eastward. For every 15 degrees longitude, add an hour. By the time you return to Greenwich, it is eight o'clock Tuesday morning. To correct for this, a day must be lost as you move eastward. As you move westward, a day must be added.
12. The International Date Line does not follow 180 degrees strictly, and it has changed over time. Kiribati, for example, "unilaterally extended the date line in an audacious 1,000 mile loop to embrace its easternmost outcropping, Caroline Island, and immediately renamed it Millennium Island." (The hope being that this could be declared the first place on Earth

to enjoy the first sunrise of the new millennium; see Seth Mydans, "A Millennial Free-For-All: Who's On First?" *New York Times*, December 8, 1999.)

13. Audoin and Guinot (2001: 43).

14. In 1987, the duties of the Bureau International de l'Heure were divided, with atomic time measurement being transferred to the Bureau International Bureau des Poids et Mesures, and astrological time measurement transferred to the International Earth Rotation Service.

15. Whitrow (1972: 65).

16. See Nelson et al. (2001: 512) and Whitrow (1972: 62).

17. Nelson et al. (2001: 524).

18. Arias and Guinot (2004: 257).

19. International Telecommunication Union Press Release, Document 7A/TEMP/16R1-E, November 11, 2005.

20. Arias and Guinot (2004: 258).

21. The Russian global navigation satellite system known as GLONASS uses Coordinated Universal Time, and is unavailable at times when leap seconds are added. See Nelson et al. (2001: 521).

22. Royal Astronomical Society PN05/41: RAS Statement on the Proposed Abolition of Leap Seconds, September 20, 2005; http://www.ras.org.uk//index2.php?option=com_content&task=view&id=830&Itemid=2&pop=1&page=0

23. I am drawing here from Barrett (2005: 262–267).

24. See Mitchell (1994).

25. See http://www.imo.org/Conventions/mainframe.asp?topic_id=247

26. See the classic article by David (1985).

27. I am drawing here from Barrett (2005: 393–397).

28. In 2000, Sudan became the first country in Sub-Saharan Africa to switch to unleaded gas, a decision based as much on economic concerns as on environmental concerns. Sudan had built a refinery, north of Khartoum, which provides gasoline for domestic consumption and an export market that demands unleaded. See Marc Lacey, "Belatedly, Africa is Converting to Lead-Free Gasoline." *New York Times*, October 31, 2004.

29. Cowan (1990).

30. Hoffert et al. (2002).

31. Caldeira et al. (2005).

CHAPTER 7

1. http://www.gatesfoundation.org/MediaCenter/Speeches/MelindaSpeeches/MFGSpeechWashWomenFdn-000406.htm

2. L. Polgreen, "War's Chaos Steals Congo's Young by the Millions." *New York Times*, July 30, 2006.

3. Kakwani and Son (2006).
4. Initially, two vaccines were licensed. The inactivated or killed vaccine was later withdrawn. The live attenuated vaccine was subsequently improved. It is often given in combination with rubella and mumps vaccine, the combined vaccine known as MMR. A small percentage of children given a single dose of the measles vaccine fail to develop an immune response, and because the disease is so highly infectious (has a high basic reproductive number), a second dose must be given to (nearly) every child to ensure that the disease is eliminated.
5. http://science.education.nih.gov/supplements/nih1/diseases/activities/ activity5_measles-database.htm
6. http://www.unicef.org/immunization/media_25308.html
7. This is based on the *Morbidity and Mortality Weekly Report* published by the Centers for Disease Control; see http://www.cdc.gov/mmwr/preview/mmwrhtml/mm5433a1.htm; http://www.cdc.gov/mmwr/preview/mmwrhtml/mm5106a2.htm; http://www.cdc.gov/mmwr/preview/mmwrhtml/mm4925a1.htm.
8. Of course, the cost per life saved would be higher than this, but the economics of vaccination are still extremely attractive. For a recent analysis of the cost-effectiveness of vaccination, see Brenzel et al. (2006). See also the case study on measles vaccination in Southern Africa reported in Levine (2004).
9. Measles eradication has been proposed before and is feasible, but because measles is so infectious, eradication would require an extraordinary effort at control—substantially greater than in the case of poliomyelitis, discussed in Chapter 2. While polio elimination requires mass vaccination to a level of around 80 percent, measles elimination requires coverage of at least 95 percent. Measles eradication is thus even more vulnerable to a weakest link. See Orenstein et al. (2000), who conclude that, measles eradication "is in our future. The question is when."
10. Mahmoud (2004).
11. At best, aid is less than fully effective in such settings. Collier and Hoeffler (2005) show that, in Africa, aid has the effect of doubling military spending.
12. According to Schneegans (2005: 4), "UNESCO had been arguing the need for an early warning system for the Indian Ocean for several years."
13. K.S. Jayaraman, "India Makes Waves Over Tsunami Warning System," December 21, 2005; http://www.nature.com/news/2005/051219/pf/4381060a_pf.html
14. Such systems can also be used for cyclones, earthquakes, floods and other disasters, many of which are more common than tsunamis.
15. Schneegans (2005: 2).

16. The Onchocerciasis Control Program, initiated by the World Bank in 1973, is unlike most World Bank activities. The Bank normally lends or uses grant financing to assist individual countries. From the start, the river blindness program was a regional program, involving a complex of partnerships that included UN agencies, businesses, and NGOs. See Benton et al. (2002).
17. The disease is also found in the Americas and in Yemen on the Arabian Peninsula.
18. I am drawing in this paragraph from Guillet (2003).
19. Levine (2004, case 6). See also Kim and Benton (1995).
20. Dadzie et al. (2003). Note that river blindness eradication, were it feasible, would be an international public good, since the disease is prevalent in more than one region. Control and elimination are location-specific interventions; when successful, they provide local or national public goods (herd immunity).
21. See Miller et al. (2006).
22. Hopkins and Withers (2002).
23. See Hopkins and Withers (2002).
24. Sachs and Malaney (2002).
25. See Wellems and Plowe (2001).
26. I am drawing here from Arrow et al. (2004: 271–272).
27. Laxminarayan et al. (2006: 328).
28. See Jambou et al. (2005: 1962).
29. See "A Pre-Emptive Strike: A Plan to Stop the Evolution of Resistance to a New Malaria Drug," *The Economist*, January 19, 2006.
30. A ban on monotherapies may only stimulate creation of a black market. And it will not help the current generation of malaria victims, unable to afford the more expensive combination drugs. Kenneth Arrow and the other members of a United States Institute of Medicine committee have therefore proposed a global subsidy of $400–$500 million per year, to bring the price of artemisinin combination therapy down to the current cost of chloroquine; funding of $10–$30 million per year to stimulate production of artemisinin; a centralized procurement process for combination drugs; policies to discourage the use of monotherapies for routine first-line treatment; improved monitoring and surveillance; and an increase in global R&D investment of $60–$80 million per year to stimulate the development of new antimalarials. As of now, this plan remains to be developed and implemented. See Arrow et al. (2004). See also Laxminarayan et al. (2006).
31. See, for example, Roper et al. (2003).
32. D.A. Henderson (1993) provides an overview of this need, and a practical proposal for filling it, by developing regional centers.

33. Chorba (2001: 143).
34. The data reported here are from UNAIDS/WHO (2005: 2).
35. The basic reproductive number is from Fraser et al. (2004).
36. See Zhu et al. (1998). HIV-2 is less virulent and harder to transmit, and is found mainly in West Africa. Most of the relatively small number of HIV-2 cases in Europe and North America are of people from Africa. HIV-2 is most closely related to a simian form of the virus found in sooty mangabeys.
37. Korber et al. (2000: 1794).
38. Keele et al. (2006: 3).
39. See Chitnis et al. (2000).
40. These values are in international dollars; see http://www.who.int/whr/2006/annex/06_annex3_en.pdf
41. Smolinski et al. (2003: 8).
42. To my knowledge, Zacher (1999) was the first to describe surveillance as a global public good.
43. Ferguson et al. (2006).
44. In addition, the belief that other countries will supply antivirals as needed would blunt the incentive for each country to build up its own stockpile.
45. Donald G McNeil Jr., "Another Death in Indonesia Deepens Fears of Bird Flu's Spread," *New York Times*, June 16, 2006, p. A14.
46. Ferguson et al. (2006).
47. Osterholm (2005a,b).
48. Osterholm (2005a). The quote is taken from the html version of the article, for which there are no page numbers.
49. Osterholm (2005b: 1841).
50. In January 2006, an international "pledging conference" was convened to promote, mobilize, and coordinate financial support for a global response to the threat of pandemic influenza. The organizers hoped to raise $1.5 billion; in the event, $1.9 billion was pledged. The United States pledged $334 million, more than any other donor, but this money was already appropriated the year before, and represents less than five percent of the overall U.S. budget for pandemic influenza.
51. See the studies cited by Kremer and Glennerster (2004).
52. Kremer and Peterson-Zwane (2005).
53. Alston et al. (1998).
54. Collins (2004: 102).
55. Vagelos (2001).
56. Knowledge is a public good only when it is not patented. The patent system, however, creates an incentive for knowledge to be created. There is thus a tradeoff: the patent's promise of a monopoly right stimulates the production of knowledge, but so long as that right is held and exercised, the distribution of the knowledge is restricted (except in the case of perfect

price discrimination). Because Merck has given ivermectin away for free, the distribution of this drug is efficient.

57. See Hellerstein (2003) for the earlier history of this decline. The low figure is from Celia W. Dugger, "Clinton Makes Up for Lost Time in Battling AIDS," *New York Times*, August 29, 2006, p. A8.

58. The two approaches are not equally efficient from a production point of view. Doing away with the "pull" incentive created by the patent (or by another device such as a prize) would increase the costs of producing new knowledge. See Kremer and Glennerster (2004).

59. In the strong words of Maskus and Reichman (2004: 307), "if nothing had been done to address the plight of millions dying of AIDS because of TRIPS patent rights, then the WTO would have contributed to the greatest health tragedy in history."

60. See Barton (2004).

61. See Berndt et al. (2005).

62. Improvement in health is calculated in terms of reductions in a "disability adjusted life year," a measure that accounts for both mortality and morbidity. Berndt and his coauthors estimate that a malaria vaccine would cost less than $15 per disability adjusted life year saved.

63. Berndt et al. (2005). See also Barder et al. (2005: 34).

64. According to Barder et al. (2005: 20), "pursuing a single candidate vaccine through the remaining phases of clinical trials, regulatory approval and production would exceed the total public and philanthropic funds presently available for the development of a malaria vaccine." Of course, more than one candidate would need to be tested.

65. Control is much harder in the tropics, where malaria can be transmitted by different species of mosquito, having different feeding habits (which matters for vector control), and possibly carrying a different form of malaria (*falciparum* malaria, common in Africa, is often fatal). Differences in climate also matter (for example, whether there is a frost).

66. Lanjouw (2002) suggests that, to address both this problem and the one raised in the previous section, companies should be required to choose between patenting their innovations in the industrialized countries or in the developing countries but not both.

67. The subject of financing is very complicated in this case, for it depends on the international property rights and trade systems.

68. See Kremer and Glennerster (2004); Barder et al. (2005); and Commission on Macroeconomics and Health (2001).

69. Jagdish Bhagwati makes this same point in a recent editorial; see his "A Global Warming Fund Could Succeed Where Kyoto Failed," *Financial Times*, August 16, 2006. See also Barrett (2005: 397).

70. Thomas Schelling (2006: 58) has made this simple point more clearly than anyone; I believe he was also the first to spot it.

CONCLUSION

1. See, for example, Besley and Coate (1998).
2. Glennon (2003).
3. http://www.whitehouse.gov/news/releases/2003/01/20030128-19.html
4. Independent International Commission on Kosovo (2000: 4).
5. On the matter of the Security Council's legitimacy and a proposal for reform, see Dervis with Özer (2005: 43–72). On the question of how to implement the emerging norm of the "responsibility to protect," see High Level Panel on Threats, Challenges, and Change (2004).
6. Members of the High Level Panel include three members of the Task Force on Global Public Goods.
7. High Level Panel on Threats, Challenges, and Change (2004: 53).
8. High Level Panel on Threats, Challenges, and Change (2004: 64).
9. High Level Panel on Threats, Challenges, and Change (2004: 64).
10. As an example, the two parties in the United States Senate agreed in 2005 not to use the filibuster except under "extraordinary circumstances" for the confirmation of judicial appointments.
11. http://daccessdds.un.org/doc/UNDOC/GEN/N06/331/99/PDF/N0633199.pdf?OpenElement
12. http://daccessdds.un.org/doc/UNDOC/GEN/N05/487/60/PDF/N0548760.pdf?OpenElement
13. The quoted passages contained in this paragraph and the next are from Woolsey (1942).
14. Address in San Francisco at the Closing Session of the United Nations Conference, June 26, 1945; http://www.presidency.ucsb.edu/ws/print.php?pid=12188

References

Abt Associates, Inc. (2003). "The Economic Impact of Nuclear Terrorist Attacks on Freight Transport Systems in an Age of Seaport Vulnerability." Executive Summary. Cambridge, MA: Abt Associate, Inc; http://www.abtassociates.com/reports/ES-economic_Impact_of_Nuclear_Terrorist_Attacks.pdf

Alesina, A. and Spolaore, E. (1997). "On the Number and Size of Nations." *Quarterly Journal of Economics*, 107(4): 1027–1056.

——Baqir, R., and Easterly, W. (1999). "Public Goods and Ethnic Divisions." *Quarterly Journal of Economics*, 114(4): 1243–1284.

Alley, R. B., Clark, P. U., Huybrechts, P., and Joughin, I. (2005a). "Ice-Sheet and Sea-Level Changes." *Science*, 310: 456–460.

——Marotzke, J., and Nordhaus, W. D. et al. (2005b). "Abrupt Climate Change." *Science*, 299: 2005–2010.

Allison, G. (2004). "How to Stop Nuclear Terror." *Foreign Affairs*; http://www.foreign-affairs.org/20040101faessay83107/graham-allison/how-to-stop-nuclear-terror.html

Alston, J. M., Pardey, P. G., and Roseboom, J. (1998). "Financing Agricultural Research: International Investment Patterns and Policy Perspectives." *World Development*, 26(6): 1057–1071.

Anderson, R. M. and May, R. M. (1991). *Infectious Diseases of Humans: Dynamics and Control*. Oxford: Oxford University Press.

——Fraser, C., and Ghani, C. A. et al. (2004). "Epidemiology, Transmission Dynamics and Control of SARS: The 2002–2003 Epidemic." *Philosophical Transactions of the Royal Society (B)*, London, B 359: 1091–1105.

Anderson, S. O. and Sarma, K. M. (2002). *Protecting the Ozone Layer: The United Nations History*. London: Earthscan.

Andorno, R. (2002). "Biomedicine and International Human Rights Law: In Search of a Global Consensus." *Bulletin of the World Health Organization*, 80: 959–963.

Annas, G. J., Andrews, L. B., and Isasi, R. M. (2002). "Protecting the Endangered Human: Toward an International Treaty Prohibiting Cloning and Inheritable Alterations." *American Journal of Law and Medicine*, 28: 151–178.

ARC Research Consultants (1997). *Global Benefits and Costs of the Montreal Protocol on Substances that Deplete the Ozone Layer*. Ottawa: Environment Canada.

Arias, E. F. and Guinot, B. (2004). "Coordinated Universal Time UTC: Historical Background and Perspectives." Mimeo, Observatoire de Paris; http://syrte.obspm.fr/journees2004/PDF/Arias2.pdf

Arita, I., Nakane, M., and Fenner, F. (2006). "Is Polio Eradication Realistic?" *Science*, 312: 852–854.

Arrow, K. J., Panosian, C. B., and Gelband, H. (eds.) (2004). *Saving Lives, Buying Time: Economics of Malaria Drugs in an Age of Resistance*. Washington, DC: Institute of Medicine of the National Academies.

Atkinson, A. B. (ed.) (2005). *New Sources of Development Finance*. Oxford: Oxford University Press.

Audoin, C. and Guinot, B. (2001). *The Measurement of Time: Time, Frequency, and the Atomic Clock*. Cambridge: Cambridge University Press.

Aylward, R. B., Acharya, A., England, S., Agocs, M., and Linkins, J. (2003). "Polio Eradication," in R. Smith, R. Beaglehole, D. Woodward, and N. Drager (eds.), *Global Public Goods for Health: Health Economic and Public Health Perspectives*. Oxford: Oxford University Press, pp. 33–53.

Baehr, J., Keller, K., and Marotzke, J. (forthcoming). "Detecting Potential Changes in the Meridional Overturning Circulation at 26°N in the Atlantic." *Climatic Change*.

Baland, J.-M. and Platteau, J.-P. (1996). *Halting Degradation of Natural Resources: Is there a Role for Rural Communities?* Oxford: Clarendon Press.

Barder, O., Kremer, M., and Levine, R. (2005). *Making Markets for Vaccines: Ideas to Action*. Washington, DC: Center for Global Development.

Barrett, S. (2001). "International Cooperation for Sale." *European Economic Review*, 45: 1835–1850.

——(2003). "Global Disease Eradication." *Journal of the European Economics Association*, 1: 591–600.

——(2004). "Eradication vs. Control: The Economics of Global Infectious Disease Policy." *Bulletin of the World Health Organization*, 82: 683–688.

——(2005). *Environment and Statecraft: The Strategy of Environmental Treaty-making*, Oxford: Oxford University Press.

——(2006a). "Making International Cooperation Pay: Financing as a Strategic Incentive," in I. Kaul and P. Conceição (eds.), *The New Public Finance: Responding to Global Challenges*. New York: Oxford University Press, pp. 357–370.

——(2006b). "The Problem of Global Catastrophe." *Chicago Journal of International Law*, 6(2): 527–552.

Barrett, S. (2006c). "Climate Treaties and 'Breakthrough' Technologies." *American Economic Review, Papers and Proceedings*, 96(2): 22–25.

——(2006d). "The Smallpox Eradication Game." *Public Choice*, 130: 179–207.

——(forthcoming). "A Multi-Track Climate Treaty System" in Joseph E. Aldy and Robert N. Stavins (eds.), *Architectures for Agreement: Addressing Global Climate Change in the Post-Kyoto World*. Cambridge: Cambridge University Press.

Barrett, S. and Hoel, M. (forthcoming). "Optimal Disease Eradication." *Environment and Development Economics*.

Barry, J. M. (2005). "1918 Revisited: Lessons and Suggestions for Further Inquiry," in Stacey L. Knobler, Alison Mack, Adel Mahmoud, and Stanley M. Lemon (eds.), *The Threat of Pandemic Influenza: Are We Ready?* Washington, DC: National Academies Press, pp. 58–68.

Barton, J. H. (2004). "TRIPS and the Global Pharmaceutical Market." *Health Affairs*, 23(3): 146–154.

Benedick, R. E. (1998). *Ozone Diplomacy: New Directions in Safeguarding the Planet*. Cambridge, MA: Harvard University Press.

Bennett, A., Lepgold, J., and Unger, D. (1994). "Burden Sharing in the Persian Gulf War." *International Organization*, 48(1): 39–75.

Benton, B., Bump, J., Sékétéli, A., and Liese, B. (2002). "Partnership and Promise: Evolution of the African River-Blindness Campaigns." *Annals of Tropical Medicine and Parasitology*, 96: 5–14.

Berndt, E. R., Glennerster, R., and Kremer, M. R. et al. (2005). "Advanced Purchase Commitments for a Malaria Vaccine: Estimating Costs and Effectiveness." National Bureau of Economic Research Working Paper No. W11288.

Besley, T. and S. Coate (1998). "Sources of Inefficiency in a Representative Democracy: A Dynamic Analysis." *American Economic Review*, 88(1): 139–156.

Bilmes, L. and Stiglitz, J. E. (2006). "The Economic Costs of the Iraq War: An Appraisal Three Years After the Beginning of the Conflict." Paper presented at the Allied Social Science Association meetings, Boston, January; http://72.14.203.104/search?q=cache:qR5dPsx2xfEJ:www2.gsb.columbia.edu/faculty/jstiglitz/cost_of_war_in_iraq.pdf+stiglitz+economic+costs+iraq+war&hl=en&gl=us&ct=clnk&cd=1.

Blaizot, J.-P., Iliopoulos, J., and Madsen, J. et al. (2003). *Study of Potentially Dangerous Events During Heavy-Ion Collisions at the LHC: Report of the LHC Safety Study Group*. Geneva: CERN 2003-001.

Bobrow, D. B. and Boyer, M. A. (2005). *Defensive Internationalism: Providing Public Goods in an Uncertain World*. Ann Arbor: University of Michigan Press.

Bodansky, D. (1996). "May We Engineer the Climate?" *Climatic Change*, 33: 309–321.

Bowland, B. J. and Beghin, J. C. (2001). "Robust Estimates of Value of a Statistical Life for Developing Economies." *Journal of Policy Modeling*, 23(4): 385–396.

Brenzel, L., Wolfson, L. J., Fox-Rushby, J., Miller, M., and Halsey, N. A. (2006). "Vaccine Preventable Diseases," in D.T. Jamison et al. (eds.), *Disease Control Priorities in Developing Countries*, 2nd edn. Oxford: Oxford University Press, pp. 389–411.

Broecker, W. S. (1997). "Thermohaline Circulation, the Achilles Heel of Our Climate System: Will Man-Made CO_2 Upset the Current Balance?" *Science*, 278: 1582–1588.

_____ and Stocker, T. F. (2006). "The Holocene CO_2 Rise: Anthropogenic or Natural?" *Eos*, 87(3): 27–29.

Bunn, G. and Timerbaev, R. M. (1993). "Security Assurances to Non-Nuclear-Weapon States." *The Nonproliferation Review*, Fall, pp. 11–21.

Bunn, M. and Weir, A. (2005). *Securing the Bomb 2005: New Global Imperatives*. Cambridge, MA: Project on Managing the Atom, Harvard University and the Nuclear Threat Initiative.

Cadsby, C. B. and Maynes, E. (1999). "Voluntary Provision of Threshold Public Goods with Continuous Contributions: Experimental Evidence." *Journal of Public Economics*, 71: 53–73.

Caldeira, K., Jain, A. K., and Hoffert, M. I. (2003). "Climate sensitivity uncertainty and the need for energy without CO_2 emission." *Science*, 299: 2052–2054.

_____ Day, D., Fulkerson, W., Hoffert, M., and Lane, L. (2005). *Climate Change Technology Exploratory Research*. Washington, DC: Climate Policy Center.

Centers for Disease Control and Prevention (2005). "Progress Toward Poliomyelitis Eradication—Poliomyelitis Outbreak in Sudan, 2004." *Morbidity and Mortality Weekly Report*, 54(4): 97–99.

_____ (2006). "Resurgence of Wild Poliovirus Type 1 Transmission and Consequences of Importation—21 Countries, 2002–2005." *Morbidity and Mortality Weekly Report*, 55(6): 145–150.

Chapman, C. R. and Morrison, D. (1994). "Impacts on the Earth by Asteroids and Comets: Assessing the Hazard." *Nature*, 367: 33–40.

Chitnis, A., Rawls, D., and Moore, J. (2000). "Origin of HIV Type 1 in Colonial French Equatorial Africa?" *AIDS Research and Human Retroviruses*, 16(1): 5–8.

Chorba, T. L. (2001). "Disease Surveillance," in J. C. Thomas and D. J. Weber (eds.), *Epidemiological Methods for the Study of Infectious Diseases*. New York: Oxford University Press, pp. 138–162.

Chowell, G., Hengartner, N. W., Castillo-Chavez, C., Fenimore, P. W., and Hyman, J. M. (2004). "The Basic Reproductive Number of Ebola and the Effects of Public Health Measures: The Cases of Congo and Uganda." *Journal of Theoretical Biology*, 229(1): 119–126.

Clark, P. U. and Mix, A. C. (2002). "Ice Sheets and Sea Level of the Last Glacial Maximum." *Quaternary Science Reviews*, 21: 1–7.

——Pisias, N. G., Stocker, T. F., and Weaver, A. J. (2002). "The Role of the Thermohaline Circulation in Abrupt Climate Change." *Nature*, 415: 863–869.

Clery, D. and Normile, D. (2005). "ITER Finds a Home—With a Whopping Mortgage," *Science*, 309: 28–29.

Cline, W.R. (1992). *The Economics of Global Warming*. Washington, DC: Institute for International Economics.

Collier, P. and Hoeffler, A. (1998). "On Economic Causes of Civil War." *Oxford Economic Papers*, 50(4): 563–573.

————(2004). "Conflicts," in B. Lomborg (ed.), *Global Problems, Global Solutions*. Cambridge: Cambridge University Press, pp. 129–156.

————(2005). "Unintended Consequences: Does Aid Promote Arms Races?" Department of Economics, University of Oxford, Oxford; http://users.ox.ac.uk/econpco/research/pdfs/Aid-promote-arms.pdf

Collins, K. (2004). "Profitable Gifts: A History of the Merck Mectizan® Donation Program and Its Implications for International Health." *Perspectives in Biology and Medicine*, 47(1): 100–109.

Commission of the European Communities (2005). "Winning the Battle Against Global Climate Change." COM (2005) 35 final; http://eur-lex.europa.eu/LexUriServ/site/en/com/2005/com2005_0035n01.pdf

Commission on Macroeconomics and Health (2001). *Investing in Health for Economic Development*. Geneva: World Health Organization.

Committee on the Assessment of Future Scientific Needs for Live Variola Virus (1999). *Assessment of Future Scientific Needs for Live Variola Virus*. Washington, DC: National Academy Press.

Committee on Oil Pollution Act of 1990 (Section 4115) Implementation Review (1998). *Double-Hull Tanker Legislation: An Assessment of the Oil Pollution Act of 1990*. Washington, DC: National Academy Press.

Cornes, R. and Sandler, T. (1996). *The Theory of Externalities, Public Goods, and Club Goods*, 2nd edn. Cambridge: Cambridge University Press.

Cowan, R. (1990). "Nuclear Power Reactors: A Study in Technological Lock-in." *Journal of Economic History*, 50(3): 541–567.

Cronkite, E. P., Conrad, R. A., and Bond, V. P. (1997). "Historical Events Associated with Fallout from Bravo Shot—Operation Castle and 25 Y of Medical Findings." *Health Physics*, 73(1): 176–186.

Crutzen, P. J. (2006). "Albedo Enhancement by Stratospheric Sulfur Injections: A Contribution to Resolve a Policy Dilemma?" *Climatic Change*, 77: 211–219.

Dadzie, Y., Neira, M., and Hopkins, D. (2003). "Final Report of the Conference on the Eradicability of Onchocerciasis." *Filaria Journal*, 2:2; http://journal.filariasis.net/media/pdfs/volume/v2_2003/1475-2883-2-2.pdf

Daggett, S. and Pagliano, G. (1991). *Persian Gulf War: US Costs and Allied Financial Contributions*. Washington, DC: Congressional Research Service, Issue Brief 91019.

Dasgupta, P. (2006). "Comments on the Stern Review's Economics of Climate Change." Comments given to the Royal Society, London, November 8.

David, P. (1985). "Clio and the Economics of QWERTY." *American Economic Review Papers and Proceedings*, 75(2): 332–337.

Davis, D. M. and Sykes, L. R. (1999). "Geologic Constraints on Clandestine Nuclear Testing in South Asia." *Proceedings of the National Academy of Sciences*, 96(20): 11090–11095.

Davis, S. J., Murphy, K. M., and Topel, R. H. (2003). "War in Iraq versus Containment: Weighing the Costs." University of Chicago; http://72.14.203.104/search?q=cache:X2NLFDZSzCAJ:gsbwww.uchicago.edu/fac/steven.davis/research/War%2520in%2520Iraq%2520versus%2520Containment,%2520Weighing%2520the%2520Costs%2520(March%25202003).pdf+davis+murphy+topel&hl=en&gl=us&ct=clnk&cd=1

Department of Health and Human Services, Centers for Disease Control and Prevention, and the National Cancer Institute (2005). *Report on the Feasibility of a Study of the Health Consequences to the American Population from Nuclear Weapons Tests Conducted by the United States and Other Nations*, Volume 1. Technical Report; http://www.cdc.gov/nceh/radiation/fallout/default.htm

Deria, A., Jezek, Z., Markvart, K., Carrasco, P., and Weisfeld, J. (1980). "The World's Last Endemic Case of Smallpox: Surveillance and Containment Measures." *Bulletin of the World Health Organization*, 58(2): 279–283.

Dervis, K. with C. Özer (2005). *A Better Globalization: Legitimacy, Governance, and Reform*. Washington, DC: Center for Global Development.

Dohrn-van Rossum, G. (1996). *History of the Hour: Clocks and Modern Temporal Orders*. Chicago: University of Chicago Press.

Doyle, M. W. and Sambanis, N. (2000). "International Peacebuilding: A Theoretical and Quantitative Analysis." *American Political Science Review*, 94(4): 779–801.

Enserink, M. (2004). "Influenza: WHO Adds More "1918" to Pandemic Predictions." *Science*, December 17, p. 2025.

Estevadeordal, A., Frantz, B., and Nguyen, T. R. (eds.) (2004). *Regional Public Goods: From Theory to Practice*. Washington, DC: Inter-American Development Bank.

Evans, D.J. (2005). "The Elasticity of Marginal Utility of Consumption: Estimates for 20 OECD Countries." *Fiscal Studies*, 26(2): 197–224.

Fallows, J. (2005). "Success without Victory." *The Atlantic Monthly*, January/February; http://www.theatlantic.com/doc/200501/fallows

Fearon, J. D. and Laitin, D. D. (2003). "Ethnicity, Insurgency, and Civil War." *American Political Science Review*, 97: 75–90.

Fehr, E. and Gächter, S. (2000). "Cooperation and Punishment in Public Goods Experiments." *American Economic Review*, 90(4): 980–94.

Fenner, F., Henderson, D. A., Arita, I., Jezek, Z. and Ladnyi, I. D. (1988). *Smallpox and its Eradication*. Geneva: World Health Organization.

Ferguson, N. M., Cummings, D. A. T., and Fraser, C. et al. (2006). "Strategies for Mitigating an Influenza Pandemic." *Nature*, 44: 448–452.

Ferroni, M. and Mody, A. (2002). *International Public Goods: Incentives, Measurement, and Financing*. Dordrecht: Kluwer.

Fidler, D. P. (1999). *International Law and Infectious Diseases*. Oxford: Clarendon Press.

——(2004). *SARS, Governance and the Globalization of Disease*. Basingstoke: Palgrave Macmillan.

——(2005). "From International Sanitary Conventions to Global Health Security: The New International Health Regulations." *Chinese Journal of International Law*.

Food and Agriculture Organization (FAO) of the United Nations (2004). *The State of the World's Fisheries and Aquaculture*. Rome: FAO.

Frank, R. H. (1997). "The Frame of Reference as a Public Good." *Economic Journal*, 107: 1832–1847.

Frankel, M. S. and Chapman, A. R. (2000). "Human Inheritable Genetic Modifications: Assessing Scientific, Ethical, Religious, and Policy Issues;" http://www.aaas.org/spp/dspp/sfrl/germline/main.htm

Fraser, C., Riley, S., Anderson, R. M., and Ferguson, N. M. (2004). "Factors That Make an Infectious Disease Outbreak Controllable." *Proceedings of the National Academy of Sciences*, 101(16): 6146–6151.

Fukuyama, F. (2002). *Our Posthuman Future: Political Consequences of the Biotechnology Revolution*. New York: Farrar, Straus and Giroux.

Gani, R. and Leach, S. (2001). "Transmission Potential of Smallpox in Contemporary Populations." *Nature*, 414: 748–751.

Glennon, M. J. (2003). "Why the Security Council Failed." *Foreign Affairs*, May/June.

Glynn, I. and Glynn, J. (2004). *The Life and Death of Smallpox*. Cambridge: Cambridge University Press.

Gough, M. (1990). "How Much Cancer Can EPA Regulate Anyway?" *Risk Analysis*, 10(1): 1–6.

Government of Canada (2005). *Moving Forward on Climate Change: A Plan for Honouring our Kyoto Commitment*; http://www.climatechange. gc.ca/english/newsroom/2005/plan05.asp

Govindasamy, B. and Caldeira, K. (2000). "Geoengineering Earth's Radiation Balance to Mitigate CO_2-induced Climate Change." *Geophysical Research Letters*, 27(14): 2141–2144.

——— and Duffy, P. B. (2003). "Geoengineering Earth's Radiation Balance to Mitigate Climate Change from a Quadrupling of CO_2," *Global and Planetary Change*, 37: 157–168.

Guillet, P. (2003). "Long Distance Migrations of Blackflies and Onchocerciasis Transmission," in Y. Dadzie, M. Neira, and D. Hopkins (eds.), "Final Report of the Conference on the Eradicability of Onchocerciasis." *Filaria Journal*, 2(2): 53–58; http://www.filariajournal.com/content/2/1/2

Haynes, R. and Bentham, G. (1995). "Childhood Leukaemia in Great Britain and Fallout from Nuclear Weapons Testing." *Journal of Radiological Protection*, 15(1): 37–43.

Hellerstein, R. (2003). "Do Drug Prices Vary Across Rich and Poor Countries?" Working paper, Social Science Research Council; www.ssrc.org/programs/gsc/themes/globalization.page

Henderson, D. A. (1993). "Surveillance Systems and Intergovernmental Cooperation," in S. S. Morse (ed.), *Emerging Viruses*. New York: Oxford University Press, pp. 283–289.

——(1999). "Eradication: Lessons from the Past." *Morbidity and Mortality Weekly Report*, 48: 16–22.

High Level Panel on Threats, Challenges, and Change (2004). *A More Secure World: Our Shared Responsibility*. New York: United Nations General Assembly A/59/565.

Hirshleifer, J. (1983). "From Weakest-Link to Best-Shot: The Voluntary Provision of Public Goods." *Public Choice*, 41: 371–386.

Hoffert, M. I. et al. (2002). "Advanced Technology Paths to Global Climate Stability: Energy for a Greenhouse Planet." *Science*, 298: 981–987.

Hopkins, D. R. and Millar, J. D. (1996). "Editorial Note," *Morbidity and Mortality Weekly Report*, 45: 538–545.

——and Withers Jr., P. C. (2002). "Sudan's War and Eradication of Dracunculiasis." *The Lancet*, Supplement, 360: s21–s22.

Independent International Commission on Kosovo (2000). *The Kosovo Report: Conflict, International Response, Lessons Learned*. Oxford: Oxford University Press.

Intergovernmental Panel on Climate Change (2001). "Climate Change 2001: Synthesis Report, Summary for Policymakers;" http://72.14.207.104/search?q=cache:pQvAnSohe-8J:www.ipcc.ch/pub/un/syreng/spm.pdf+ipcc+2001+climate+change+summary+policymakers&hl=en&gl=us&ct=clnk&cd=2

International Conference (1884). *International Conference Held at Washington for the Purpose of Fixing a Prime Meridian and a Universal Day: Protocols of the Proceedings*. Washington, DC: International Conference.

International Task Force on Global Public Goods (2006). *Meeting Global Challenges: International Cooperation in the National Interest*, Final Report. Stockholm, Sweden: International Task Force on Global Public Goods.

Irwin, A. (2002). "The Molina-Rowland Chemical Equations and the CFC Problem," in G. Farmelo (ed.), *It Must Be Beautiful: Great Equations in Modern Science*. London: Granta.

Jambou, R. et al. (2005). "Resistance of Plasmodium Falciparum Field Isolates to In-Vitro Artemether and Point Mutations of the SERCA-Type PfAT-Pase6." *The Lancet*, 366: 1960–1963.

Johnson, N. and Mueller, J. (2002). "Updating the Accounts: Global Mortality of the 1918-1920 'Spanish' Influenza Pandemic." *Bulletin of the History of Medicine*, 76: 105–115.

Kakwani, N. and Son, H.H. (2006). "New Global Poverty Counts." International Poverty Centre, United Nations Development Programme, Working Paper No. 29.

Kaul, I. and Conceição, P. (eds.) (2006). *The New Public Finance: Responding to Global Challenges*. New York: Oxford University Press.

——Grunberg, I., and Stern, M. (eds.) (1999). *Global Public Goods: International Cooperation in the 21st Century*. New York: Oxford University Press.

——Conceição, P., Le Goulven, K., and Mendoza, R. U. (eds.) (2003). *Providing Global Public Goods: Managing Globalization*. New York: Oxford University Press.

Keele, B. F., Van Heuverswyn, F., Li, Y. et al. (2006). "Chimpanzee Reservoirs of Pandemic and Nonpandemic HIV-1." *Sciencexpress*; www. sciencexpress.org/25May2006/Page1/10.1126/science.1126531

Keen, M. and Strand, J. (2005). "The Public Economics of Coordinated Indirect Taxes on Aviation." IMF Working Paper, Fiscal Affairs Department, Washington, DC: International Monetary Fund.

Khanna, J., Sandler, T., and Shimizu, H. (1998). "Sharing the Financial Burden for U.N. and NATO Peacekeeping, 1976–1996." *Journal of Conflict Resolution*, 42(2): 176–195.

Kim, A. and Benton, B. (1995). "Cost-Benefit Analysis of the Onchocerciasis Control Program (OCP)." World Bank Technical Paper No. 282.

King, D. A. (2004). "The Scientific Impact of Nations." *Nature*, 430: 311–316.

Knobler, S. L., Mack, A., Mahmoud, A., and Lemon, S. M. (2005). "Summary and Assessment," in S. L. Knobler, A. Mack, A. Mahmoud, and S. M. Lemon (eds.), *The Threat of Pandemic Influenza: Are We Ready?* Washington, DC: National Academies Press, pp. 1–56.

Korber, B., Muldoon, M., Theiler, J. et al. (2000). "Timing the Ancestor of the HIV-1 Pandemic Strains." *Science*, 288: 1789–1796.

Kremer, M. and Glennerster, R. (2004). *Strong Medicine: Creating Incentives for Pharmaceutical Research on Neglected Diseases*. Princeton: Princeton University Press.

——and Peterson-Zwane, A. (2005). "Creating Incentives for Private Sector Involvement in Poverty Reduction: Purchase Commitments for Agricultural Innovation," in I. Kaul and P. Conceição (eds.), *The New Public Finance: Responding to Global Challenges*. New York: Oxford University Press.

Landes, D. S. (2000). *Revolution in Time*. Cambridge, MA: Harvard University Press.

Lanjouw, J. O. (2002). "Beyond TRIPS: A New Global Patent Regime." *CGD Brief*. Washington, DC: Center for Global Development (CGD).

Laxminarayan, R., Over, M., and Smith, D. L. (2006). "Will a Global Subsidy of New Antimalarials Delay the Emergence of Resistance and Save Lives?" *Health Affairs*, 25(2): 325–336.

Lee, J.-W. and McKibbin, W. J. (2004). "Estimating the Global Economic Costs of SARS," in S. Knobler, A. Mahmoud, S. Lemon, A. Mack, L. Sivitz, and K. Oberholtzer (eds.), *Learning from SARS: Preparing for the Next Disease Outbreak*. Washington, DC: National Academies Press, pp. 92–109.

Lembke, J. (2001). "The Politics of Galileo." European Union Center, Center for West European Studies, University of Pittsburgh, University Center for International Studies, European Policy Paper No. 7.

Levine, R. (2004). *Millions Saved: Proven Successes in Global Health*. Washington, DC: Center for Global Development.

Levy, M. A. (1993). "European Acid Rain: The Power of Tote-Board Diplomacy," in P. M. Haas, R. O. Keohane, and M. A. Levy (eds.), *Institutions for the Earth: Sources of Effective International Environmental Protection*. Cambridge, MA: MIT Press.

Lieber, K. A. and Press, D.G. (2006). "The Rise of U.S. Nuclear Primacy." *Foreign Affairs*, March/April, pp. 42–54.

Longini Jr., I. M., Halloran, M. E., Nizam, A., and Yang, Y. (2004). "Containing Pandemic Influenza with Antiviral Agents." *American Journal of Epidemiology*, 159(7): 623–633.

Madrian, B.C. and Shea, D.F. (2001). "The Power of Suggestion: Inertia in 410(k) Participation and Savings Behavior." *Quarterly Journal of Economics*, 116(4): 1149–1187.

Mahmoud, A. (2004). "The Global Vaccination Gap." *Science*, 305: 147.

——and Lemon, S. M. (2004). "Summary and Assessment," in S. Knobler, A. Mahmoud, S. Lemon, A. Mack, L. Sivitz, and K. Oberholtzer (eds.), *Learning from SARS: Preparing for the Next Disease Outbreak*. Washington, DC: National Academies Press, pp. 1–39.

Mandelbaum, M. (2005). *The Case for Goliath: How America Acts as the World's Government in the 21st Century*. New York: Public Affairs.

Marshall, S. J. (2005). "Governments in a Dilemma over Bird Flu." *Bulletin of the World Health Organization*, 83 (5): 325–326.

Maskus, K. E. and Reichman, J. H. (2004). "The Globalization of Private Knowledge Goods and the Privatization of Global Public Goods." *Journal of International Economic Law*, 7(2): 279–320.

Mason, B. (2004). "Climate Change: The Hot Hand of History." *Nature*, 427: 582–583.

Medalia, J. (2002). "Nuclear Weapons: Comprehensive Test Ban Treaty." United States Congressional Research Service; http://usinfo.state.gov/usa/infousa/laws/treaties/nucleart.pdf

Meltzer, M. I., Cox, N. J., and Fukuda, K. (2005). "The Economic Impact of Pandemic Influenza in the United States: Priorities for Intervention," in S. L. Knobler, A. Mack, A. Mahmoud, and S. M. Lemon (eds.), *The Threat of Pandemic Influenza: Are We Ready?* Washington, DC: National Academies Press, pp. 316–339.

Mendelsohn, R., A. Dinar, and L. Williams (2006). "The Distributional Impact of Climate Change on Rich and Poor Countries." *Environment and Development Economics*, 11: 159–178.

Milani, A. (2003). "Extraterrestrial Material—Virtual or Real Hazards?" *Science*, 300: 1882–1883.

Miller, M., Barrett, S., and Henderson, D. A. (2006). "Control and Eradication," in D. T. Jamison et al. (eds.), *Disease Control Priorities in Developing Countries*, 2nd edn. Oxford: Oxford University Press, pp. 1163–1176.

Mills, C. E., Robins, J. M., and Lipsitch, M. (2004). "Transmissibility of 1918 Pandemic Influenza." *Nature*, 432: 904–906.

Mitchell, R. (1994). *Intentional Oil Pollution at Sea: Environmental Policy and Treaty Compliance*. Cambridge, MA: MIT Press.

Morrison, D. (2005). "Defending the Earth Against Asteroids: The Case for a Global Response." *Science and Global Security*, 13: 87–102.

Morton, O. (2002). "Europe's New Air War: Why Are US Allies Building Their Own Global Positioning System? Call It a Declaration of Independence." *Wired*; http://www.wired.com/wired/archive/10.08/airwar.html

Near-Earth Object Science Definition Team (2003). "Study to Determine the Feasibility of Extending the Search for Near-Earth Objects to Smaller Limiting Diameters." National Aeronautics and Space Administration; http://neo.jpl.nasa.gov/neo/neoreport030825.pdf

Nelson, R. A., McCarthy, D. D., Malys, S. et al. (2001). "The Leap Second: Its History and Possible Future." *Metrologia*, 38: 509–529.

Nordhaus, W. D. (2002). "The Economic Consequences of a War with Iraq." Mimeo, Yale University; http://www.econ.yale.edu/~nordhaus/iraq.html

——(2006). "The *Stern Review* on the Economics of Climate Change." Mimeo, Yale University.

——Boyer, J. (2000). *Warming the World: Economic Models of Global Warming*. Cambridge, MA: MIT Press.

North, D. C. (1990). *Institutions, Institutional Change and Economic Performance*. Cambridge: Cambridge University Press.

Nozick, R. (1974). *Anarchy, State, and Utopia*. New York: Basic Books.

OECD Consultative Group on High-Energy Physics (2002). "Report of the Consultative Group on High-Energy Physics." June; http://www.oecd.org/dataoecd/2/32/1944269.pdf

Officer, L. H. (1994). "An Assessment of the United Nations Scale of Assessments from a Developing-Country Standpoint." *Journal of Money and Finance*, 13: 415–428.

Offit, P. A. (2005). *The Cutter Incident: How America's First Polio Vaccine Led to the Growing Vaccine Crisis*. New Haven: Yale University Press.

Olson, M. (1965). *The Logic of Collective Action*. Cambridge, MA: Harvard University Press.

——and Zeckhauser, R. (1966). "An Economic Theory of Alliances." *Review of Economics and Statistics*, 48: 266–279.

O'Neill, B. C. and Oppenheimer, M. (2002). "Dangerous Climate Impacts and the Kyoto Protocol." *Science*, 296: 1971–1972.

Orenstein, W. A., Strebel, P. M., Papania, M. et al. (2000). "Measles Eradication: Is It in Our Future?" *American Journal of Public Health*, 90: 1521–1525.

Oshinksy, D. M. (2005). *Polio: An American Story*. New York: Oxford University Press.

Osterholm, M. T. (2005a). "Preparing for the Next Pandemic." *Foreign Affairs*, July/August.

——(2005b). "Preparing for the Next Pandemic." *New England Journal of Medicine*, 352(18): 1839–1842.

Ostrom, E. (1990). *Governing the Commons: The Evolution of Institutions for Collective Action*. Cambridge: Cambridge University Press.

Pacala, S. and Socolow, R. (2004). "Stabilization Wedges: Solving the Climate Problem for the Next 50 Years with Current Technologies." *Science*, 305: 968–972.

Patz, J. A., Campbell-Lendrum, D., Holloway, T., and Foley, J. A. (2005). "Impact of Regional Climate Change on Human Health." *Nature*, 438: 310–317.

Pearce, D.W. (2005). "The Social Cost of Carbon," in D. Helm (ed.), *Climate Change Policy*. Oxford: Oxford University Press, pp. 99–133.

Phillips, H. and Killingray, D. (2003). "Introduction," in H. Phillips and D. Killingray (eds.), *The Spanish Influenza Pandemic of 1918–19: New Perspectives*. London: Routledge, pp. 1–25.

Popp, D. (2005). "R&D Subsidies and Climate Policy: Is There a 'Free Lunch'?" The Maxwell School, Syracuse University.

Portney, P. R. and Weyant, J. P. (eds.) (1999). *Discounting and Intergenerational Equity*. Washington, DC: Resources for the Future.

Posner, R. A. (2004). *Catastrophe: Risk and Response*. New York: Oxford University Press.

Power, S. (2002). *A Problem from Hell: America and the Age of Genocide*. New York: Basic Books.

Preston, R. (1994). *The Hot Zone*. New York: Anchor Books.

Rees, M. (2003). *Our Final Hour*. New York: Basic Books.

Richards, P. G. and Kim, W.-Y. (1997). "Testing the Nuclear Test-Ban Treaty." *Nature*, 389: 782–783.

Roberts, L. (2006). "Polio Eradication: Is it Time to Give Up?" *Science*, 312: 832–835.

Robock, A. (2002). "The Climatic Aftermath," *Science*, 295: 1242–1243.

Royal Society (2005). *Ocean Acidification Due to Increasing Atmospheric Carbon Dioxide*. London: The Royal Society.

Roper, C. et al. (2003). "Antifolate Antimalarial Resistance in Southeast Africa: A Population-Based Analysis." *The Lancet*, 361: 1174–1181.

Ruddiman, W. F. (2005). *Plows, Plagues, and Petroleum: How Humans Took Control of Climate*. Princeton: Princeton University Press.

Sachs, J. and Malaney, P. (2002). "The Economic and Social Burden of Malaria." *Nature*, 415: 680–685.

Sagan, C. and Ostro, S. J. (1994). "Dangers of an Asteroid Deflection." *Nature*, 368: 501.

Sagan, S.D. (1996). "Why Do States Build Nuclear Weapons?" *International Security*, 21(3): 54–86.

Samuelson, P. A. (1954). "The Pure Theory of Public Expenditures." *Review of Economics and Statistics*, 36(4): 350–356.

Sandler, T. (1992). *Collective Action: Theory and Applications*. Ann Arbor: University of Michigan Press.

——(1997). *Global Challenges: An Approach to Environmental, Political, and Economic Problems*. Cambridge: Cambridge University Press.

——(2004). *Global Collective Action*. Cambridge: Cambridge University Press.

——(2005). "Collective Versus Unilateral Responses to Terrorism." *Public Choice*, 124(1–2): 75–93.

——and Hartley, K. (2001). "Economics of Alliances: The Lessons for Collective Action." *Journal of Economic Literature*, 39: 869–896.

SARS Epidemiology Working Group (2003). *Consensus Document on the Epidemiology of Severe Acute Respiratory Syndrome (SARS)*. Geneva: World Health Organization.

Schelling, T. C. (1955). "International Cost-Sharing Arrangements." *Essays in International Finance*, No. 24, Princeton University, pp. 1–25.

——(1960). *The Strategy of Conflict*. Cambridge, MA: Harvard University Press.

——(1966). *Arms and Influence*. New Haven: Yale University Press.

——(1995). "Intergenerational Discounting." *Energy Policy*, 23(4/5): 395–401.

——(2002). "What Makes Greenhouse Sense?" *Foreign Affairs*, 81(3): 2–9.

——(2006). *Strategies of Commitment*. Cambridge, MA: Harvard University Press.

Schneegans, S. (2005). "Killer Wave." *A World of Science*, 3(2): 2–8.

Schneider, S. H. (2001). "Earth Systems Engineering and Management." *Nature*, 409: 417–421.

Scholz, J. T. and Lubell, M. (1998). "Trust and Taxpaying: Testing the Heuristic Approach to Collective Action." *American Journal of Political Science*, 42(2): 398–417.

Schweickart, R. L. (2003). "The Need for a United Nations Asteroid Deflection Treaty to Establish a System for Trustworthy Mission Design and Execution." B612 Foundation Occasional Paper 0301; http://72.14.203.104/search?q=cache:KiM_-AdEapoJ:www.b612foundation.org/papers/OECD_trustworthy.pdf+b612+foundation+paper+0301&hl=en&gl=us&ct=clnk&cd=2&ie=UTF-8

Schweickart, R. L., Lu, E. T., Hut, P., and Chapman, C. R. (2003). "The Asteroid Tugboat." *Scientific American*, November, pp. 54–61.

Secretary General of the United Nations (2000). *We the Peoples: The Role of the United Nations in the 21st Century*. New York: United Nations Department of Public Information, p. 56; http://www.un.org/millennium/sg/report/index.html

——(2005). *In Larger Freedom: Towards Development, Security and Human Rights for All*. New York: United Nations General Assembly A/59/2005.

Sencer, D. J. and Axnick, N. W. (1973). "Cost Benefit Analysis." *International Symposium on Vaccination Against Communicable Diseases, Monaco 1973; Symposia Series in Immunobiological Standardization*, 22: 37–46.

Shimizu, H. and Sandler, T. (2002). "Peacekeeping and Burden-Sharing, 1994–2000." *Journal of Peace Research*, 39(6): 651–668.

Simon, S. L. (1997). "A Brief History of People and Events Related To Atomic Weapons Testing in the Marshall Islands." *Health Physics*, 73(1): 5–20.

Skarbinski, J., Eliades, M. J., and Causer, L. M. et al. (2006). "Malaria Surveillance—United States, 2004." *Morbidity and Mortality Weekly Report, Surveillance Summaries*, 55/SS-4: 23–35.

Smith, R., Beaglehole, R.,Woodward, D., and Drager, N. (eds.) (2003). *Global Public Goods for Health*. Oxford: Oxford University Press.

Smolinski, M. S., Hamburg, M. A., and Lederberg, J. (eds.) (2003). *Microbial Threats to Health: Emergence, Detection, and Response*. Washington, DC: National Academies Press.

Solomon, S. (1999). "Stratospheric Ozone Depletion: A Review of Concepts and History." *Reviews of Geophysics*, 37(3): 275–316.

Stern, N. (2006). *Stern Review: The Economics of Climate Change*. London: HM Treasury; http://www.hm-treasury.gov.uk/independent_reviews/stern_review_economics_climate_change/sternreview_index.cfm

Stiglitz, J. E. (2006). "A New Agenda for Global Warming." *Economists' Voice*, July; http://www.bepress.com/ev

Swan, J. (2002). "Fishing Vessels Operating Under Open Registers and the Exercise of Flag State Responsibilities: Information and Options." *FAO Fisheries Circular* No.980. Rome: FAO.

Tanser, F. C., Sharp, B., and le Sueur, D. (2003). "Potential Effect of Climate Change on Malaria Transmission in Africa." *The Lancet*, 362: 1792–1798.

Task Force on Potentially Hazardous Near Earth Objects (2000). *Report of the Task Force on Potentially Hazardous Near Earth Objects*; http://www.nearearthobjects.co.uk/report/resources_task_intro.cfm

Taubenberger, J. K. and Morens, D. M. (2006). "1918 Influenza: the Mother of All Pandemics." *Emerging Infectious Diseases*, 12(1): 15–22.

Tedeschi, W. and Teller, E. (1994). "A Plan for Worldwide Protection Against Asteroid Impacts." *Space Policy*, 10(3): 183–184.

Teller, E., Hyde, R., Ishikawa, M., Nuckolls, J., and Wood, L. (2003). "Active Stabilization of Climate: Inexpensive, Low Risk, Near-Term Options for Preventing Global Warming and Ice Ages Via Technologically Varied Solar Radiative Forcing." Lawrence Livermore National Library, 30 November.

Terasawa, K. L. and Gates, W. R. (1993). "Burden Sharing in the Persian Gulf: Lessons Learned and Implications for the Future." Mimeo, United States Naval Postgraduate School.

Toon, O. B., Zahnle, K., Morrison, D., Turco, R., and Covey, C. (1997). "Environmental Perturbations Caused by the Impacts of Asteroids and Comets." *Reviews of Geophysics*, 35(1): 41–78.

Travis, D. J., Carleton, A. M., and Lauritsen, R. G. (2002). "Contrails Reduce Daily Temperature Range." *Nature*, 418: 601.

Tucker, J. B. (2001). *Scourge: The Once and Future Threat of Smallpox*. New York: Atlantic Monthly Press.

UNAIDS/WHO (2005). *AIDS Epidemic Update*, December; http://www.who.int/hiv/epiupdates/en/index.html

U.S. Department of Defense (1992). "Conduct of the Persian Gulf War." Final Report to the US Congress, April.

United States Environmental Protection Agency (1988). *Regulatory Impact Analysis: Protection of Stratospheric Ozone*, August. Washington, DC: EPA.

United States General Accounting Office (GAO) (2002a). "Review of Studies of the Economic Impact of the September 11, 2001, Terrorist Attacks on the World Trade Centre," GAO-02-700R. Washington, DC: GAO; http://www.gao.gov/new.items/d02700r.pdf

——(2002b). "UN Peacekeeping: Estimated US Contributions, Fiscal Years 1996–2001," GAO-02-294. Washington, DC: GAO.

——(2003). "Emerging Infectious Diseases: Asian SARS Outbreak Challenged International and National Responses," GAO-04-564. Washington DC: GAO.

——(2006). "Peacekeeping: Cost Comparison of Actual UN and Hypothetical U.S. Operations in Haiti." GAO-06-331.

Vagelos, P. R. (2001). "Social Benefits of a Successful Biomedical Research Company: Merck." *Proceedings of the American Philosophical Society*, 145(4): 575–578.

Vaughan, D. and Spouge, J. (2002). "Risk Estimation of Collapse of the West Antarctic Ice Sheet." *Climatic Change*, 52: 65–91.

Velders, G. J., Slaper, H., Pearce, D. W., and Howarth, A. (2000). "Technical Report on Stratospheric Ozone Depletion in Europe: An Integrated Economic and Environmental Assessment." Rijksinstituut voor Volksgezondheid en Milieu, Bilthoven, the Netherlands, RIVM Report 481505011.

Viscusi, W. K. (2006). "Regulation of Health, Safety, and Environmental Risks." National Bureau of Economic Research Working Paper No. 11934, January.

Viscusi, W. K. and Aldy, J. E. (2003). "The Value of a Statistical Life: A Critical Review of Market Estimates Throughout the World." *Journal of Risk and Uncertainty*, 27(1): 5–76.

Wallsten, S. and Kosec, K. (2005). "The Economic Costs of the War in Iraq." Working Paper 05-19, AEI-Brookings Joint Center for Regulatory Studies, September.

Wellems, T. E. and Plowe, C. V. (2001). "Chloroquine-Resistant Malaria." *Journal of Infectious Diseases*, 184: 770–776.

Whitrow, G. J. (1972). *What is Time?* Oxford: Oxford University Press.

Wigley, T.M.L. (1998). "The Kyoto Protocol: CO2, CH4 and Climate Implications." *Geophysical Research Letters*, 25(13): 2285–2288.

Wong, R. S. and Hui, D. S. (2004). "Index Patient and SARS Outbreak in Hong Kong." *Emerging Infectious Diseases*, 10(2): 339–341.

Woolsey, L.H. (1942). "War Between the United States and the Axis Powers." *American Journal of International Law*, 36(1): 77–83.

Working Group 2, Commission on Macroeconomics and Health (2002). *Global Public Goods for Health: The Report of Working Group 2 of the Commission on Macroeconomics and Health.* Geneva: World Health Organization.

World Bank (2005). "Spread of Avian Flu Could Affect Next Year's Economic Outlook." World Bank East Asia and Pacific Region; http://www.worldbank.org/eapupdate

WHO (World Health Organization) (2003). *The World Health Report 2003 — Shaping the Future.* Geneva: World Health Organization; http://www.who.int/whr/2003/en/

World Meteorological Organization (2002). "Scientific Assessment of Ozone Depletion: 2002, Executive Summary." Global Ozone Research and Monitoring Project, Report No. 47, World Meteorological Organization, Geneva.

Zacher, M. W. (1999). "Global Epidemiological Surveillance: International Cooperation to Monitor Infectious Diseases," in I. Kaul, I. Grunberg, and M. A. Stern (eds.), *Global Public Goods: International Cooperation in the 21st Century.* New York: Oxford University Press, pp. 266–283.

Zerubavel, E. (1982). "The Standardization of Time: A Sociohistorical Perspective." *American Journal of Sociology*, 88(1): 1–23.

Zhou, P. and Leydesdorff, L. (2006). "The Emergence of China as a Leading Nation in Science," *Research Policy*, 35(1): 83–104.

Zhu, T., Korber, B. T., Nahmias, A. J., Hooper, E., Sharp, P. M., and Ho, D. D. (1998). "An African HIV-1 Sequence from 1959 and Implications for the Origin of the Epidemic." *Nature*, 391: 594–597.

Index